CAMBRIDGE SOUTH ASIAN STUDIES

SIR WILLIAM JONES:

A STUDY IN EIGHTEENTH-CENTURY BRITISH ATTITUDES TO INDIA

CAMBRIDGE SOUTH ASIAN STUDIES

These monographs are published by the Syndics of Cambridge Univesity Press in association with the Cambridge University Centre for South Asian Studies. The following books have been published in this series:

William Jones by Sir Joshua Reynolds

SIR WILLIAM JONES:

A STUDY IN EIGHTEENTH-CENTURY BRITISH ATTITUDES TO INDIA

BY

S. N. MUKHERJEE

*University Assistant Lecturer in
the History of South Asia,
University of Cambridge*

CAMBRIDGE
AT THE UNIVERSITY PRESS
1968

Published by the Syndics of the Cambridge University Press
Bentley House, P.O. Box 92, 200 Euston Road, London, N.W.1
American Branch: 32 East 57th Street, New York, N.Y.10022

© Cambridge University Press 1968

Library of Congress Catalogue Card Number: 68-10689
Standard Book Number: 521 05777 9

Printed in Great Britain
at the University Printing House, Cambridge
(Brooke Crutchley, University Printer)

CONTENTS

ILLUSTRATIONS

PREFACE

A biography of a scholar like Sir William Jones could be written in two ways; as a review of his works and an analysis of his ideas or as a straightforward story of his life. In this work I do not wish to write a definitive biography of Jones, or a review of his works, but aim to study the complex personality of Jones, analyse his ideas about India and her civilization, and finally describe the far-reaching effects of his works on British attitudes towards India.

Originally I intended to make a complete survey of early British attitudes towards India but I soon realized that this would be a lifetime's work, so I concentrated my attention on Jones, who is perhaps the most interesting person in the history of eighteenth-century British policy in India. He came to Calcutta in 1783, less than two years before Warren Hastings left India. In 1786 Cornwallis arrived with a very different view on the British administration of India. Jones shared with Hastings his admiration for India and her tradition, yet his Whig philosophy found much in common with Cornwallis. He worked with, and was loved and admired by, both of them.

This study is based on Jones's private correspondence. I have drawn heavily on his unpublished letters now retained at Althorp Park, Northampton. I am most grateful to the present Earl Spencer for kindly allowing me to study them; also for his permission to reproduce the two portraits. I am grateful to the present Marquis of Landsdowne for allowing me to consult the Jones items among the Landsdowne papers at Bowood. I have also used some official records in the India Office Library. Among the private papers there I used the Orme collection. I am most grateful to the Librarian and the staff of the India Office Library for their kind co-operation. I am also most grateful to the Trustees of the British Museum, and to the Keepers of Manuscripts and the staff of the following libraries: the National Library of Wales, Aberystwyth: the National Library of Scotland, Edinburgh; the Central Library, Sheffield; the Bodleian Library, Oxford; the University Library, Cambridge; the Royal Asiatic Society; the University Library, London; the Library of the Institute of Historical Research, London; County Record Office, Warwick; the

Preface

National Szechenyi Library, Budapest; the William L. Clements Library, Ann Arbor, Michigan, U.S.A.; the American Philosophical Library, Philadelphia; the National Archives of India, New Delhi; the Bar Library, Calcutta; the Asiatic Society of Bengal, Calcutta; and the University Library, Leiden.

I am also grateful to the librarian and staff of the library of the School of Oriental and African Studies, particularly to Miss N. Matthews and Mr J. D. Pearson.

This work is based on my London Ph.D. thesis. My gratitude is due to the School of Oriental and African Studies Scholarship Committee for awarding me a Forlong Exhibition for the session 1960–1, and to the University of London Scholarships Committee for awarding me a University of London Post-graduate Studentship for the sessions 1961–2 and 1962–3. The Central Research Fund of the University of London have been most generous in assisting me towards the cost of research incurred in Aberystwyth and Althorp Park. The research fund of the Faculty of Oriental Studies, Cambridge, paid the cost of typing the manuscript. My parents have been most generous throughout.

During the course of my research I have received the guidance of my teacher Professor A. L. Basham. I am deeply grateful for his patience and advice. My gratitude is also due to Dr K. A. Ballhatchet, Dr J. G. de Casparis, Mr Ian R. Christie, Dr E. Hobsbawm, Dr C. C. Davies, Dr T. G. P. Spear, for their help and criticism, to Miss B. Schutz, Miss J. Domanska and Mr H. Muhammadi for help in translation, and to Mrs Zell and Mrs Davies for typing. This script would never have reached the publisher without the active encouragement of Mr B. H. Farmer, the Director of the Centre of South Asian Studies, Cambridge. My wife's help throughout has been invaluable. I wish to acknowledge the help given by Mr Iain White and the staff of the Cambridge University Press in proof-reading and the production of the book.

INTRODUCTION

The history of modern India has so far been presented to us as the history of British activities in India. It is either an account of the administrative reforms, the revenue systems, the growth of British institutions in the subcontinent, or the story of conflicts and coalitions of interests (among the officers and among the various pressure groups with interests in India in the House of Commons). However, there is now a tendency among some British historians to pay more attention to ideas and policies than to conflicts and coalitions of interests. It has been suggested that 'British policy moved within an orbit of ideas primarily determined in Europe'; thus 'the transformation of the Englishman in India from Nabob to Sahib was fundamentally an English transformation not Indian'.[1] The British policies in India are now studied by some historians with direct reference to the intellectual movements in Europe and as an integral part of the European body of political thought. The books of Dr K. A. Ballhatchet and Dr E. Stokes are pioneering works in this field.[2] The history of India in the modern period is still regarded in Britain as the history of British India;[3] but the English political thought which reached India through various channels is an important factor in the history of modern India; it helps us to understand the nature of the administrative reforms, especially the land-laws, which so fundamentally changed the way of life in India and above all it helps us to understand the modern Indian mind.

Ever since the famous 'Namierite Revolution' in historical scholarship it has become fashionable among a group of scholars to neglect the role of ideas in history. It has been suggested that the ideas have no validity of their own. They are merely a rationalization of human activities which are motivated by the thirst for power. According to Sir Lewis Namier, men in the eighteenth century went to parliament 'to make a figure' and they 'no more dreamt of a seat in the House in order to benefit humanity than a child dreams of a birthday cake that others may eat it'.[4] It is not for me to say whether all politicians in the eighteenth century went to the House of Commons only to 'make a figure', but it is certainly true that ideas and ideals played a significant part in the history of modern

India. Men went to India for a variety of reasons, to make money, for adventure, and as a help up the social ladder in Britain, but the majority of men also had a definite missionary zeal to shape the future of the country. Moreover, men in political power in India were open to intellectual influences from Europe. The political activities of such men as Philip Francis, Cornwallis, Macaulay and Bentinck were moulded according to their ideological convictions. It will be futile to suggest that the transformation of the rural life in Bengal was solely due to the application of Whig and Physiocratic economic ideas to the Indian situation. The transformation took place owing to many other deep-rooted social and economic causes, but the ideas, which set politicians in motion to reform the administrative system, left a definite mark upon Indian society.

A comprehensive study of the British ideas and administrative policies must take into account the history of the development of Indian studies. It is often forgotten that all Oriental Studies in the eighteenth century had a political slant, and all political pamphleteers writing on East Indian affairs based their theories of Indian politics on Oriental researches, or so they thought. In textbooks[1] the history of Indian studies has been presented as a story of a series of discoveries by the British officers, who spent part of their leisure in revealing the history and culture of the country. The scholarly activities of the British administrators and the European missionaries and travellers (as most of the early Orientalists were) are presented in isolation, almost without reference to the society in which the Orientalists were born and to the British administration which they served (or to which, as in the case of some French scholars, they were actively hostile). For a better understanding of the British response to Indian civilization we should study it within the context of the British and European economic system, social structure and intellectual movements and with reference to the problems of the British administration in India. Early Orientalists were not an isolated group. They were involved in the political conflicts of the time and their 'theories' about Indian history and culture were influenced by their respective political positions and intellectual convictions.

Sir William Jones was a key figure in the development of both the Oriental studies and the British policies of the eighteenth century. He founded the Asiatic Society of Bengal, which for the first time made an organized effort to study the history, society

Introduction

and culture of India; his works on Indian civilization captured the post-Revolutionary European mind and stimulated further research on the subject. He was involved in politics; in England he was an ardent supporter of America and the movement for parliamentary reform, and in India he developed a definite theory of law and government for the British Raj in Bengal. He was constantly in touch with men in power and was often consulted by them.[1] Thus his 'digest' of Indian Laws was considered as complementary to Cornwallis's Permanent Settlement. In fact, Jones occupies a larger place in the history of the British attitudes towards India than has hitherto been recognized. He is one of the most interesting figures in the history of British India, but not because he was an erudite scholar who knew twenty-eight languages and made numerous 'great discoveries' in Indian studies, nor because he was a pious man who treated Indians kindly. Some of his so-called 'great discoveries' were already known to other scholars, as we shall see later, while others, like that on orthography, were of small importance. His treatment of Indians was not as exceptional as is often made out; in the eighteenth century British officers had a close social contact with Indians, although Indians were never treated as equals, not even by Jones. However, some of his discoveries were of great significance. His *śakuntalā* had a profound effect in India. By saving Kālidāsa from the medieval commentators he ushered in what has been called 'an Indian Renaissance'. But I think his career is important because it shows more clearly than anything else the dichotomy of the attitudes of some of the British officers in India; many were radicals at home and they were attracted by India, her 'glorious past' and her 'simple people', yet they had to uphold an authoritarian rule. Jones epitomizes this dichotomy in his life and works.

In this work I attempt to study the ideas of Sir William Jones from the published and unpublished sources, with reference to the British administrative policies, European attitudes towards India, the growth of Indian studies, and English Whig philosophy.

CHAPTER I

INDIA AND THE WEST

It is conventional in textbooks on the history of ideas to identify the eighteenth century with the Age of Reason. However, Horace Walpole had a different view; writing in the middle of the century he said: 'A century had now passed since Reason had begun to attain that ascendant in the affairs of the world to conduct which it had been granted to men six thousand years ago.'[1] This is not an accurate statement and the historians of ideas rightly place the Age of Reason in the eighteenth century before the French Revolution. But in one sense Horace Walpole was right, for much of the groundwork for the eighteenth-century *Aufklärung* was already prepared in the seventeenth century. The cult of Reason was based on Newtonian physics and Lockian psychology; Newton had shown that the existing myths were not in accord with scientific facts and Locke disproved the Cartesian doctrine that ideas are innate and clearly showed that they are derived from experience.[2] The faith in Revealed Religion was already shaken by the Scientific Revolution and by voyages and discoveries.[3] The Scientific Revolution had shown that man can shape his own destiny and the voyages and discoveries proved that the knowledge of the ancients regarding the shape and nature of the earth was very limited. Men began to question the validity of Divine Right, the doctrines of Revelation, the chronology of Genesis and the rituals practised by the churches. The religious wars had left a scarred Europe which now preferred to settle down in peace and tolerate different faiths.[4] This loss of faith in the accepted myths, the urge for toleration and the growing knowledge about civilizations outside Europe led to the development of a new faith—Deism. The universe was no longer limited to the boundaries of Christendom so God was no longer a tribal god of the Christians but Father of all; as Pope[5] said in his Universal Prayer:

> Father of all in every age,
> In every clime adored.
> By saint, by savage and by sage,
> Jehovah, Jove or Lord.

4

The universe worked according to the laws of nature, but the Creator had an important part to play. Newtonian astronomy provided the basis for the Deist 'theology'. Nature worked like a clock and the Creator was the clockmaker who had set it to work at the beginning, but subsequently it worked according to its own laws. If the law of gravity held the physical world together, then the law of Reason kept the moral world together. The *philosophes* divorced ethics and philosophy from Christianity, and tried to demonstrate that natural morality based on the law of Reason was far superior to Christian morality.

Similarly the political ideas of the *philosophes* of the Enlightenment were based on the assumption that human institutions can be justified if they are based on Reason. They argued passionately against what they considered irrational institutions, and developed an exaggerated view of the power of the legislators to shape the future of the world. Probably this led some of the *physiocrats* to advocate legal absolutism, to re-establish 'the natural legal code' which they thought should rightfully 'regulate economic and social existence'.[1] However, as champions of human liberty, the majority of the eighteenth-century thinkers detested absolutism in any form. To them the most ideal constitution was a 'mixed state' which found its practical expression in the English constitution. Montesquieu[2] used it as his model for the Theory of the Separation of Powers and Voltaire was inspired by it.

They were no democrats. They were rather contemptuous of the ordinary people, their 'superstitions', beliefs and their inelegant way of life. They upheld the institution of private property, which in their mind was closely related to human liberty and the prosperity of the whole community. If Hobbes's *Leviathan* represents the fear of disorder and anarchy, it was shared by the Rationalist philosophers. They would agree with John Locke that 'the great and chief end'[3] of men's uniting into commonwealths and putting themselves under government, 'is the preservation of their property'.[4]

This Europe, with its faith in Reason and its distrust of disorder, looked at China with admiration. It was natural that China should be so admired, as according to the Jesuit reports she had an orderly government with scholar-governors—the Mandarins—and above all Confucian political philosophy. The *philosophes* found in China a great civilization which owed nothing to the Graeco-

Roman heritage or to the Christian tradition.[1] The Chinese had a philosopher with similar ideas two thousand years ago.[2] They managed the affairs of their state much more rationally and without Christianity. The German philosopher Leibniz was greatly impressed by China; he worked hard to establish the Berlin Society with the idea of the opening up of China and the interchange of civilizations between Europe and that country.[3] Voltaire too admired China, particularly her political organization and her ethics based on Reason. His *Orphelin de la Chine* was largely written to prove Rousseau wrong. Rousseau thought that science and art are destructive of morals. Voltaire in his *Orphelin de la Chine* made an attempt to show that this was not so in China.[4] In fact there was in Europe, in the eighteenth century, a cult of China; and Asia, as seen by the Rationalist thinkers, meant, primarily, China.

India, by contrast, appeared disorderly, chaotic and superstitious. Her heterogeneous culture, her diverse customs and her loosely knitted empire were to the *philosophes* difficult to put into a rational order. The cunning and ritual-ridden Brahmins were no match for the Mandarins, the scholar-governors. India never occupied such a position in the European mind as did China. In d'Herbelot's *Bibliothèque Orientale*, in Diderot's *Encyclopédie* and in Voltaire'e *Essai sur les Mœurs* fewer pages are devoted to India than to China. In fact it was not until the beginning of the nineteenth century that a group of intellectuals were attracted by India and then for a very different reason. The men who harked back to the Middle Ages in search of what they called the 'lost harmony' between man and nature also looked for guidance to 'spiritual India'. India provided an escape from the spiritual narrowness of nineteenth-century Europe.[5] There were also a group of English officers who were inspired by the works of Burke and Rousseau (the two leading figures of the so-called Romantic revolt—an intellectual movement which challenged the very principles which were upheld by the eighteenth-century Rationalists) and were eager to defend Indian institutions and block the way of anglicization of Indian administration.[6] On the other hand, to the narrow-minded Victorian rationalists India was a backward country which provided them with an area to try out the political principles of Jeremy Bentham and James Mill for social reform and political 'emancipation'.[7]

However, it would be wrong to assume that the *philosophes* neglected India altogether. In fact India provided an example of the Oriental form of state and government; her religion, with innumerable gods, Brahmanic philosophy and the claim of a great antiquity, was a weapon for the Deists against the accepted chronology and Christian morality. As Voltaire put it rather ironically, 'there is no mention of Adam or Noah or any of our sacred history in the ancient books of the Hindus'.[1] Thus, although India was never looked upon in the same light as was China, Europe had similar problems of response to an alien culture in her attitudes towards India. There was the same debate on the nature of the political society and the same arguments on the nature of the religions. The existence of Islam was an additional point in their talks on India.

In the eighteenth century, India was not a strange country. Knowledge about the subcontinent had been growing ever since the late medieval period. To late medieval and early modern Europe the term 'India' conveyed a picture of a 'farre-distant'[2] country, rich in spices and gems, embracing much of Asia and part of Africa, which was invaded and conquered by Alexander. His stories of thrilling adventures were handed down to the common people in the form of romances[3] and letters, which purported to be written from India by Alexander to his mother, and his preceptor Aristotle.[4] Christians believed that this rather fabulous and remote land was ruled by a Christian king called Prester John.[5] The legend of Prester John developed from the twelfth century, though his 'letter' was first printed in 1500. There was another Christian tradition which was concerned with India: St Thomas the Apostle was supposed to have preached the Gospel among the Indians.[6] This tradition was confirmed by Marco Polo, who visited his reputed tomb in South India. Since the days of Henry the Navigator, the Portuguese had been making continuous efforts to discover the sea route to India in order to capture the lucrative spice trade from the Venetians who had previously monopolized it. They also wanted to find Christian allies in Asia to help them against their traditional enemy, the Moors. Although by the fifteenth century, with the Portuguese penetration in Ethiopia, the reputed area of Prester John's empire was cut down to a plausible size, most non-Muslim Asiatics were thought to be some kind of fallen Christians. When Vasco da Gama landed in Calicut on

20 May 1498, he and his men entered a temple with the impression that it was a church.[1]

The European ideas of India changed rapidly with the increasing number of voyages after 1498 and especially from the seventeenth century when the Portuguese monopoly in the Indian seas was broken by the Dutch, the English and the French. Among those besides traders who went on these voyages, were travellers, adventurers and missionaries. Soon Europe was flooded with travellers' tales, adventure stories and missionary reports. Since the advent of printing, the reading public had increased greatly, and thrived on stories of the exotic. They were eager to read accounts of the seafaring activities of their sons, and of the strange and distant lands they visited. Such stories came from almost all quarters of the world. India provided a fertile field for travellers' tales. Her heterogeneous culture with uncommon and varied customs soon attracted the reading public in Europe. So the travellers and adventurers filled their journals with stories of *satī*, child marriage, the matrilineal system of the Nāyars, untouchability, and the caste system. They may have been genuinely shocked by such practices as *satī* but yet they were not hesitant in describing in detail the grotesque custom of girls jumping on to their husbands' funeral pyres. Similarly the naked mendicant (*nāgā sanyāsi*), whom Ralph Fitch described as the 'monster among the rest',[2] figured well in travellers' journals.

But most of these travellers had very little real contact with the Indians. This is manifested in their explanations of Indian customs and manners. Edward Terry, the chaplain who accompanied Thomas Roe, thought out an incredible explanation for the Brahmin's *sikhā*: 'They usually shave off all the haire from their heads reserving only a locke on the crowne for Mahomet to pull them into heaven.'[3] The Jains were thought to be followers of Pythagoras.[4] The Aśokan Pillars and other such columns were explained as posts erected by Alexander commemorating his victory over Porus. Thomas Coryat was certain that the inscription on the iron pillar in Delhi was written in Greek.[5] If they had had any real contact they would have had a very different explanation for the Brahmins' *sikhā* and the Aśokan pillars (though the prevalent Indian ideas of those columns were equally incredible).[6] However, there were other visitors whose efforts were not solely devoted to describing the strange customs of India. Edward Terry himself was sympathetic and genuinely interested. Although he did not stay long in the country he learnt some Persian, which enabled him to communicate with the Indians. Terry was one of the first Europeans to admit that India possessed some great literature, although he could not appreciate Indian music. He praised the religious toleration of the Mughals.[1] He found that nature was merciful to India; there were fruits in the trees, crops in the fields.

But he raised a note of caution: 'but lest this remote country should seem like earthly Paradise without any discommodities, I must need take notice there of lions, tygres, wolves, jackals (which seem to be like wild dogs) and many other harmful beasts.'[2]

Sir Thomas Roe, the ambassador at Jahangir's court, was a keen observer and drew serious conclusions about the future of India, 'All in these kingdoms will be in combustion'.[3] The complicated system of land tenure, *Mansabdari* administrative machinery was hardly understood, but Roe concluded, 'Laws they have none written. The kyngs judgment bynds who sits and gives sentence with much patience once weakly both in capital and criminal causes.'[4] There was no property in land for the king is owner of all land. 'He is every man's heir when he dyeth.'[5] He warned against the absence of a stable nobility and the increasing poverty of peasants. He thus laid down the very foundation of the theory of Oriental despotism.

Apart from satisfying the interest in exotic customs and unusual social and political institutions, and being one of the main sources of economic prosperity, India provided a great field of activity for Christian missionaries. From the very early period of contact, priests travelled to Asia. They looked for converts, especially among those whom they took to be degraded Christians. Various orders were at work in Asia but the most important of them all was the Jesuits. From the onset, Ignatius Loyola,[6] the founder of the Society of Jesus, looked for converts in the East rather than in the West; his Spanish origin made him more interested in the Muslim world than in heretic Germany.

The Jesuits had a great organizing capacity and they often sent men of great calibre to the East. In India they showed an amazing zeal especially after the arrival of Francis Xavier in 1542. Their system of reporting to their superiors has left us an enormous literature in the form of letters. Such letters contain not only reports on the progress of their missionary works, but also accounts of the social and religious customs of the people. In fact at times they had penetrated further in understanding Indian culture than the merchant-travellers. At an early period they recognised the importance of learning local languages; Thomas Stevens learnt Marathi and Sanskrit; De Nobili mastered Sanskrit and Tamil, in spite of the reluctance of the Brahmins to teach them their sacred language;[1] and Roth was supposed to have written a Sanskrit grammar which was never published. But very few of the missionaries brought back any Sanskrit works to Europe. The only genuine translation from Sanskrit was done by a Dutch priest-scholar, Abraham Roger. His version of Bhartṛhari's proverbs was the first direct translation of a Sanskrit text into a European language before the works of William Jones and Charles Wilkins.[2] However, the missionaries from Madurai started sending Sanskrit manuscripts to Europe from 1730 onwards, but they collected dust in the great libraries and remained unread for a very long time.

Jesuit and other missionary activities raised two problems to which Europe was very alive even at the end of the eighteenth century. One of these problems was how to reconcile a new religion with a traditional culture. This led men like De Nobili to identify themselves totally with the local culture.[3] They recognized the differences between the two cultures and the danger of asking the Indians to give up their way of life while embracing a new religion. This was perhaps the first understanding, however vague it might have been, of the problems arising out of imposing one culture upon another. The other problem which baffled the missionaries and delighted the Deists was the professed antiquity of the Brahminic civilization and its numerous gods. Attempts were made to explain the gods and reduce the Indian chronology to the limits set by Genesis. This was often done by identifying an Indian mythological figure with a name in Genesis, like Manu with Adam or Noah.[4]

So, by the second half of the eighteenth century, India was comparatively familiar to Europe. Men had already taken notice of her civilization, her religions, languages and her political system. The contemplative Rationalist philosophers, who speculated on the nature of Indian polity, based their theories on missionary reports, travellers' tales and merchants' accounts. However, there was one man who influenced them more than all the others. He was François Bernier.

Bernier was a French physician who was very much a product of his age. He was well acquainted with the new mathematics and the new anatomy of the latter half of the seventeenth century.[1] He was a precursor of the *philosophes*. His scepticism, his faith in Reason and in private property as a source of prosperity and good government, made his works essential reading for the eighteenth-century thinkers. He visited India in 1656 and lived there for thirteen years. He observed from close quarters the civil war and the Mughal court during the first years of Aurangzeb's rule. He gathered a great deal of information on Indian religions and society from Brahmin pandits, some of whom had worked for Dara Shikho (the unfortunate Mughal prince), and from the high Mughal officials.

He has been praised by modern historians as a penetrating and thoughtful observer.[2] But a close examination of his works shows that he failed to grasp the basic tenets of Brahmanism. The Vedantic monism was beyond the limits of his intellectual horizon. He failed to see that it is possible for the Brahmins to pay homage to numerous gods yet believe in one creator. Bernier suspected that the Brahmins, who proclaimed their faith in one God to him, framed their answers to suit the tenets of Christianity.[3] He had not much respect for them.

The Brahmins encourage and promote these gross errors and superstitions to which they are indebted for their wealth and consequence. As persons attached and consecrated to important mysteries they are held in general veneration and enriched by the alms of the people.[4]

However, he summarized the Hindu mythology fairly accurately and his accounts of such exotic Indian customs as *sati* were comparatively free from prejudice. He sought to find a rational basis for the Brahmanic obsession with vegetarianism and ablution; he suggested that this was due to climatic conditions in India. As a scholar he did not fail to recognize the similarities between the Indian and the Greek philosophies.

If Bernier's views on Indian religions were limited by his time, his views on the Indian political system have to be judged in the context of the rise of Mercantilism, the accumulation of capital and the development of private property in Europe in the seventeenth century. Bernier found that the political organization in India and in other parts of Asia was quite unlike the European system. Asiatic nations are ruled by powerful autocrats who manage the affairs of the state through a group of bureaucrats, who are entirely dependent on the whims of their masters. The monarch in Asia exercises a type of absolute power over his subjects, which Europe had never experienced. The despotic rule is wicked. As in Asia there is no nobility or propertied class to challenge the authority of the rulers:

It must not be imagined that the omrahs or lords of the Moghul's court are members of ancient families as our nobility in France. The King is proprietor of all the lands in the empire, there can exist neither dukedoms nor marquisates, nor can any family be found possessed of wealth arising from a domain and living upon its own patrimony.[1]

The lack of private property was the sole reason for the general decline of the Asian powers:

It is owing to this miserable system of government that most towns in Hindustan are made up of earth, mud and other wretched materials; that there is no city or town which, if it is not already ruined and deserted, does not bear evident marks of approaching decay.[2]

If the right of private property was recognized and acted upon, then the land would be carefully cultivated and the country would be prosperous.[3]

It is true that in India, in the seventeenth century, private property in land did not exist as an integral single right, but there were various rights over the land, especially the *zemindari* right. The *zemindari* right was, as Habib has shown recently, an article of property, in the sense that it was inheritable and to a certain extent alienable.[4] Bernier failed to understand the real nature of such rights, largely because his ideas about property in land were based on the seventeenth-century concept of private property. Seventeenth-century Europe not only recognized the 'natural right' of the individual to inherit and enjoy the fruits of property in land, but stressed the unlimited right of the individual to acquire and alienate landed property at his will without any reference to authority or the community. John Locke was the greatest seventeenth-century exponent of the theory of private property.[5] It seems that Bernier was trying to establish a case for private property in France; he used India as an example. There is no private property; hence there is gradual 'decay' in that country. This comes out very clearly in his letter to Colbert, the famous minister of Louis XIV: 'Yes, my dear Lord, to conclude briefly I must repeat it; take away the right of private property in land and you introduce as a sure and necessary consequence tyranny, slavery, injustice, beggary and barbarism.'[1]

Bernier's ideas received wide attention in the eighteenth century. Montesquieu was most impressed. In fact he worked out the ideas of Sir Thomas Roe and Bernier into a definite political theory. Montesquieu recognized three types of states, republic, monarchy and despotism. Each type rules according to certain principles, virtue for republic, honour for monarchy and fear for despotism.[2] Under despotism the ruler managed the affairs of state not according to fixed and accepted laws, but according to his caprice.[3] Under such a state no new ideas are encouraged to grow. Men live under fear of severe punishment and torture. The object of the state is the pleasure of the prince, who treats his subjects as his slaves and all land as his own personal property.[4] The examples of despotism are invariably from Asia. This is largely because of the climatic condition in those parts of the world. In Asia, men are indolent, slow to change, live under customs which existed from time immemorial. Asians are more speculative than active and have no desire to resist absolute rule. This led Montesquieu to declare that feudalism is an 'event' which only happened in Europe. Like many other eighteenth-century thinkers, Montesquieu used 'feudalism' to mean fragmentation of political authority. In Asia he found no fragmentation of authority.[5]

Montesquieu was supported by others. In 1762 Nicolas-Antoine Boulanger, a writer of the d'Holbach group, published an essay as an 'introduction and key' to the *Esprit des Lois*.[6] He suggested that despotism in Asia was not only due to the climatic conditions in those countries but also due to the religious faiths. 'Despotism', he said, 'has established itself through man's desire to model the government of the universe as it is reigned over by the Supreme Being; magnificent but fatal project.'[7] He thought that the Oriental form of government was some kind of theocracy.

Alexander Dow in 1772, in vol. III of his *History of Hindostan*, added a 'Dissertation on the origin and nature of despotism in Hindostan'. Following Montesquieu he suggested that the inherent manners of the people determine the 'spirit and genius' of a government.[8] Such manners are largely influenced by the climatic conditions and by the religious beliefs. The climate in India has made the Indian people 'phlegmatic', 'slothful' and easily submissive to despotic power.[1] Indian religions, both Islam and Hinduism, also encourage despotism; 'the faith of Mahommed is peculiarly calculated for despotism: and it is one of the greatest causes which fix for ever the duration of that species of government in the East'.[2] Hinduism, on the other hand, is 'productive from its principles of the greatest degree of subordination to authority'.[3] But Dow found that despotism in India is not so harmful to the people as it is in other parts of Asia. He presented the Mughal princes as benevolent despots, 'humane' and 'engaging'. He followed Bernier and Montesquieu and suggested that there was no private property in land in India, but the lack of private property was, he thought, compensated by the *zemindari* right, which, according to Dow, was a form of tax-farming system.[4] His views were supported by others including Robert Orme, the historian.

This view on the nature of Oriental governments did not pass unchallenged. The *physiocrats*, in direct contradiction to the traditional view, proclaimed that despotism as known in the East was an agreeable form of government. In fact they suggested that legal despotism is essential to establish a good society based on natural laws.[5] Voltaire, on the other hand, challenged the fundamental concepts of the *Esprit des Lois*. As an admirer of Asian civilizations, he could not agree that the rulers were tyrannical and that private property in land was absent in India and other parts of Asia. He argued that despotism did not become a prominent watchword of political thought until late in history. The term was not authorized by Latin usage and the Greek term *despotes* was applied exclusively to the head of the household.[6] Voltaire was entirely right in claiming that despotism was a comparatively new concept in Europe in the eighteenth century. It was used by Milton, Locke and by the French authors writing during the reign of Louis XIV to mean a tyrannical absolutism. However, Voltaire overlooked the fact that already two thousand years ago it was used by Aristotle to mean tyrannical absolutism. In fact the Greek philosopher had recommended to Alexander that the conqueror should rule over the Greeks as their leader and over the conquered Barbarians as a *despotes*, as a master over slaves.[7] However, Voltaire further argued in his *Fragments sur l'Inde* that 'everyone who is quite well-informed knows that the Moghul government was, since Chenghiz Khan and possibly a long time before that, a feudal government almost the same as that in Germany'.[1] He suggested that 'feudalism is not an event; it is a very ancient form of government which exists in three-quarters of our hemisphere with different administration. The Grand Moghul is like the German emperor. The Subadors are the princes of the Empire'.[2] This kind of comparison between the European nobility and Indian aristocracy was not entirely new, for it had been made by Hawkin, a seventeenth-century English traveller and by the Jesuits.[3] But Voltaire claimed that India had experienced private property in land. He suggested that Bernier and Roe were dazzled by the Mughal splendour and misunderstood the Indian system. He thought that Scrafton was far more reliable than Bernier and Roe. Scrafton had claimed that India had private property in land and that the Indian courts of justice followed established precedents. He also thought that India was happy and prosperous until she was invaded by Nadir Shah.[4]

Voltaire was also impressed by the Indian religions. He was aware of the 'superstitious' practices of the common people in India but he also learnt that the Indian had 'sublime ideas' about the Supreme Being. This, he suggested, India had inherited from an age when Greek philosophers like Pythagoras visited the subcontinent for instruction but that such 'sublime ideas' were only known to a small *élite* whereas the *petit peuple*, as in Europe or China, practised horrible rituals: 'This horrible excess of religion and greatness of soul still exist side by side, with faith of Brahmans that God only desires of us charity and good works'.[5] There were many English authors who provided Voltaire with evidence to support his Deistic interpretation of Brahmanic religion. The medieval tradition of prejudice against Islam survived right down to the end of the eighteenth century,[6] and this prejudice can be traced in the works of Scrafton, Dow and Holwell. Hinduism on the other hand appeared as an antithesis of Islam. They agreed that, in spite of the horrible rituals of the Brahmins, the Hindus were aware of a pure morality and one supreme God.[7] Holwell wrote,

It is worthy of notice that metempsychosis, as well as the three grand principles taught in the Greater Eleusinian mysteries; namely, the unity of Godhead, His general providence over all creation and a further state of rewards and punishments, were fundamental doctrines of Bramah, Chartah Bhade, Shastah and were preached by the Bramins from time immemorial to this day throughout Indostan.[8]

In fact he claimed that Hinduism was one of the three religions which 'manifestly carry the divine stamp of God',[1] the other two being Judaism and Christianity.

The British were particularly interested in the debate on the nature of the Indian system of land revenue and government. Since 1757 they were virtually the kingmakers of Bengal, and in 1765 the East India Company took the charge of the Diwani of Bengal from the Mughal emperor Sha Alam I. This was a part of Clive's larger plan of the dyarchical system of government which masked the true nature of power politics in Bengal and allowed the Nawab to function as the governor of the province, while the company got a very large share of the revenue.[2] There was then an urgent need to know the true nature of the rights in land, the Indian form of government and the nature of the relationship between the state and the landholders. In England many men were perturbed that a merchants' company should exercise sovereign power over millions of people; there was a continuous demand that parliament should control the affairs of the East India Company. A public debate in England on East Indian affairs followed and was conducted in the House of Commons and through pamphlets and articles in the *Monthly Review* and the *Gentleman's Magazine*.[3]

Thus by the latter part of the sixties of the century, when Jones was approaching his manhood, India was comparatively familiar to Europe. Although there was no cult of India among the intellectuals, as there was a cult of China, India received the attention of the great *philosophes*, who debated heatedly on the nature of Indian polity and Indian religions. The British were particularly interested for pragmatic reasons to find a workable administrative policy for India. The theories on India were based on second-hand sources, from the Indian informers and Persian works. Although Holwell claimed that he had read the Shastras in the original language, he had no real knowledge of Sanskrit. Dow had a dubious knowledge of Persian.[4] The Orientalists of the universities took no part in the development of Indian studies. Oriental studies had ceased to be a branch of theology in the seventeenth century, and now Orientalists' interest was focused on Asian culture and society,[5] but most men who learnt Asian languages and wrote books on India and other parts of Asia were amateurs, travellers, company officials and missionaries. They worked independently without an organization and without a scientific or methodological approach.

CHAPTER 2

'A PHILOSOPHER AMONG COURTIERS'

William Jones was born a commoner; his father came from a yeoman family,[1] settled in the island of Anglesey. His mother's father was a cabinet maker in London. Whatever glory his Welsh forefathers might have gained,[2] Jones himself had very little interest in his remote ancestry. During one of his visits to Wales, he had a view of Anglesey; he described the island as 'the ancient rock where my ancestors presided over a free, but uncivilised people'.[3] In fact Wales was a foreign country to him. After a visit to a town in North Wales he wrote, 'I could not help fancying myself in a Flemish town; it was at least wholly unlike an English one as the language, manners, dress and countenances of the people are entirely different from ours'.[4]

This did not prevent him from becoming a Cymmrodorian in 1778 and from learning Welsh. He wrote some of his rather romantic poems, which conveyed pagan motifs, along the river Wye and by Cardigan Bay during his annual visits to Wales as a lawyer.[5] When, in February 1780, Burke proposed a bill, at the House of Commons, to abolish the Welsh circuit, Jones took up the cause of the Welshmen, 'I hope the Welshmen will petition against the Bill and if they please they may employ me to support their petition at the bar of the House'.[6] But he never considered himself to be a Welshman and took little interest in the cultural history of his ancestors.[7] George Nix, the maternal grandfather of Jones, had been a rival of Chippendale. He had made his way to the dinner table at Lord Macclesfield's house, though very little is known about him and his work.[8]

William Jones (1680–1749), the father of the Orientalist, was a man of exceptional ability. He showed an early talent in mathematics. After a brief period of adventure in the West Indies, William Jones settled in London as a tutor in mathematics. He had already made his mark in the high society of London; he struck up a friendship with Lord Anson, whom he had taught mathematics in the West Indies, and in 1702 he published a work on navigation. In 1706 he published his second work, a book on mathematics.[9]

He soon got himself appointed as tutor to Philip Yorke (afterwards Lord Hardwicke) and later to Thomas and George Parker, the first and second earls of Macclesfield. The second earl became his lifelong friend and patron. He came to know such celebrities as Isaac Newton, Samuel Johnson, and Edmund Halley. Newton took particular interest in Jones and allowed him to edit many of his minor works. In 1712 William Jones was elected a Fellow of the Royal Society for his exceptional ability in mathematics.

When Macclesfield retired to Shirburn Castle in Oxfordshire, William Jones went to stay with the family. Here he met Mary Nix, and soon married her. They had three children; the first, George, died in infancy, the second, Mary, was born in 1736, married a rich merchant named Rhinsford, and died in 1802. On 28 September 1746, on the eve of St Michael's day, William, the third child, was born in London. The father died when William was three years old, leaving behind him his fame, a small fortune, a group of friends who were well known in their time, and his books on Newtonian mathematics.[1]

The onus of bringing up the children fell upon the widow. From all accounts she appears to have been a remarkable woman. Though born in the age of patronage and sinecure, she was very independently minded and declined the countess of Macclesfield's repeated requests to stay in Shirburn Castle. She remained in London and managed with the small fortune left by her husband. Her ideas of education were considered remarkable by her contemporaries. She had probably read John Locke's work on the subject, which saw its twelfth edition in 1752.[2] It was an age when the middle classes gave great importance to education and children were brought up under strict discipline. This discipline was often achieved by heavy corporal punishment; Susanna Wesley, who used the rod even for a baby in the cot, was no exception.[3] John Locke, although prescribing strict discipline in bringing up children, discouraged corporal punishment.[4] Perhaps following Locke, Mrs Jones discarded corporal punishment and 'to his incessant importunities for information on casual topics of conversation which she watchfully stimulated, she constantly replied, read and you will know'.[5] Thus Jones grew up in a family where Newton and Locke loomed large.

It is no wonder that Jones could quote Shakespeare and Gay's fables from memory at the age of four. Born in an age of child prodigies, he was no exception; as a junior boy at Harrow he could write *The Tempest* from memory from the first line to the last.[1] His mother had indefatigable energy in stimulating him to work hard. He was not allowed to spend his vacations in idleness, for she helped him to improve his English and taught him the rudiments of drawing. The boy had an accident at the age of four which permanently damaged his eyesight. Even in 1788 we find him complaining of the strain of reading by candlelight and of the glaring Indian sun.[2] But this physical disability, instead of making him nervous, made him all the more determined to read and learn. Once at Harrow he was advised by a doctor to leave the school to save his eyesight. At this he was most upset and urged that he should be allowed to stay, and he arranged to have his friends read to him.[3]

This accident, which was followed by another at the age of nine when he broke his thigh and spent a year in bed, perhaps made his mother more protective towards her son and she came to live near him when he was at Harrow and at Oxford.[4] The relationship between the mother and son was very close; he spent many evenings at her house in Oxford,[5] where he could bring his friends, and he would take her with him during his holidays.[6] During his stay in London as a lawyer, he used to spend at least a day every week at his mother's place at 54 Red Lion Street, where he would invite the closest friends to a 'domestic party'.[7] On her death in 1780 he wrote

I have no parent left but my country, and I am in a disposition to serve that second parent at any hazard, especially as my dear departed mother loved and taught me to love the rights and liberties of my countrymen while she detested and taught me to detest the abettors of unconstitutional power.[8]

He joined Harrow at Michaelmas 1753. The public school left a deep mark on his character. His progress was slow at first and even slower when he joined his old form after a year of absence because of his broken thigh. The year in bed was not totally wasted, as he read the works of Pope and Dryden and was encouraged by his mother to write verses imitating them. But when he went back to school he was expected to keep pace with his old classmates, and, when he failed to do so, he was severely punished. The story of the rather brutal corporal punishment which Jones underwent on this occasion was remembered in the school tradition well into the nineteenth century.[1] It had much more lasting effect on the boy than the master intended. Jones grew up alienated from authority and he himself was conscious of it. Shore writes that,

the accumulation of punishment for his inability to soar before he had been taught to fly (I use his own expression) might have rendered the feelings callous; and a sense of the injustice attending the infliction of it was calculated to destroy the respect due to magisterial authority and its influence over the scholar.[2]

But Jones's alienation was never complete; he did not grow up to hate the system altogether. Later, he became fond of Harrow and he recommended a public school education for his pupil and friend George John Spencer, Viscount Althorp: 'Take my word for it, my dear Lord, you will always have reason to be glad that you were bred at the public school and you will thank me for the part I took in recommending that *mode* of education.'[3]

After the initial difficulties he soon excelled in Latin and Greek; he composed verses imitating Virgil and Sophocles, and his master, Dr Sumner, who followed Thackeray as the Headmaster at Harrow, was heard to declare that Jones knew more Greek than himself.[4] The study of the classics left a deep imprint on the boy's mind; he was charmed by the old literature and was inspired by the 'ancient wisdom'. 'From my earliest years I was charmed with the poetry of the Greeks; nothing, I then thought, could be more sublime than the Odes of Pindar, nothing sweeter than Anacreon, nothing more polished or elegant than the Golden Remains of Sappho.'[5] Among the works he recommended his young pupil and friend, Althorp, to study were those of Cicero and Demosthenes: 'If all the ancient books were destroyed except Demosthenes and Cicero I should be contented with them both.'[6]

But the formal education did not satisfy the curiosity of the boy and soon he turned his attention to books and subjects outside the curriculum. During the vacations he improved his French, arithmetic and Italian, and at Harrow he taught himself Hebrew and the Arabic script. His leisure time was spent in inventing games which involved intellectual rather than physical exercise. While other boys liked the usual amusements, he spent his time in arranging his 'army' as the 'King of Arcadia', disputing in syllogism or displaying oratory in the fields of Harrow.[7] At the age of thirteen he wrote a drama, a tragedy called 'Meleager'.[1] This was staged at Harrow, with Jones cast as the hero. It is not surprising to find him flattered by the title of 'Great Scholar', probably given to him by his fellow pupils.[2]

Among his friends at Harrow were William Bennet, bishop of Cloyne; Samuel Parr, prebendary of St Paul's and curate of Hutton, and John Parnell, chancellor of the Exchequer of Ireland. They were all known at Harrow for their exceptional abilities, and they all loved and admired Jones. 'He was always an uncommon boy... I loved him and revered him and though one or two years older than he was, was always instructed by him from my earliest age.'[3] This was what William Bennet wrote to William Shipley, the Dean of St Asaph in November 1795. Similarly John Parnell wrote to the widow of Sir William Jones: 'He gave very early proof of his possessing very extraordinary abilities...His time being employed to his study, prevented him joining those plays and amusements which occupied the time of his other school fellows.'[4]

Perhaps the admiration of his fellow pupils and the encouragement of his mother stimulated his independent spirit and gave him a self-confidence which later allowed him to move freely in fields unknown and to become a manager of men. But this independence and self-confidence made him ambitious and somewhat indifferent to personal pain and pleasure. To him life was not worth living without tangible achievements. So he thought it better to die before falling from fame.

I cannot help thinking [he wrote to his sister on the death of a friend] any grief upon a person's death, very superfluous, inconsistent with sense...How happy must he be who takes the reward of his excellences, without the possibility of falling away from them and losing the virtue which he professed, on whose character death has fixed a kind of seal, and placed him out of reach of vice and infamy.[5]

When in 1780 he was urged by his schoolfellow Samuel Parr to take steps to save the life of their French master, Henri, who had been sentenced to death in France, Jones wrote:

To a man who is poor and wise without any chance of being richer, or a man who is rich and foolish without any chance of being wiser, life can administer no comfort and consequently is no advantage; but a man who is both poor and mad without any hopes of becoming easy in his circumstances or of recovering his understanding can receive no greater benefit than death.[6]

This did not prevent him from being kind to others. He took up the cause of a poor musician in Bath, who had been sent to prison for an unpaid debt of seven pounds. He repeatedly declared that he followed his profession in order to serve the cause of the poor: 'I may say truly and I hope not arrogantly that while I wear gown, no helpless or injured person of any nation shall want an advocate without fee in any of our courts.'[1] This led him to take up the cause of imprisoned debtors in India.[2] But such kindness was impersonal, the urge to 'do good' to the downtrodden rather than love for them. After he had managed to save the life of his Syrian friend, Mirza, he wrote to Lady Georgiana Spencer, mother of his pupil, George John: 'I assure your ladyship, that I look upon it as a cause gained and take it as a favourable omen for my future labours as an advocate in the course of which it will be my chief happiness to dedicate my imperfect talents to the relief of the distressed.'[3]

In 1764, when he was seventeen, Jones went to Oxford; he was admitted to University College as a commoner. His father's legal friends advised against sending him to Oxford, and would have preferred him to study for the Bar. But the boy had no interest in Law at this stage. He much preferred to study classics and his master Dr Sumner encouraged him in this pursuit.[4]

For the greater part of the eighteenth century the history of Oxford is very dull. It is the history of a small society 'where disillusioned Jacobites and half-hearted Hanoverians contended with each other'.[5] To men with new ideas and dissenting views it was a stifling place; in 1768 even the followers of John Wesley were expelled.[6] Most men found the university lifeless and the teaching uninteresting. Gibbon described his stay in Oxford as 'the most idle and unprofitable of my whole life'.[7] Samuel Johnson, who was at Pembroke, thought that his tutor's lectures in logic were not worth half the twopenny fine imposed for missing them. Such sentiments were echoed by Adam Smith and Jeremy Bentham.[8]

At first Jones was not happy with the situation in Oxford; he complained that he was required to attend dull lectures on artificial ethics and logic, delivered in such barbarous Latin that he professed to know as little of it as he knew of Arabic.[9] However, later he was allowed to pursue his studies independently, and he widened his horizon. After gaining further knowledge in classics he turned his attention to Oriental Studies.

The university was famous for Oriental scholarship, which goes back to the days of Edward Pococke, who became the first professor of Arabic in 1636. At the time of Jones perhaps the best-known Oriental scholar was Joseph White of Wadham, who in 1774 became professor of Arabic and later of Hebrew. Among his works the *Institutes of Temour* is well known.[1] But in spite of this tradition the students did not get much help in their Oriental pursuits. Gibbon bitterly complained of how he was discouraged from learning Arabic.[2] Jones was first incited to learn this language by a fellow student, though he needed little encouragement as he had already learnt the Arabic script at Harrow and was inclined to traverse unknown fields. But he learnt Arabic, not from the university teachers but from Mirza, a Syrian whom he had met in London and whom he brought to Oxford. A part of each morning was spent with Mirza in retranslating *One Thousand and One Nights*.[3] His attention was soon drawn to Persian as he found 'a near connection between the modern Persian and Arabic'.[4] He soon mastered the two languages and by 1768 he had become well known as an Orientalist.[5]

But learning classical and Oriental languages was not the end of his education; he regularly attended classes in riding and fencing and his vacations were spent in improving his mastery over modern languages. This is how Milton wanted young men to be educated, a combination of the education of a gentleman and that of a man of letters, to learn as much about things that matter as about the 'wisdom of the ancients'. This is the education which Jones was to recommend for his pupil and which he himself tried to follow.[6]

Independently minded as he was, he was often at odds with the authorities at Oxford. In 1768, when he received his B.A., he had to endure the convocation ceremony, which he called 'the most ridiculous thing imaginable'.[7] Yet he went through the ceremony as custom required. In 1773 during the four days of the *encaenia* celebrations Jones was asked to address the university but

when I showed them my oration, they thought it not flattering enough and I soon found that they expected a very different kind of speech from what I intended to give them, which determined me not to speak at all, and I had no cause to repent of my silence, for most of the compositions, that were repeated, were so full of flattery that my bold strain would hardly have met with a favourable reception.[8]

This shows that he was unable to adapt himself fully to the accepted norms of the university. Yet he was not totally alienated from Oxford society; he disliked the ridiculous ceremonies and he complained of the lack of freedom in the university yet he defended the university whenever he felt it necessary. He attacked Anquetil Duperron, the French Orientalist who ridiculed Oxford scholarship, chiefly to discredit 'the French nation' and to defend Oxford.[1] He made a number of friends at Oxford; Robert Chambers, John Paradise, and William Warburton Lytton were his best friends, and together they formed a club called the 'Grecian' in which informal dinners were held in alternate members' rooms and interesting literary subjects were discussed.[2] He even thought of residing permanently in Oxford, had he failed to obtain his judgeship in Bengal, and he intended to donate all his Oriental manuscripts to the university.[3] In 1780 he wanted to represent the *Alma Mater* in Parliament.[4]

The pursuit of the education of a gentleman and a scholar proved to be too expensive. He was elected a Bennet scholar in 1764 but the stipend was a modest sum and hardly met his expenses, which included fees for fencing and riding lessons, and maintaining Mirza in Oxford. In 1765 he was offered a post as a tutor in the Spencer family, to teach young George John, then seven years old. Jones had no alternative but to accept the offer, and in the summer of that year he went to stay at Wimbledon Park to take charge of the boy. A year later he was elected to the Bennet Fellowship at University College, but he had then grown fond of George John and so he continued at the same time as his tutor.[5] The relationship between tutor and pupil was friendly and informal. From the very start Jones discarded all formalities—'drop all formalities' was a much repeated phrase in his correspondence. The mother, Lady Georgiana Spencer, recognized this. 'He now loves you as his friend,' she wrote to Jones, 'which is surely much better than fearing you as a master.'[6]

Thus started a friendship which lasted until the end of Jones's life. He drafted a plan for the education of his pupil, which was to include the study of words (meaning, languages and literature) and the study of things (material affairs).[7] He continued to put his plan into practice even after he had ceased to be his tutor. His early correspondence was more a mode of instruction than a matter of mere courtesy.

His letters were written in the same way as Cicero wrote to his friend Atticus. 'Cicero's letters are the most beautiful models of epistolary writing...you will be charmed with them. I was going to say you are my Atticus but you will be a man as superior to Atticus as I shall be inferior to Cicero.'[1] His repeated advice to his young pupil was to distinguish himself: 'from the mob of noblemen and consider birth, fortune and so forth as nothing more than steps by which you may climb more rapidly into the temple of virtue which is far above them all'.[2] He discouraged Althorp from indulging too much in ordinary recreations such as hunting, dancing and music.[3] These recreations should never be permitted to engage too much of an Englishman's time, since he 'has so many accomplishments to learn and so many duties to perform to his friends, to his country and to the whole race of man'.[4] Therefore he advised his pupil that

when you are not in the field or in company, you run eagerly into [the] library, *abdiste in bibliothecum* (as Tully did, when he was a hunter not of foxes but of Catiline's wolves and bloodhounds) and that you make the improvement of your mind keep pace with the strength and activity of your body.[5]

The importance of the enlargement of mind comes only after the 'exercise of religion' and the 'practice of virtue'.[6] For the 'improvement of mind', Jones suggested that Althorp should read as many books as he could for 'there are few books from which we may not receive some instruction or amusement',[7] although the most important authors for instruction were Demosthenes and Cicero.[8] Three other authors whom he especially recommended to Lady Georgiana for her son were Euclid, Locke and Blackstone, for 'the first will open to him the principles of all natural knowledge, the second will show him the natural extent of human reason and the third will offer to him a specimen of that reason reduced to practice in the admirable laws of our country'.[9]

His love for classical literature led him to love what he called the 'ancient wisdom', which, he believed, found expression in contemporary Whig philosophy and the English constitution. What he considered most sacred was the 'Englishman's liberty'. He persuaded George John to his ideas about the English constitution, liberty and the American Revolution. He also hoped that the time would come,

when there will be less interruption to our friendship, when we shall be able to confer together about the great interest of our country, when you in the Senate and I at the Bar shall endeavour to deserve well of mankind by ensuring and promoting their happiness. The difference of twelve years will soon disappear and we shall both be young men together.[1]

But to be a senator or barrister one must be first an eloquent orator; hence Jones stressed that Althorp should pay attention to oratory:

I rejoice that you are to begin with your oratorical exercises this summer, believe me my dear lord, you will learn nothing at school so useful and agreeable...What made Pitt a minister and afterwards a peer? His eloquence. What made Murray Chief Justice and him [*sic*] the title of Mansfield? Eloquence.[2]

This is the reason why Jones liked Isaeus, the famous Greek orator, 'I am quite in love with him for the solidity of his reasoning and the manly sense which appears in his speeches'.[3] He could not be very enthusiastic about Charles James Fox, for Fox would not compose his speeches in 'manner of the ancient': 'he is a man of very quick and lively parts, but I think he wishes rather to display them than to convince his audience'.[4]

Jones had a definite faith in Christianity but his advice was to avoid controversies over theology and metaphysics; 'I am sure enough to answer every purpose of knowledge, and I am equally sure of Christianity, but if you think with me you will not trouble yourself with such objections as Gibbon or anybody else can make',[5] he advised his friend. To Jones the best way to serve God was through one's work and not by entering into theological controversy;

surely the elegance of ancient poetry and rhetoric, the contemplation of God's works and God's ways, the respectable task of making boys learned and men virtuous may employ the forty and fifty years you have to live, more serenely, more laudably, more profitably, than the vain warfare of controversial divinity.[6]

These instructions were carried out in person even after Jones left the Spencer family. He used to visit George John at Harrow, where the boy had been sent in 1769. There they would eat a fowl together at the King's Head and discuss George John's prospects in Parliament.[7] The young man lived up to Jones's expectations and became First Lord of the Admiralty during the Napoleonic

Wars. In later life he left politics and spent his time as Jones would have liked, 'in a studious and tranquil retirement'.[1]

The connection with the Spencer family proved to be very fruitful for Jones's career. He moved freely among the higher orders of society. At Wimbledon in the summer of 1766 he was offered a post as interpreter of Oriental languages by the duke of Grafton, but he declined it.[2] Again in spring 1768 Sutton, the under-secretary of the duke, contacted him with the request that he should translate a Persian manuscript, a history of Nadir Shah brought to England by Christian VII of Denmark.[3] This translation established him in Europe as an Orientalist. Through the Spencer family he met Count Reviczki,[4] a Hungarian diplomat and Orientalist, in the spring of 1768. This was the beginning of a friendship which lasted till the end of his life.

In summer 1766 he met Anna Maria Shipley, the daughter of Jonathan Shipley, dean of Winchester and later bishop of St Asaph. She was a regular visitor to the family, being related to Lady Georgiana. Lord Macartney, the Governor of Madras, met her[5] at Wimbledon. Jones was soon attracted to her, but being cautious and ambitious he knew he would not have enough income 'to be independent and married'.[6] He had to wait until October 1782, when he had some prospect of gaining the judgeship in India, to propose to her. He found in Anna Maria all the qualities he wanted in a woman:

I look upon equality to be the best foundation of happiness in private as well as national society, good sense and good temper, agreeable manners, a feeling heart, domestick affections, knowledge of the world and contempt of what is wrong in it—these were the qualities which I ever sought, and have not I trust, sought in vain. I believe some years ago, that I found them in Miss Shipley.[7]

From 1766 onwards he grew very fond of the Shipley family and was a regular visitor to their home in Chilbolton. Through the bishop of St Asaph he came to know the radicals and the supporters of the American Revolution, among whom was Benjamin Franklin, the 'sage of Passy' as he was called. Jones visited him several times in Paris.

But, nonconformist and outsider as he was, he did not fit well into the upper strata of society. He described his position as a 'philosopher among courtiers', a 'lark or nightingale in a menagerie of peacocks or Indian peafowls'.[1] He avoided social occasions and spent most of his time in his study, reading until late at night and drinking coffee.

You are now sleeping and I hope dreaming of your verses or something agreeable, as for me, though it is midnight, the briskness of my fire and the still silence of the house tempt me to sit reading an hour longer.[2]

In Althorp, the home of the Spencer family, he spent most of his time within the walls of the library, away from the usual amusements that went with life in high circles. It is natural that he should be described 'as one who locked himself up all day and took no part in the amusements that usually employ young men'.[3] This was also noticed by Reviczki, who advised his friend to take more interest in life. Jones, however, disagreed that he was shy and unworldly:

Do not however imagine that I despise the usual enjoyments of youth; no one takes more delight in singing and dancing than I do, nor in the moderate use of wine, nor in the exquisite beauty of the ladies, of whom London affords an enchanting variety.[4]

He enjoyed riding and fencing and found dancing quite agreeable. He frequented the residences of Mrs Montagu, Lady Lucan and Mrs Vesey, who according to Horace Walpole, used to collect 'all graduates and candidates to fame, where they vie with one another, till they are as unintelligible as the good folks at Babel'.[5] The duchess of Devonshire, the sister of George John, was also among his friends. But he would soon grow tired of parties and other social occasions, and would long to get away from them. His holidays in Bath and Margate were spent reading law, classics and logic, or in riding and bathing alone. He generally avoided meeting people:

My days are constantly spent in bathing in the sea, riding on the shore or reading in my study; as for dancing it is almost incompatible with swimming which would hardly be safe if the body were not cool and though I still love a good dance yet I must confess that I prefer the company of Nereids to the ladies at a dance.[6]

In 1769, when most of the higher orders gathered at Stratford on Avon to celebrate the bicentenary of Shakespeare's birth, he went alone to visit Milton's desolate house at Forest Hill, near

Oxford. Milton was another of his heroes, the 'most perfect scholar' and 'sublimest poet that our country ever produced'.[1] A month earlier he told his friend he was inclined to go to Stratford,

for I want very much to hear Mr Garrick speak the recitation part of his ode but to say the truth I have no great inclination to take as much trouble as I shall be forced to take about dress and other foppishness.[2]

As the private tutor of young Lord Althorp he accompanied the family on their trips to the continent. The last one was to Nice, during the winter of 1769–70. He soon grew tired of merely teaching George John and escorting the ladies on their walks and sightseeing trips. He wrote to Nathaniel Halhed, who later became famous as the author of *Gentoo Laws*: 'I cannot describe to you how weary I am of this place, nor my anxiety to be again at Oxford when I might jest with you and philosophise with Poore.'[3] This feeling of loneliness was a persistent mood in Jones's correspondence from Nice. 'I am disgusted with the odious rattle of French gaiety and the calm serenity of an Italian sky has something gloomy in it', he wrote to Reviczki. He would much rather have been in Vienna, 'where I might enjoy your conversation, philosophise with you, trifle away our idle hours or explore with you the hidden treasures of poetry'.[4] A storm, which had been brewing, broke and abruptly brought an end to his career as a tutor. It was not 'French gaiety' nor the 'gloomy Italian sky' which bothered him, but it was his position as a domestic tutor which really irritated him most. 'I never would listen to any proposals of being a domestic tutor in any family, a character which I always thought far below one whose natural freedom of mind renders him incapable of bearing the least restraint of inattention.'[5]

The quarrel with the Spencers broke over the interruptions in the career of young George John at Harrow. Lady Georgiana was rather protective towards her son; she was unwilling to send Lord Althorp back to school when she thought that he was not fully fit and well, and that the weather at Harrow would not suit him. Jones insisted that the boy should attend the school regularly as the public school education gave the highest advantages. Failing that, he should be given a private education under Jones's supervision. He proposed that a house should be built where 'I may pursue my plan without being turned from it by the avocations of a family'.[6] This was not possible so Jones resigned.

My love for liberty is such that I would not only quit my private family to preserve it, and would even leave my country if I felt my freedom endangered and should be happier with liberty in a desert or rock than with any other advantage in the palace of a King.[1]

In fact this 'love of liberty' and his dislike of his position as a 'domestic tutor' perhaps induced him to contemplate leaving the Spencers even before the quarrel over the question of sending George John to Harrow started. On 19 September 1770 he enrolled at the Middle Temple, nine days before he abruptly left Wimbledon, where he never returned as a tutor.[2] Luckily for Jones and for us this quarrel did not result in a complete break with the Spencer family; he remained friendly with both mother and son and corresponded with them regularly until the end of his life. This act of resignation was considered very extraordinary by the men of the eighteenth century, accustomed to a world of sinecure and patronage.[3]

The four years which followed were years of both hard work and success. Most of his time was spent in Oxford and London studying and writing many works including *Histoire de Nader Chah* and *A Grammar of the Persian Language*. Jones was then determined to be a lawyer; he spent less and less time on literature and more and more time on law:

I pass the summer at Oxford, whence I frequently make a little excursion to the neighbouring places and ride constantly every day upon my little grey horse, who has really been a most serviceable beast to me. I study law and history seven or eight hours a day, it is scarce credible how much I read and write from seven in the morning till twelve at night as I never go to rest earlier.[4]

He now found law an agreeable subject and chose the Bar and politics for his career. This was the career Demosthenes and Cicero had chosen for themselves. Jones modelled his life on Cicero; 'If you wish to know my occupations', he wrote to Bennet, 'read the beginning of Middleton's Cicero.'[5] Cicero's life was to be followed closely. A typical day in London included a visit to Parliament, meetings with friends at Alice's Coffee House, at Westminster Hall, where the lawyers and the Members of Parliament met regularly, a call at Lady Spencer's house at St James's Place, and an hour's study of law at the Temple, where he had his chambers: 'Thus have I passed my day and thus did Cicero at my age pass his.[1] His friends were aware of his love for Cicero; Lord Althorp presented him with a set of twenty volumes of works of Cicero,[2] which, according to Pollard, Jones used to read through once every year.[3]

His books like the *Histoire de Nader Chah* brought him fame and many friends. On 30 April 1772 he was elected a Fellow of the Royal Society, as a linguist and an Orientalist.[4] Nearly a year later, on 2 April 1773, he was admitted to that most exclusive club of Samuel Johnson, which met regularly at the Turk's Head in Soho. Jones had no difficulty in gaining admission at this club, whereas even Garrick, the famous actor, had trouble.[5] Jones was already known to most of the original members of the club. He had known Johnson and Goldsmith at least since 1769 when he had dined with them at Oxford.[6] Robert Chambers was an old friend from University College days. He also had known Sir Joshua Reynolds since 1768 and often dined at his place, where he met many other original members of Johnson's club, including Burke, Nugent and Langton.[7] He was at once popular among them; they respected his scholarship, his linguistic ability and his modesty in company. Sir Joshua Reynolds sought his criticism of the early drafts of his annual discourses to his Royal Academy.[8] Burke praised him for his translation of *The Speeches of Isaeus*:

I do not know how it has happened that orators have hitherto fared worse in the hands of the translators than even the poets; I never could bear to read a translation of Cicero...I am satisfied that there is now an eminent exception to this rule.[9]

Johnson presented Jones's *A Grammar of the Persian Language* to Warren Hastings. He wrote to the Governor-General, 'that literature is not forsaking us and that your favourite language is not neglected will appear from the book'.[10] Edward Gibbon was awed by Jones's scholarship:

He is perhaps the only lawyer equally conversant with the year-books of Westminster, the commentaries of Ulpian, the Attic pleadings of Isaeus, and the sentences of Arabian and Persian cadhis.[11]

Jones took an active part in the club; he became president of the club on 11 March 1780 and on 9 May of that year Jones presided over an extraordinary meeting when the rules of the club were changed largely through his own initiative.[12] He persuaded his friends, Jonathan Shipley, the bishop of St Asaph, and Viscount

Althorp to join the club, which he thought unique in Europe; 'There is no branch of human knowledge concerning which we could not collectively give the world good information'.[1]

In 1774 he was called to the Bar and in the spring of 1775 he left London to attend the circuit in Oxford and Wales as a junior pleader. In the circuit he met Dunning (Lord Ashburton), whom he knew already from Johnson's club. Throughout he enjoyed his 'forensick campaigns' and saved four men from capital punishment. He wrote in a moment of undue optimism 'my profession will in due time give as great a share of the labour and advantage of this world as I shall know what to do with'.[2] These 'campaigns' in Oxford and Wales were carried out every spring and summer of his last years in England, and Jones remained a very busy man. He found such 'expeditions' 'extremely pleasant', for 'fine weather' 'excellent business' and for 'speeches, gold and fame'.[3] But, although he saved many more lives and gained pleasure in helping the distressed, he generally found that his income was not enough to meet all his expenses.[4] This was so even after 1776 when he was made a commissioner of the Bankrupts by Lord Bathurst, the Lord Chancellor. Jones was not successful as a practising lawyer. He used to speak in a highly declamatory tone and with studied action, and he aimed at impressing his audience 'who had ever heard of Cicero or Hortensius, with the belief that he had worked himself up into the notion of his being one or both of them for the occasion'.[5]

However to the later scholars and legal historians he was an 'eminent lawyer'. His 'life' appeared along with the lives of Coke, Blackstone and Mansfield.[6] But this was largely because of his scholarship as he did not make any mark as a lawyer or as a judge in Calcutta. He brought to law his 'exact mind,' 'orderly method' and 'logical manner'.[7] His extensive knowledge of the legal works of all periods and of many countries impressed most people. His *Speeches of Isaeus in Causes Concerning the Law of Succession to Property at Athens* was the best English rendering of the original Greek work to date. In his preface and commentary he showed his immense knowledge on the subject. In it he pleaded for better land-laws in England and for the comparative study of law: 'The laws of England are the proper study of Englishmen; but they always shine with greater lustre when they are compared with those of other nations.'[8] In 1781 he brought out his second and most important work on law, *An Essay on the Law of Bailments*.

This was a pioneering work in comparative law, and was most useful for generations of lawyers. It has been praised by modern scholars[1] as an outstanding achievement. In this work Jones tried to bring together all decisions 'ancient and modern' on bailments 'to illustrate our laws by a comparison of them with those of other nations, together with an investigation of their true spirit and reason'; this would not be wholly unacceptable to the student of English law,[2] since Blackstone had neglected it. In his *Essay* Jones treated law analytically, to trace 'every part of it up to the first principles of natural reason'; historically—'to show with what perfect harmony those principles are recognised and established by other nations'; and synthetically—'to expound such rules, as in my humble apprehension, will prevent any further perplexity on this interesting title, except in cases very peculiarly circumstanced'.[3] Jones's concept of law was based on the eighteenth-century idea that all good laws must be founded on 'natural reason';

The great system of jurisprudence, like that of the universe, consists of many subordinate systems, all of which are connected by nice links and beautiful dependencies, and each of them, as I have fully persuaded myself, is reducible to a few plain elements either the wise maxims of national policy and general convenience or the positive rules of our forefathers, which are seldom deficient in wisdom or utility; if law be a science, and really deserve so sublime a name, it must be founded on principle and claim an exalted rank in the empire of reason.[4]

He claimed that 'all nations' whatever seas or mountains may separate them, based their good laws on 'natural reason'.[5]

He promised to write a large treatise on English law using similar methods,[6] a promise he could not fulfil. But his works on Isaeus and Bailments gave him a permanent place among the great lawyers of the eighteenth century.

Jones's last years in England were marked by frustrating attempts to alleviate his financial difficulties and to raise his social status. No doubt he was by then the best-known English Orientalist, whose works were read throughout Europe, and he was a formidable authority on English law. It is also true, as Thomas Maurice had said, 'To know Jones was to know the whole literary world'.[7] In fact Jones knew many prominent men in all walks of life, from Garrick to Fox. But his ambitions were not satisfied. He wished to be an eighteenth-century Cicero—a philosopher, statesman and scholar. The modest income from his profession was not enough to match his project. He complained that as a lawyer he must content himself 'with thorns without roses and with a very distant prospect of fruit'.[1] He was aware of this difficulty even before he started his career as a lawyer: 'The profession of the law, without some other is a tree that bears fruit only in twenty years.'[2] So Jones searched in high places for secure posts. Early in 1775 when he learned that Eden, the secretary to Lord Suffolk, was to resign, he immediately wrote to Lady Spencer asking her to use her influence to secure the post for him.[3] Again on 16 May 1775 when he heard at a dance that the duke of Devonshire wanted an auditor, he left the ball at 2 a.m. and wrote a long letter urging Lady Spencer to put in a good word for him.[4] Unfortunately he was not successful in gaining a post. His other 'courtier' friends like Lord Bathurst, or the duchess of Devonshire, failed to get a secure and lucrative post for him in England.

As an outsider he was unable to integrate fully into any circle, literary or political. Although he was enthusiastic about Johnson's club, he did not attend it regularly.[5] He was often tired of Johnson.[6] He wrote to Samuel Parr: 'My ideas of philology are so faded, and other habits of study begin so strongly to prevail, that I have no great pleasure in his conversation.' The political views of Johnson also strained their friendship: 'Captain Langton is one of the tallest men in the kingdom; but he and his Socrates, Dr Johnson have such prejudices in politics that one must be upon one's guard in their company if one wishes to preserve their good opinion.'[7] He was disappointed with Burke and considered him to be 'an angry man'. Likewise he told his friend that he was 'delighted' with his profession but was 'disgusted' with the professors, 'very few of whom have any publick principle or any view but that of exposing to sale in the best market their faculties and their voices'.[8]

Perhaps it was in desperation that in 1780 he made his unsuccessful attempt to gain a seat in Parliament to represent Oxford. So it was natural that he should look to an Indian judgeship, which was offered to him by Lord Bathurst in 1778, with a hope of seeing money and gaining prestige.

Although my professional gains are very handsome and are continually increasing, yet I must be twenty years in England before I can save as much as in India. I might easily by in five or six [*sic*]; and on my return (if it please God to permit me) I might still be a young man with thirty thousand pounds in my pocket. So I might proceed at the Bar or in Parliament with ease to myself and perhaps with advantage to others.[9]

CHAPTER 3

THE POET AND THE ORIENTALIST

Two forces ultimately led Jones to India. One was his ambitious character which made him wish to be independent of patronage. He left the Spencers, took up law to alleviate his financial difficulties, and tried to raise his social status by gaining a seat in Parliament. But, failing to gain much success in either of these pursuits, he turned to an Indian judgeship with a hope of saving money and gaining social prestige.[1] The other force which induced him to go East was his love of Oriental literature. He saw that he would have scope to improve his Oriental studies if he could live in an Asian country. As early as 1771 he expressed his desire to his friend Count Reviczki,[2]

whenever the war with Russia is at an end, I propose to making an open and direct application for the office of minister at Constantinople; at present I can only privately whisper my wishes. The king is very well disposed towards me; so perhaps are the men in power; and the Turkish company wish much to oblige me; all I have to apprehend is the appearance of some powerful competitor who may drive me off the stage. If I shall succeed in my wishes how shall I bound for joy! First I shall enjoy your company at Vienna, then I shall explore the Turkish manners in their most hidden sources.

Whether in fact he applied or not we do not know, but this letter shows that, as early as 1771, he entertained the idea of going East to improve his knowledge of Asian literature.

The period of thirteen years between 1770 and 1783 was very fruitful both in the number of works[3] produced and in gaining a recognition in literary circles. He wrote many works and at least nine of them were connected with Orientalism, and it was his fame as an Orientalist which made it easy for him to become a member of Johnson's exclusive literary club in 1773, and a Fellow of the Royal Society of London. So we should not attach much importance to the following rather dramatic statement,

but my friend the die is cast and I have no longer a choice, all my books and manuscripts with an exception of those only which relate to law and oratory are locked up at Oxford and I have determined for the next twenty years at least to renounce all studies but those which are connected with my profession.[1]

These years are in fact very important in the evaluation of Jones's ideas of the East and its culture and history, as they are related to his conception of history, culture and poetry in general.

We have already noticed how Jones was influenced by the works of Cicero, how he imitated his style of correspondence in his letters to his friends and how he modelled his life on the Roman statesman.[2] In his historical writings he also tried to follow the rules for the perfect historian, as laid down by Cicero in his treatise *On Oration*.[3] According to this, a historian should not only be truthful and free from bias, but also a shrewd judge of all public transactions, and should write elegantly and copiously. Jones realized that this was just an ideal 'to which the works of human genius are constantly tending, though like the logarithmick spiral, they will never meet the point to which they are infinitely approaching'.[4] This is the reason why no historian satisfies all the rules laid down by Cicero. Jones found that the very essence of history, 'truth', is not present in the writings of so many historians, ancient or modern, European or Asiatic—'which we can read without asking in almost every page, "is this true"?'. Most historians do not possess all the qualities that go to make a perfect one,

some of them are grave and judicious, some bold and impartial, others polished and elegant; but none of them seem to have possessed all those qualities, a perfect union of which is required in the character of a finished historian.[5]

Thus, though Herodotus was an example of a noble simplicity, his accounts of Persian affairs are 'at least doubtful if not fabulous'.[6] Thucydides on the other hand described facts which were in general 'authentick', and his observations were 'deep' and 'sagacious' but he wrote in a poor language.[7] The defective style of Tacitus, 'prevents us from considering him as a consummate historian though his wisdom and penetration would otherwise give him a just claim to that title'.[8] Among the moderns he found Voltaire most agreeable, 'his style is lively and spirited, his descriptions animated and striking, his remarks always ingenious, often deep', but his periods are not sufficiently expanded, he is inclined to unnecessary brevity and his wit is often ill-placed, 'he cannot give an abstract of the Newtonian philosophy without interspersing it with strokes of humour'.[1]

About Gibbon's *History of the Decline and Fall of the Roman Empire* he said, 'it is written in elegant and easy style but hath very little nerve or vigour'.[2]

Jones was well aware that, judged by Ciceronian standards of a complete historian, he himself could hardly claim the title of historian.

I am like the drop of water, in the fable of Sadi, which fell from a cloud into the sea, lost in the consciousness of its own insignificance. The chief merit of the book—[that is, his English version of the *History of the Life of Nader Shah*]—if it has any, consists in exhibiting in one view the transactions of sixty years in the finest part of Asia.[3]

This desire to write rather the essence of history than to give minute descriptions of facts is also reflected in his other works such as *A Short History of Persia, or The History of the Persian Language* or *A Prefatory Discourse to an Essay on the History of the Turks*.[4] *A Short History of Persia* was an abstract of the history of Persia, following the extinct plan of Atticus as mentioned by Cicero. In it Jones's aim was to catch the general and striking features of truth in history.[5] He discarded facts which he considered dull or false 'as nothing should be related merely because it is true if it be not instructive or entertaining'.[6] He divided the history of Persia into four periods, ruled by four celebrated dynasties. It seems implicit that Jones considered these the four most enlightened periods in history because they are connected with four stages in the growth of Persian literature.[7] In this respect he followed Voltaire and what Collingwood[8] called the 'historiography of the Enlightenment'. Like Voltaire Jones divided history into 'periods' and was interested more in the 'truth' or 'essence' in history than in the facts. The only facts which mattered in history were the instructive ones like the story of Sheik Sefi who by the use of his charms freed the Carmathian slaves from Timur.[9]

In the *Prefatory Discourse* to his proposed history of the Turks, he suggested

that among the numerous events which must be recorded in the general history of any nation, there are very few which seem capable of yielding either pleasure or instruction to the judicious reader who desires to be acquainted with past transactions, not because they have happened, but because he hopes to derive from them some useful lesson for the conduct of his life.[1]

To him, as to Voltaire, history was essentially the history of civil society; it has to deal with the manners and customs of the people.[2]

This *Short History* and the *History of the Persian Language* are full of errors and Jones did not live up to his own standard. He rejected the existence of any literature before the Sassanian kings and called the work of Anquetil Duperron fraudulent. This attack was originally made in a letter published anonymously in defence of the Orientalists of Oxford University.[3] It was renewed in his *History of the Persian Language*. It is now universally recognized that Jones was wrong in rejecting Anquetil Duperron's *Zend Avesta* and in not recognizing the existence of a pre-Sassanian Persian literature, and his attitude was not in the best of taste.[4] He rejected the historicity of Zoroaster not only because he was blinded by his dislike of Anquetil Duperron's attack on Oxford, but also because the theory did not fit in with his idea of history. In the first two periods the language was not polished, though the Persians were not entirely strangers to the art of composition either in verse or in prose, but it only reached maturity and elegance in the Sassanian period when an academy was founded in Gandisapor (a city in Khorasan).[5] One can trace a vague conception of evolution in this, a gradual growth of language from unpolished to polished; in this process, there are four landmarks making four distinct periods of history. He rejected Anquetil Duperron because he could not bear the idea that an elegant and ancient language could be actually spoken by people who did not lead an enlightened life:

From this we may reasonably conclude that the gibberish of these swarthy vagabonds whom we often see brooding over a miserable fire under the hedges may as well be taken for old Egyptian and the beggars themselves for the priests of Isis as the jugglers on the coast of India for the disciples of Zoroaster, and their barbarous dialect for the ancient language of Persia.[6]

From Cicero he also learnt to suspect the accumulation of power in one hand. This appealed to his rather rebellious nature and to his dislike of authority. He deplored the cult of great conquerors or warriors, as these men are not great by any standard, their achievements are the effect of the united effort of the multitude, wrongly attributed to one single person, and true virtue does not consist in destroying our fellow creatures but in protecting them, not in seizing their property but in defending their rights and liberties even at the hazard of our own safety.[1]

The boy who grew up to believe that life is not worth living without some tangible achievements and that death is preferable to a worthless life, did not consider love of power and territorial conquest as tangible achievements.[2] He praised the works of industry and mental ability rather than those of arms and power. This love of power together with a lust for dominion has filled the world with terror and misery from Sesostris,[3] who invaded Africa and Europe, to the

three mighty potentates who are ravaging Poland. How much more splendid would their glory have been if instead of raising their fame on the subversion of kingdoms they had applied their whole thoughts to the patronage of arts, science, letters, agriculture, trade; had made their nations more illustrious in wisdom, extensive in commerce, eminent in riches, firm in virtue, happy in freedom and had chosen rather to be benefactors than the destroyers of the human species.[4]

Since wars and military victories are insignificant and conquerors cannot be called great, one would have thought that the life of Nadir Shah would have been the last thing for Jones to translate.

In 1765 Carsten Niebuhr, the Danish traveller and writer, visited Shiraz. There he purchased a manuscript copy of *Tārīkh-i-Nādirī*, an official history written by Muhammad Mahdi. This manuscript was deposited at the Kongelige Bibliothek at Copenhagen.[5] During his visit in 1768 Christian VII, king of Denmark, brought this manuscript to England. He wanted an Englishman to translate it into French. The task fell upon Jones, who accepted it very reluctantly after declining it once, 'as it was hinted to him that this will be some mark of distinction to him, and above all it will be a reflection upon his country if the King should be obliged to carry the manuscript to France'.[6] The task could not have been as disagreeable as Shore's account, and Jones's own utterances in his letters[7] and works made out, as Jones brought out an English edition of the history in 1773, and in the French translation of 1770[8] there was no mention of his theory of history and his dislike of conquerors and warriors. In 1773 Jones stated in the preface to *The History of the Life of Nader Shah* that the idea that war and

39

military victories are insignificant, and the lives of the conquerors dull, should have deterred him from writing the history unless it had been for the sake of exposing the 'most infamously wicked' and of 'displaying the charms of liberty' by showing the 'odiousness of tyranny and oppression'. In this English version, which was mostly his own work based on Mahdi's *Tārīkh-i-Nādirī*, the main character does not appear to be the most 'infamously wicked' person and Jones only partially succeeded in showing the 'odiousness of tyranny and oppression'.[1]

Unlike a modern English historian, Jones did not find in the career of Nadir Shah an example of a peculiar 'characteristic of the East' which 'has been the periodic bursting forth (appearance is too mild a word) there of great conquerors who overran vast stretches of country ravaging, killing, and destroying'.[2] For Jones the territorial conquests, the ravaging, the killing and the destruction were not a specifically Eastern characteristic. These were common to any power anywhere, in Europe and Asia. He rather stressed the similarities among human civilizations than the differences. That is why he purposely played down the cruelties of Nadir Shah, and had no sympathy for the notion that despotism was peculiar to the Oriental nature. In this he was much nearer to Voltaire and other admirers of Asia, who believed that the Oriental system of state and society was similar to the European feudal system. Jones could not agree with Bernier and Montesquieu that Asia never experienced feudalism and private property.[3] He thought that India was ruled under some kind of feudalism[4] and he did not yet pronounce that Indians are precluded from the very idea of freedom.[5] In his *Essay on the Law of Bailments* he found that, in spite of differences in other respects, 'in the great system of contracts and the common intercourse between man and man, the "Pootee" of the Indians and the "Digest" of the Romans are by no means dissimilar'.[6] He further suggested that laws in every nation are based on the 'wisdom' of the ancients and 'natural reason'.[7]

Jones's Nadir does not appear to be an Oriental despot, an embodiment of absolute power who ruled without any respect for the populace and the nobility. He compares well with the European rulers in the art of war. Had he lived in better times he would have been a greater patron of arts and learning. Thus Jones's comment on Nadir's appointment of Indian musicians in Persia was, we cannot help admiring the remarkable disposition of this singular man, who with the fierceness of a warrior had yet a taste for the polite and ornamental arts, and while he was conquering the Empire, had the calmness to think of improving the musick of his own nation.[1]

Nadir was in fact his hero; his conquest of India is comparable to that of Alexander. He ransacked the country but treated the Mughal emperor and the princes of Sind mildly and installed them in their old positions.[2] Like Alexander he used the artifice of foreseeing victory in dreams to inspire his soldiers and officers.[3] This comparison between Alexander and Nadir Shah had already been made by earlier European writers on the subject.[4] But there is nothing to show that Jones had read these works, although he might have got the idea from Mahdi himself, who often compared Nadir with Sikandar Shah (Alexander) and Dara (Darius). Here his attitude can be contrasted with that of Vincent Smith. In Indian history, Smith made the Greek conqueror his hero and seized upon any opportunity he could to exaggerate the cruelties of the Eastern rulers and to prove that they ruled in a very despotic manner.[5] Jones, on the other hand, found Nadir no more or no less cruel than many of his European counterparts. When he described how Nadir gave orders to tear out the eyes of one of his sons who conspired against him, Jones's only comment was that this action was a 'common but inhuman punishment for high crimes in Asia'.[6] Jones's Nadir had a mission in life, which was to be the 'deliverer of Persia' and the 'conqueror of India'.[7]

If we throw a veil over his latter years in which he was rather to be pitied than condemned, we shall see nothing in his life but what was noble and laudable, he had neither the rashness of Alexander, the indefatigable ambition of Caesar, the inflexible obstinacy of Charles the Twelfth, nor the wiles of his illustrious rival, Peter the Great, he resembled rather that real hero Gustavus Vasa, who to use the words of an excellent writer 'left the forest where he lay concealed and came to deliver his country'.[8]

But like all military victories Nadir's conquests were in vain, and after his death Persia was left in a worse mess than before: 'such are the fruits of military glory and such the state of those kingdoms whose rulers prefer the pride of conquest to the calmer joys of peace and to the welfare of their people.'[9]

If in his historical works Jones followed the familiar eighteenth-century model of history with the emphasis on style and 'truth', then his attitudes towards Asia were shaped according to the standard set by the French *philosophes*. He read Voltaire assiduously,[1] he was well acquainted with the work of Diderot and the contributors to the *Encyclopédie*. He particularly admired Voltaire, whom he quoted in his works, and tried to meet the old philosopher on one occasion.[2] He described him as one 'who excells all writers of his age and country in the elegance of his style and the wonderful variety of his talents'.[3]

Many modern scholars have considered Jones as a precursor of the Romantic movement. It is easy to detect a love for the simple life, a yearning for the primitive and a search for the noble savage in his early writings on the Arabs.[4] He admired the Arabs, for they had been able to retain the simplicity of their ancestors for three thousand years, and they were never subdued by another nation. Arabia, he claimed, was the only country left in the world which was simple, free and happy, especially since the Mughal conquest of Kashmir. He was charmed by the seven Arab poets, with their nomadic life, violent love, and thrilling adventures, and 'the dramatic pastoral poems'.[5] This passion for the simplicity of tribal life is understandable in November 1780, when Jones had lost all his chances to win a seat in Parliament. 'In these rambles into the wilds of Asia I soften the anguish which I feel whenever I reflect on the melancholy times in which we live.'[6]

It would be natural for a man with Jones's temperament to be attracted towards the uncommon and towards a mode of life entirely different to that of Europe. But he would not share the same enthusiasm for the 'spiritual' India as some of the nineteenth-century Romantic intellectuals had.[7] He was no lover of the 'irrational', nor did he think that the most 'happy and free' Arabs were to be emulated by the Europeans. He had already read Rousseau's works and found them 'wonderfully absurd'.[8] His love and sympathy for the Arabs was shared by Gibbon, a man who could hardly be called a Romantic.[9]

It is not easy to draw a clear line between the men of the Enlightenment and those of the Romantic movement, especially in their attitudes towards non-European cultures. It was Candide, the hero of Voltaire's famous novel, who went in search of happiness outside Europe, but his creator had no urge for the 'primitive'. On the other hand modern research has shown that Rousseau was no such 'primitivist' as his English followers took him to be.[1]

In the eighteenth century literary ideas were determined by neo-classical tenets; the epics dominated the field of poetry, art was considered to be imitative and there was a tremendous emphasis on style and decorum. However from the middle of the century a new trend could be noticed; Edmund Burke in his *Philosophical Inquiry into the Origin of our Ideas of the Sublime* discarded imitation:

poetry and rhetoric do not succeed in exact description so well as painting does; their business is to affect rather by sympathy than imitation, to display rather the effect of things on the mind of the speaker of others than to put a clear idea of things themselves.[2]

The second half of the eighteenth century saw a gradual shift of emphasis from style to feeling at least in poetry. Jones in 1772 followed Burke: in his Essay 'on the arts commonly called imitative', which was appended to his *Poems Consisting chiefly of Translations from the Asiatick languages*, he attacked the traditional Aristotelian concept that art should imitate nature. To Jones poetry and music have a 'nobler origin':

It seems probable (then) that poetry was originally no more than a strong and animated expression of the human passions of joy and grief, love and hate, admiration and anger, sometimes pure and unmixed sometimes variously modified and combined.[3]

This he found true in every nation. In fact he went further than Burke and other English authors and installed lyric as the centre of poetry. In this he was closer to Herder and Leopardi.[4]

His poem 'A Persian song of Hafiz' which first appeared in his *Grammar* and was later published in his *Poems* gave him a place among the minor eighteenth-century poets. It was undoubtedly a forerunner of the Romantic movement. It had all the qualities, subjectivity, emotion, reference to uncommon names and far-away places which appealed to the Romantic poets like Southey and Byron,

> Sweet maid, if thou would'st charm my sight,
> And bid these arms thy neck infold;
> That rosy cheek, that lily hand,
> Would give thy poet more delight
> Than all Bokhara's vaunted gold,
> Than all the gems of Samarcand.

A similar Romantic trend could be noticed in his other occasional poems 'To the nymph of the spring', or 'The damsels of Cardigan'

> No longer then pore over dark gothic pages,
> To cull a rude gibberish from Neathen or Brooke,
> Leave your books and parchments to greybearded sages,
> Be nature and love, and fair woman, our book.

But it would be a mistake to portray Jones as a Romantic poet. In the same volume where he published his 'Persian song' he published his 'An ode to Petrarch', 'Laura', an 'Elegy from Petrarch', and 'Arcadia', which show marks of the eighteenth-century neo-classical spirit.[1] His rather popular poem 'Caissa or the Game of Chess' was written in imitation of Ovid, and he planned to write an epic, in classical fashion, called 'The Britain Discovered'. In his *Poems* he was still faithful to the classical standards: 'I am convinced that whatever changes we make in our opinions, we always return to the writings of the ancients as to the standard of true taste.'[2] So, although he had advanced new ideas on art and literature and some of his poems were no doubt forerunners of the Romantic Movement, his literary opinions and tastes were for the most part of the eighteenth-century world. He may be described as Burke has been described, as 'a classicist who appealed to nature before the rules'.[3]

At this stage Jones was only eager to make Asia appear more acceptable to Europe. Hence the emphasis on the similarities between the two cultures. So Nadir was no more cruel than many European rulers and the political system in Asia was not dominated by tyrannical despotism. Asia had also produced a great civilization, rich in literature and art: 'it is certain (to say no more) that the poets of Asia have as much genius as ourselves.'[4] They have a Homer in Firdusi, a Virgil in Hafiz, and some of the Persian songs have a striking resemblance to the sonnets of Petrarch'.[5] To Jones poetry was originally 'a strong and animated expression of the human passions',[6] pure and unmixed. So the finest parts of the poetry, music, and painting 'are expressions of the passions and operate on our minds by sympathy'.[7] In this the Asian mind is most fertile. The climate and the environment in Asia enable the Asiatics to write poetry with passion and animation. Thus Yemen is the 'only country in the world in which we can lay the scene of pastoral poetry', because 'no nation at this day can vie with the

Arabians in the delightfulness of their climate, and the simplicity of their manners'.[1] Persia too possesses a mild and temperate climate and the Persians have much leisure to write fine poetry. The Persians sleep on the rooftops and observe 'the figures of the constellations and the various appearances of the heavens',[2] and this may in some measure account for the use of allusions in their poetry to the heavenly bodies. Voltaire thought that these were examples of the bad taste of the Asiatics, but they only show 'that every nation has a set of images and expressions peculiar to itself which arise from the differences of its climate, manners, and history'.[3]

The manner of life also helps in producing sublime poetry. Thus Persia has produced more writers of every kind but chiefly poets, than all Europe put together, 'since their way of life cannot be cultivated to advantage without the greatest calmness and serenity of mind'.[4] The Arabs have not only climatic advantages and natural beauty but they have been able to retain the simplicity of their ancestors for three thousand years. What he regretted most was the lack of general interest in Asia, which was considered to be strange and remote,

The very sound of which, they say, conveys the idea of something savage, but they would be at a loss to assign a reason why the Aras and Forat are words less melodious than Dnieper and the Bogh...the accounts of the northern kings are read with pleasure, are thought to abound with a variety of interesting events, while the historians of the East are neglected and the Asiatick languages considered as inharmonious and inelegant.[5]

In his *Grammar* he lamented that there was no Medici family to encourage Oriental learning to usher in a new renaissance in Europe.[6] Asian poetry can revitalize European literature, which has subsisted too long on the perpetual repetition of the same images and the incessant allusions to the same fables. He thought that Firdusi might be versified as easily as the *Iliad* and he saw no reason 'why the delivery of Persia by Cyrus should not be a subject as interesting to us as the anger of Achilles or the wanderings of Ulysses'.[7] Earlier he had put forward similar arguments in his 'Traité sur la poésie orientale' and *Dissertation sur la Litérature Orientale*, and he came back to it again in 1774 in his Latin work *Poeseos Asiaticae comentariorum*. He further argued that Asian studies have some pragmatic value for the Europeans. Thus the study of Asian history gives insight into European history, showing, for instance, how the career of Nadir Shah affected the affairs of Europe.

If Persia had not been delivered by this daring genius, the Russians would still have possessed the rich provinces, which border on the Caspian lake, we would, no doubt, have attacked the Turks on the side of Georgia, which might have given them the dominion of the Black Sea and might have opened a passage to Constantinople itself,

or

If India had not been drained of its treasures in 1738, the Mughul Empire would not have been weakened and divided, the Nawabs or Viceroys would not have declared themselves independent of the Emperor, and consequently our settlements on the Ganges would still have depended for protection on the court of Delhi.[1]

In this period Jones's knowledge of India was not very sound. His chief sources were European works on India. He drew heavily on Herbelot's *Bibliothèque Orientale*, Dow's *History of Hindostan* and Robert Orme's work on wars in India, which he persuaded his young pupil and his sister to read. Among the Persian works on India he read the *Babur Nāma*, *Akbar Nāma* and Haidar Ali's work on Kashmir. The Persian author wrote some eighty-four pages on the pre-Muslim history of Kashmir and took that part largely from Kalhāna's *Rājataraṅgiṇī*.[2]

In Jones's *Description of Asia* the part of India was taken mostly from Herbelot's article on Hend (India). He divided India into three parts as Herbelot did, and put Assam as a part of the Malayan peninsula. He thought that the word Porus signified a town and that Sanskrit had become like Greek 'to be respected rather than known'.[3] In his description of the Gangetic valley he followed Herbelot almost line for line; 'all the territories were governed by Rai's or Rajas, who held their lands of a supreme lord called Balhar, the seat of whose residence was the city of Cannouge, now in ruins'.[4] From this he concluded that 'the ancient system of government which prevailed [in India] was perfectly feudal'.[5]

It seems that he took very little interest in India until he thought of going there as judge in 1778. In May 1777 he was approached by R. Griffiths, the editor of *Monthly Review*, to review his friend Halhed's book *The Gentoo Laws*. Jones declined: 'I am so totally engaged in forensick occupations and professional studies that I have not even time to read my friend's work much less to review it.'[1] He had only a very vague idea of pre-Muslim India, which was a 'dark period' to him, for, though India produced the fables of Bidpai and invented the game of chess, she had no poetry. The Mughals carried Persian poetry to India and 'the Indian poets to this day compose their verses in imitation of them'.[2] He had no sympathy for Indians:

The Indians are soft and voluptuous, but artful and insincere, at least to the Europeans, whom, to say the truth, they have no great reason of late years to admire for the opposite virtues.[3]

When in 1778 he was offered a post of judgeship in India by Lord Bathurst, the Chancellor, who had already made him a Commissioner of the Bankrupts in 1776, Jones turned his attention to India. He listened carefully to the debates on India and studied the laws of the country. Soon he came to be recognized as an authority on India. Burke invited him to breakfast to discuss the Bengal Bill: 'The natives of the East, to whose literature you have done so much justice, are particularly under your protection for their rights.'[4] There were others besides Burke who thought the same about Jones:

I have for a week or ten days passed, been an assiduous attendant in your gallery on the different India Bills, principally that concerning the Bengal judicature, on which I have been consulted by the promoters and the opposers of it. I have steered a middle course, as I really think parts of the bill wise and salutary, though I have strong objections to other parts, many amendments have been made and one whole clause struck out on my remonstrance.[5]

Like many Englishmen of the age Jones had little sympathy for the East India Company. He shared the general suspicion that British rule in India might corrupt 'freedom-loving' Britons and endanger freedom in Britain. In Pembrokeshire in the summer of 1780, he saved a man who was prosecuted for raising a false alarm. One of the two magistrates who prosecuted the man 'was an Indian' (meaning an Englishman from India). In his speech Jones mingled 'many bitter reflections on the state of his country at the time of the alarm, and on the attempt...to import the Indian laws into England by imprisoning and indicting an honest man'.[6] Such sentiments can be traced in his marginal notes on Orme's copy of

The Extract of a Letter from the Governor and Council at Fort William to the Court of Directors.[1] In this letter, Hastings suggested that the children of criminals should be enslaved to eradicate crime in India as in that country the 'slaves are treated as the children of the families to which they belong, and often acquire a happier state by their slavery than they could have hoped by the enjoyment of liberty'. Jones commented, 'this is the most spurious argument for despotism which all despots use'.

He looked forward to going to India, to be able to mitigate the misery of the Indians, to purchase Oriental books and manuscripts, and to earn enough to be able to return to England to live independently.[2]

CHAPTER 4

MR JONES—'A STAUNCH WHIG, BUT VERY WRONGHEADED'

John Shore, in his efforts to depict Jones as an Evangelical hero, an embodiment of public and private virtues, either deliberately suppressed Jones's political views or made them acceptable to the establishment of his time.[1] Professor Arberry and others, during the bicentenary celebration of his birth, have done a great deal to undo this whitewashing by Shore. But so far no attempt has been made to assess the political ideas of Jones against the background of the eighteenth-century reform movement. Arberry, after considering a few quotations from some unpublished correspondence, came to the conclusion that Jones was not guilty of being a republican 'in the literal sense of the term'.[2] But it seems such judgements are superfluous as, in the eighteenth century, republicanism did not exclude monarchy. In fact the classical republicanism of the extreme Whigs was easily reconciled with the Hanoverian dynasty.[3] To most, the term 'republic' meant the body politic as such, and not a form of government. Jones himself confessed that he was 'no more republican than a Mahomedan or a Gentoo'.[4] To his contemporaries Jones was known either as a 'staunch Whig but very wrongheaded'[5] or as an eighteenth-century leveller.[6] Later critics in the nineteenth century complained that his political writings lack philosophical capacity and deal mostly with particulars rather than things general.[7] What follows is an attempt to evaluate Jones's political ideas against the eighteenth-century background. We hope to examine Jones's views on the basis of civil society, the nature of law and limited democracy in relation to his intellectual heritage, and the circle of reformers with whom he was in contact.

The origins of the eighteenth-century radical movement can be traced in the popular discontent in the metropolitan area during the last decades of the reign of George II. This discontent was further stimulated by the so-called 'Palace Revolution' in 1761 and it gained momentum during the troubled years of 1768 with John Wilkes and the Middlesex election. In the early stage of the movement its aims were ill-defined and its organization inarticulate. But since 1769 the people connected with it began to display dissatisfaction with the existing political institutions, and in the early seventies of the century the dissatisfaction took a definite shape in the form of a political programme.[1] The movement included not only the 'country party' and the city merchants, whose opposition to the government was traditional, but also the freeholders and the unenfranchised 'lower orders' of society, the type of people who had hitherto taken little interest in politics. But, apart from the fact that they all felt a certain antipathy towards the crown for its 'undue influence', the reformers had very little in common. In fact they often held contradictory views on the nature of reform and on the ways of achieving it. The customary division for the reformers between the 'economic' and the 'political' was illogical, but they could be broadly divided into two groups, moderates and extremists.

There were again various types of moderates. There were those who agreed with Burke that purely economic reform, such as the reduction of the civil list, would curtail the 'undue influence' of the crown and safeguard the independence of parliament, and others like Shelburne and the younger Pitt who suggested additional county representation as the remedy for the discontent.[2] There was yet another group led by Christopher Wyvill and tacitly supported by Charles James Fox. Wyvill advocated economic reforms such as the elimination of placemen from the House of Commons as a measure to reduce the influence of the crown, but also thought that by shortening the duration of parliaments and increasing the representation from the counties the nation could guarantee its safety against the corrupting influence of the executive.[3] Almost all of them rejected universal suffrage.

It was a group of extremists which consisted of men like John Wilkes, Richard Price, John Cartwright, John Jebb and Charles Lennox, the third duke of Richmond, who advocated both universal suffrage and annual parliaments. They appealed to the 'inferior' set of people to 'restore' their 'natural right' to share in the legislature. They identified the English struggle against tyranny with the American efforts for independence. Most of the extremists belonged to the Society for Constitution Information which was founded by John Cartwright in April 1780 to propagate the cause of parliamentary reform.[4]

They considered themselves as the 'real' or 'honest' Whigs carrying on the tradition of fighting against tyranny and for toleration, individual freedom and the natural rights. Their ideas were shaped according to the basic tenets set out by the seventeenth-century political thinkers and by the political experience of the civil war and the 'glorious revolution' of 1688.[1]

It seems natural that Jones should be attracted towards this group of 'real' Whigs. He shared with Richard Price and his friends their enthusiasm for Englishmen's liberty, faith in Reason, an admiration for classical republicanism and the veneration for John Locke, Milton and other seventeenth-century political thinkers. The study of the classical literature and the Roman laws made him an admirer of the 'ancient statesmen' and the political system of Athens and Rome. In Cicero he discovered a fighter against tyranny and oppression. He never forgave Augustus for the death of Cicero and the death of the Roman Republic: 'I have not Christian charity for him.'[2]

In his *Oration*, which he was unable to deliver to Oxford in 1773, he described Locke's *Treatise on Government* as a 'perpetual testimony of his wisdom, learning, virtue and a full confutation of the audacious charge against men of letters, that instead of being friends of liberty they are flatterers of power and high priests of oppression'.[3] John Milton was also one of the 'greatest men' 'who ever adorned this island'.[4] On 5 December 1779 he dined with Captain Langton, but Jones was cold to him since Langton abused liberty and Milton: 'whom of all men I most admire'.[5] The political arguments were further sharpened by his own complex personality and by his mother, who encouraged his passion for liberty. The boy who was brutally punished by a rather sadistic master grew up to fear uncontrolled power in one person: 'Distrust in power is the very nerve of wisdom',[6] he once told his friend.

He came to know the radicals at Bishop Shipley's house, where the friends of parliamentary reform and the American cause used to meet. He was not a formal member of any of the reform organizations until 1782 when he was elected as an honorary member of the Society for Constitutional Information.[7] But he had always been sympathetic to its cause ever since it was born in 1780,[8] and he was in close touch with the Cartwrights, especially Edmund the inventor of the power loom, who was a co-student of Jones in

4-2

Oxford. He knew Wilkes, although he did not always agree with him and was shocked by his morals.[1] He was also a friend of Price and Priestley, he shared their political and religious views and worked as their emissary carrying messages and books to and from Benjamin Franklin and other Americans living in France.[2] He was connected with the County Association Movement and addressed their meetings although he did not agree with their plans:

I wish the associated counties, instead of stooping to petty reformations in the King's kitchen, would insist on the saving of millions of guineas and myriads of lives by a speedy union with America.[3]

In 1779 he had already suggested to Althorp and Pitt that 'the young supporters of liberty' should form a union to defend the Constitution: 'That is the only hope for England.'[4] Later in 1780 he thought it would be a mistake to drop petitions.[5]

However, he made very little direct impact on the movement. His plan[6] for peace in America had no relevance to the realities of war and politics there. Similarly his plan for the English militia was too radical even for his friends. But he still deserves a place in the history of the reform movement and the history of political ideas. This was largely due to his most controversial and most popular pamphlet, *The Principles of Government*.

In summer 1782 William Jones went to France, with his friend John Paradise. They wanted to proceed to America, where Jones would help Paradise in some property dispute and have an opportunity to see for himself the new state where he had been invited to settle. But John Paradise was a weak man; he was afraid to make the arduous journey across the Atlantic, and backed out at the last moment. Jones had no alternative but to postpone his much desired visit to the States. However, this last visit to France was an important landmark in his life. During this trip he had another chance to meet his old friend Benjamin Franklin in Paris. Through Franklin he also met Vergennes, the French Minister. At Franklin's house in Paris one evening the three entered into a political argument in which Jones maintained that 'the first principles of government could be made intelligible to plain illiterate readers' [*sic*].[7] This Vergennes thought impossible, and Franklin was doubtful about it. Jones was prompted to write a pamphlet on the principles of government in the form of a Socratic dialogue, between a fictitious scholar and a fictitious peasant. The scholar asks the peasant to sign a petition for parliamentary reform. His arguments are based within the framework of the peasant's terms of reference; so the village club is compared to the state. After reading the pamphlet, Franklin and Vergennes agreed with Jones that the first principles of government can be made simple enough to be understood by common folk. But this pamphlet *The Principles of Government* which Jones later described as a mere *jeu d'esprit*, did more than prove his point in an argument.[1] The Society for Constitutional Information found that many of their ideas, for example the active participation of the citizens in state affairs and the people's choice in the formation of the legislative branch of government, were echoed in this pamphlet, and what is more they were put very clearly. Therefore the Society published ten thousand copies of the pamphlet and distributed them gratis.[2] Some idea of the popularity of the *Dialogue* may be obtained from the number of editions published. There were in fact nine editions, one of which was published by John Cartwright, the radical reformer.[3] *The Principles of Government* was one of the most influential books of the movement for parliamentary reform in the late eighteenth and early nineteenth centuries, and so gave Jones an undeniable position in the history of the reform movement. However, though the pamphlet contained sufficient explosives to invite the wrath of the conservatives of the day, and so made it all the more popular among the reformers, it would not have been quite so popular had it not been given involuntary publicity by Fitzmaurice, the sheriff of Flintshire, who took upon himself the task of defending the good cause of loyalty towards the King and God.

He prosecuted the Rev. William Shipley, the dean of St Asaph, a friend of Jones and later his brother-in-law, when in 1783 the dean published an edition of the *Dialogue* in Flintshire. The trial that followed was a long-drawn-out affair, but the dean was finally acquitted of the charge of publishing a libellous pamphlet on 16 November 1784, largely through Thomas Erskine, the lawyer for the defence, who successfully arrested the judgement against Shipley.[4] The success of Erskine and Shipley was celebrated throughout the country with bonfires and illuminations especially at Twyford, where Bishop Shipley was living at the moment.[5]

The historians of English law have rightly shown how this trial focused the public attention to the problems of trial by jury

Conftitutional Information.

At a Meeting of a new Society for *propagating* Conftitutional Principles, lately held at G------, in the County of D------, Mrs. *****, a certain jolly, Epifcopal Newfmonger in that Neighbourhood, having been unanimoufly voted into an eafy Chair, the following Refolutions were propofed and carried, nem. con. viz.

RESOLVED, That the Letter figned *Veritas*, lately publifhed in the Chefter Chronicle, contains too true a Reprefentation of the Dean of St. Afaph's triumphal Entry into the County of Denbigh; and that every poffible Means be ufed by the Members of this Society to induce the Public to difbelieve the Facts therein ftated.

Refolved, That the *Denbigh 'Squire*, the Grand Puffer, Fabricator, and *Retailer* General of Falfehoods, to this Society, having in a Letter fome Time fince publifhed under the Signature of Philo-Juris, attempted to make the Public believe that *fome Thoufands* of real and independent Gentlemen had attended the Dean's Cavalcade; and it being too well known in the County, that only *One* Gentleman of that Defcription, and of *Refpect and Underftanding*, attended upon that Occafion, and he only for a few Minutes; it is become abfolutely neceffary to have another Account publifhed, which will have a little more the Appearance of Truth, and confequently be more likely to be credited, viz. that the Number of the Dean's Attendants amounted only to *Five Hundred*, confifting of Hirelings, Reverend Dependants, and Gentlemen Butchers of the Diocefe of St. Afaph, with Bob Knock at their Head.

Refolved, That no Pains be fpared by the Members of this Society, to invent fuch Falfehoods as may have a Chance of throwing a Stigma upon all thofe who have had any Hand in the Profecution, particularly the Honourable and truly loyal Character, who fo confcientioufly difcharged his Duty as Sheriff, in inftituting the Profecution; the fixteen refpectable Grand Jurymen, who found the Bill at Wrexham; the twelve refpectable Characters who ferved as Special Jurors upon the Trial of the Indictment at Shrewfbury, when the Dean was found *Guilty*; and the two learned and much refpected Judges who prefided at the Hearing of the Bufinefs at both thofe Places.

The *Motions* for the above Refolutions were *firft* made to the Chair by Capt. *Bob-adil*; and feconded by ------ of St. A----. *They* were *carried* without a diffenting Voice, when the Meeting at laft broke up, but with Liberty for the *Members* to have a private Audience with, and free Accefs *into*, the Chair, upon *Conftitutional Principles*, whenever a convenient Opportunity offers.

Signed by Order of the Meeting,

MAJOR *WOODCOCK*, Sec.

N. B. The gallant C----- was *faft afleep* when thefe feveral *Motions were made*; but it is well known that he never yet has taken, nor is he ever likely to take, a very *active* Part in *Conftitutional Struggles*.

54

Two examples (see also facing page) from the Thomas Pennant collection at the National Library of Wales of contemporary publications satirizing the rejoicing on Shipley's return

in cases of libel and how this eventually led Charles James Fox to introduce a bill in 1792 which gave the jury the right to decide on the libellous tendency of a thing published.[1] The far-reaching effect of the trial on the legal history of England has somewhat overshadowed the importance of the pamphlet and its author in the history of the movement for parliamentary reform. But to his contemporaries the contents of the pamphlet and the political views of the author were important and familiar. The Society for Constitutional Information took a keen interest in the trial, as they appointed Erskine to defend Shipley. To the Society the defence of Shipley was the defence of their cause. They circulated an advertisement defending the contents of the tract at Wrexham, where the trial was originally going to take place. The radicals upheld Jones's ideas as an expression of political wisdom; one edition of his works was brought out after the notorious Peterloo Massacre to prove the prudence of Jones's political philosophy, which, if accepted, would avoid such occurrences.[2] The fame that Jones gained as an Orientalist was useful to the radicals. They made him an honorary member of the Society; John Cartwright in 1820 cited his friendship with Jones to prove the respectability of his early activities.[3] Sir William Jones was equally recognized as a figure to be reckoned with by those who disagreed with him. Josiah Tucker, dean of Gloucester, who had already made his rather unusual viewpoints known, as he had dared to challenge Locke, the patron saint of eighteenth-century Whiggish radicalism,[4] was prompted to write a sequel to Jones's *Dialogue* to prove the dangerous nature of its views.

It was rather the boldness and simplicity of Jones's style than any originality of thought which made his works so popular. Even by eighteenth-century standards Jones's frankness and independence of character were remarkable. When he wrote his famous *Dialogue* he put the ideas that were already prevalent among most eighteenth-century reformers, simply and boldly, without much thought for the consequences. Consider the following quotation:

Scholar:... recollect your opinion about your club in the village and tell me what ought to be the consequence, if the King alone was to insist on making laws or altering them at his will and pleasure. Peasant: He too must be expelled. Scholar: Oh! but think of his standing army, and of the militia, which now are his in substance though ours in form. Peasant: If he were to employ that force against the nation they would and ought to resist him or the state would cease to be a state...We ought always therefore to be ready, and keep each of us a strong firelock in the corner of his bedroom.[1]

Surely this in itself would sound most revolutionary in the eighteenth-century context, and the prosecution made much of it during the trial. In the innuendoes of the Indictment it was suggested that the king in the pamphlet meant the king of England, hence the tract called upon the people to arm and rise against the king.

In fact in this pamphlet Jones was trying to establish his concept of state and law. To him, the state consists of the whole community living in it. This is a free society where the people are assembled freely 'to be as merry as they can without hurting themselves or their neighbours but chiefly to relieve their wants'.[2] In this respect it is comparable to a village club where the residents of the village assemble freely and are governed by a set of equal rules agreed upon by the members. The president and other officers are elected by the members of the club and they, like the other members of the community, are subject to the set of rules. This was undoubtedly the Lockian civil society where the king and the community had entered into a social contract. Jones agreed with Locke that originally there was a social contract, but it was an 'implied' contract and the individual had 'the right of removing from one community and becoming [a] member of another, whenever the first shall cease to deserve the name of country'.[3]

In his poem 'An ode in imitation of Alcaeus' Jones put his conception of state and law in the form of verse:

> Men who their duties know
> But know their rights, and, knowing, dare maintain,
> Prevent the long aimed blow,
> And crush the tyrant while they rend the chain.
> These constitute a state,
> And sovereign law, that state's collected will,
> O'er thrones and globes elate,
> Sits Empress, crowning good; repressing ill;[4]

The state consists of the whole people and the law is the aggregate will of the people and not the wish of a sovereign: 'I differ from Blackstone, he defines law "a rule prescribed by a superior power". I define it the will of the whole community as far as it can be collected with convenience.'[1] The aggregate will of the people is the supreme authority; King, Lords and the Commons are all ruled by it:

I am delighted with the reflection that you should so early be warmed with the flame of genuine patriotism and declare your opposition to all power not deduced from its true fountains, the will of the aggregate community which alone is and ought to be called law.[2]

Jones had admired Blackstone, he recommended his works to his pupil[3] and probably he had attended his lectures at Oxford. But with years the two began to differ:

Sir William Blackstone whose learning, taste and judgment I admire, though I cannot harmonise with him in his ideas of laws in general was here yesterday and seemed much out of order.[4]

However it should be noted that Jones criticized Blackstone not on utilitarian grounds as did Gibbon[5] and Bentham, but on the nature of the final authority of law in a society.

To Blackstone, law

in its most general and comprehensive sense signifies a rule of action, and is applied indiscriminately to all kinds of actions...And it is the rule of action which is prescribed by some superior and which the inferior is bound to obey.[6]

Blackstone recognized that there were two foundations of human law, the law of nature and the law of revelation, but he also admitted that the Creator did not only lay down the rules, he had also enabled 'human reason to discover' them 'so far as they are necessary for the conduct of human actions'.[7] So far Jones would not disagree; he would perhaps stress the importance of 'natural reason' as a foundation of all good laws.[8] But he disagreed with Blackstone when the Professor of Law decided that the function of civil law could only be guaranteed by a self-perpetuating sovereign to which all men had originally agreed. Man was

formed for society and he is neither capable of living alone nor indeed has the courage to do it. So he is assembled in society where municipal or civil law governs. This law is a rule of civil conduct prescribed by the supreme power in a state commending what is right prohibiting what is wrong.[9]

Men in civil society cannot live without a supreme power, for though the state is a collective body of a multitude of individuals the will and inclinations of those individuals are so diverse that they cannot be 'disposed into a uniform will of the whole'. So men submit all their will to a superior power who prescribed the 'rule of civil conduct' which is law.[1]

This idea of state and law clearly stems from the Hobbesian fear of disorder and Blackstone agreed that a self-perpetuating sovereign was essential for an orderly society. Jones disagreed and went rather to John Locke and his theory of social contract. Like the village club the state is governed by law, the collective will of the people. This will is not expressed by a group of people in a given day but is handed down to them through the ages as a heritage from forefathers whose wisdom and reason have approved such a set of rules. This collected will of the people is the real sovereign:

The papers of this morning ascribe to you many noble sentiments but they put into your mouth one word, one only, which I must be frank enough to say I cannot approve. I mean sovereign as applied to the king. Now the king is constitutionally (that is in the old sense derived from the abrogated feudal relation) our lord, but legislature only is our sovereign. Shakespeare and the liturgy are equal authority in this case that is, of no authority. I speak as a constitution lawyer.[2]

The king ought to obey the true sovereign, the law. If he violates the law the people have a right to expel him, and if he employs force to perpetuate his position the people shall use force in reply. Hence they should be prepared and learn to use firelocks. Jones never thought that this could be interpreted as seditious and create such a stir. He wrote to a friend: 'Had I dreamt that the dialogue would have made such a stir I would certainly have taken more pains with it.'[3]

The counsel for the prosecution in the case against Shipley thought otherwise; he attacked the *Dialogue* for it had asked the farmer not to uphold the 'sound doctrine' of fearing God and honouring the King, but on the contrary to defy authority.[4] Erskine on the other hand maintained that

if any one sentence from the beginning to the end of it is seditious or libellous, the Bill of Rights (to use the language of the advertisement prefixed to it) was seditious libel; the Revolution was wicked rebellion, the existing government is a traitorous conspiracy against the hereditary monarchy of England; our sovereign whose title I am persuaded we are, all of us, prepared to defend with our own blood, is an usurper of the crown of these kingdoms.[5]

What the counsel were debating here was clearly an important part of eighteenth-century political polemics. The question was whether the 1688 Revolution established the right of the people to choose their own government and resist and expel if need be an oppressive monarch. To Jones and to the early radicals it did, but to men like Dean Tucker it only established a new dynasty. According to the dean

the government is indisputably the ordinance of God, for the benefit of mankind; in that sense it is *jure divino*, and therefore ought never to be attempted to be annihilated or even to be rendered too excessively weak and impotent as not to be able to answer those good ends which providence had graciously proposed.[1]

Richard Price raised the question of the king's status again during the French Revolution; in his last sermon he maintained that the English king 'is the only lawful king in the world because the only one who owes crown to the choice of the people'.[2] This provoked Burke to write his *Reflections* attacking the doctrine of popular choice and Thomas Paine gave his reply to Burke in his famous tract the *Rights of Man*.

However, it would be a mistake to portray Jones as a revolutionary who wanted to do away with monarchy and nobility. It is true that some of his contemporaries thought he did:

The flame of liberty burns very ardently in his mind and has I fear consumed everything monarchical or aristocratical it found there. I do not, I own, like to part with king or nobles and of course differ a little with Sir William as to the present European politics.[3]

No doubt he sympathized with the French and the Americans who armed themselves to throw away tyrannical systems:

I say nothing of politics except that I heartily wish success to the French and Flemings and should depart in peace from this world if I see an end of all tyrannies which laziness and vices of nations have suffered to be established in it.[4]

He also thought that Burke's *Reflections* was 'weak' and 'wicked'.[5] But Jones was not willing to part with monarchy or nobility. He did not attempt to establish a democratic form of government. He had firm faith in 'mixed government' and in the English constitution. To him the 'true spirit of the constitution' was in the English Common Law, which was the 'collected wisdom of many

centuries, having been used and approved by successive generations'.[1] So the collected will of the people was not the same as
Rousseau's General Will. He might have borrowed the phrase
from Rousseau since he had read the French philosopher's works.[2]
But Jones identified 'the collected will of the people' with the
common laws and in this he shared the general eighteenth-century
veneration for common laws.[3] Edward Coke had, in the seventeenth
century, successfully created a myth that the common laws had
remained unchanged since the days of the ancient Britons, and
hence the common laws are the ultimate authority on constitutional
matters.[4] Jones agreed with this view but he tried to read his own
views on 'nearly universal suffrage' and 'the balance of powers' in
the common laws. He claimed that he did not carry his 'system' to
law but had 'found it in law'.[5]

This law and constitution have to be defended since the king of
England had misused his prerogatives and was threatening the
very existence of 'our Republic'—the English constitution. Against
such tyranny the vigilant citizens should gather to defend liberty:

Let you and me therefore be Philosophers now and then but citizens
always; let us sometimes observe with eagerness the satellites of Jupiter
but let us incessantly watch with jealousy the satellites of the King.[6]

This vigilance was to

prevent the introduction among us of a government similar to that of
France or Russia, for which England is almost ripe. Let no man talk
to me of a mild monarchy. I will not be governed by a single man
whatever.[7]

He shared the Whig view that the aim of George III was to usurp
power and wreck the Constitution. To him, as to most Whigs and
the king, the English Constitution was the *summum bonum* of
human wisdom and aspiration for political liberty since the days of
Athens and Rome:

The original part of our Constitution is almost divine; to such a degree
that no state of Rome or Greece could even boast of one superior to it
nor could Plato, Aristotle nor any legislator even conceive of a more
perfect model of a state. The three parts which composed it are so
harmoniously blended and incorporated that neither the flute of
Aristoxenus nor the lyre of Timotheus ever produced more perfect
concord.[8]

This concord is to be maintained. The monarchy, aristocracy or commons should not upset this balance by crossing the limit drawn by the law. This conception, very Ciceronian, stems from the fear of concentration of power in one man. Burke and the Whigs of the opposition agreed with such principles.

But Jones parted company with the Whigs when it came to assessing the role of the aristocracy. He had a certain dislike for the nobility. Perhaps he partly inherited his mother's dislike of patronage and partly he found the nobility lacking in virtue, which he thought the most essential quality in a politician in a corrupt age. He disagreed with Burke's views[1] that the aristocracy had a special role to play in the British Constitution. There was no conception of trusteeship in Jones. This was one of the reasons why he disliked Burke.

I have been much with Burke on this business and have heard many animated speeches from him in the House, we are good friends, but in serious truth, he is too aristocratical (as most of his countrymen are) for me. His system about America is to me incomprehensible and his system of national liberty still more sublime, that is, obscure.[2]

With the years he grew to fear the aristocracy more than he feared the king. 'Care must now be taken lest by reducing the regal power to its just level we raise the aristocratical to a dangerous height', he wrote to Thomas Yeates,[3] the Secretary of the Society for Constitutional Information. Similar sentiments are echoed in his correspondence to others.[4] This was also clear from his dislike of rank.

This I know that I should think very ill of any society in which rank was considered as a substitute for virtue, for if that were the case such men as the late Lord Baltimore who was sovereign prince of Maryland, such men as the late Duc de Villars and hundreds more whose profligacy has made their names stink in our nostrils would be very respectable characters.[5]

His fear of the aristocracy was strengthened by his readings of English history. In setting forth a plea for constitutional reformation, Jones invoked history. He considered the history of England since the Norman Conquest as the history of a struggle between two forces, feudalism and commerce. The forces of commerce and trade were trying to replace the feudalism, there has been a continued war in the constitution of England between two jarring principles: the evil principle of the feudal system with his dark auxiliaries, ignorance and false philosophy; and the good principle of increasing commerce, with her liberal allies, true learning and sound reason.[1]

This idea of the fight of two principles had already found expression among the early radicals:

Did we not know that, at this day it consists of a mixture of the old or first establishment and the new or that which took place at (and since), what is commonly called the conquest by William the First.

These two forms of government, the first founded upon the principles of liberty and the latter upon the principles of slavery being so diametrically opposite, 'it is no wonder that they are continually at war with the other'.[2]

The conception of English history as the history of the continued struggle of the English people to free Anglo-Saxon institutions from the Norman yoke was a popular one, and was used as a weapon for parliamentary reform by the early radicals.[3] There was nothing new in Jones's detecting two struggling forces in history. But what was new, was a vague notion of interrelationship between the system of property and the system of government:

What caused the absurd yet fatal distinction between property, personal and real? The feudal principle...what prevented the large provision in the Act of Henry IV by which all freeholders were declared electors, from being extended to all holders of property, however denominated, however inconsiderable? The same infernal principle which subdued and stifled the genuine equalising spirit of our constitution.[4]

To Jones, feudalism was a force of reaction whereas commerce was the source of prosperity and happiness.

The idea that feudalism was a result of historical evolution had not yet gained ground. To Montesquieu it was a 'unique event'[5] which happened in Europe only. On the other hand Voltaire[6] had used it to mean fragmentation of authority, which was a more desirable form of government than despotism. In England Blackstone[7] had used it in a very strict legal sense in connection with the Land Tenure system. John Millar had been working out a new theory of the feudal system.[8] Earlier, Jones had followed Voltaire when he described the political system of India during the early period in her history. Now he was following Blackstone in attacking the 'feudal fiction' in connection with the ownership of land, although he was presupposing some of Millar's ideas, like the interconnection between the system of property and the system of government and the struggle between commerce and feudalism.

He was against the feudal system but not against the nobility within the limits of the constitution. He would tolerate the nobility so long as they did not interfere with the rights of the people to choose their representatives in parliament, and the extension of commerce and learning. But he would not tolerate the feudal system, which prevented the prosperity of the nation and deprived the people of their liberty:

If we find that this demon [the feudal system], was himself in process of time subdued, as he certainly was by the extension of commerce under Elizabeth, and the enlarged conceptions which extended commerce always produces, by the revival of learning which dispelled the darkness of Gothick ignorance and by the great transactions of the last century, when the true theory and genuine principles of freedom were unfolded and illustrated, we shall not hesitate to pronounce that by the spirit of our constitution all Englishmen having property of any kind or quantity are entitled to votes in chusing Parliamentary delegates.[1]

This spirit of the constitution is to be evoked to kill the feudal system, which was only 'scotched' by the Revolution.[2]

The 'feudal system' must be killed to restore the balance, by curtailing the king's prerogatives, by annual parliaments and the extension of suffrage. Jones could not agree to a universal adult suffrage. He adhered to the then commonly held view that an individual is not free unless he is owner in his own personal capacity. In other words the freedom of the individual was related to his possessions.[3] Jones agreed but he took the Lockian idea that 'everyman has a property in his own person'[4] to the extreme. He argued that a man is independent if he is capable and willing to use his own labour, since labour is the source of property:

I consider a fair trade or profession as valuable property; and an Englishman who can support himself by honest industry, though in a low station, has often a more independent mind than the prodigal owners of large estate.[5]

But the franchise should not be given to men who are unable or unwilling to support themselves 'by honest industry or labour', 'but live on alms'. These men have no free will.[1] So his civil society excluded a large number of people. In fact his political works had a twofold function: they attacked too much concentration of power in few hands, and they also encouraged honest propertied citizens to arm themselves in defending liberty and their property against any encroachments from the 'inarticulate' 'rabble' or 'populace'. The term 'populace' was used by Jones to mean vulgar lower orders who do not wish to live on their honest industry. The term 'people' was used to mean the community collectively. These ideas are nowhere better illustrated than in his attitude to the Gordon riots.

The Gordon riots like most other urban riots in the eighteenth century were an expression of, as Rudé has put it, 'a groping desire [of the poor] to settle accounts with the rich, if only for a day, and to achieve some kind of social justice',[2] though they started with quite different aims. During this period Jones was preoccupied with his campaigns in the Oxford election where he was a candidate. While the city was subjected to nightmarish experiences of fire and looting Jones was at Lamb's building in the Temple, making various lists of patrons who had substantial influence among the Oxford voters. Suddenly he became aware of the riots. On 7 June, rumour had it that a gang was planning to attack the Temple. Jones was alarmed, he sent his valuables to a safe place and together with others prepared to defend the Temple. Such efforts proved unnecessary as soldiers moved in. But this clearly showed that he was determined to resist 'the rabble' with force.[3]

Some of his thoughts during this period were expressed in letters to Lady Georgiana. He condemned the politicians who had misused the name of liberty and incited the populace, 'by pretending that the will of the rabble is the law; that liberty is the power given to the populace of acting according to their will'.[4] To him, 'law is the will of the people, and liberty is freedom from all political restraint such as is imposed by laws enacted by the people'.[5] So Jones was not hesitant to take up arms against the 'rabble' in defence of property. But on the other hand he also feared that the government had used the riots as a pretext to strengthen their power: 'what I as a lover of my country chiefly dread is the pretext for strengthening the prerogative (already too strong for the freedom of Parliament)'.[6] So he put his faith in a citizen's militia; to set an example he gathered a party of volunteers from among the students and barristers to defend the Temple. Dean Shipley, who was converted to Jones's ideas, did a similar glorious deed in 1796, when he helped to put down unrest in Wales and received thanks for that from the duke of Portland.[1] In March 1768 Jones expressed his dislike of riots. He then condemned Wilkes for the folly of inciting the people instead of holding them in, 'I cannot therefore restrain my indignation against Wilkes, bold and able, but turbulent man, the very torch and firebrand of sedition'.[2] The Gordon riots confirmed his views and frightened him enough to write a plan to suppress such occurrences in future. This was his tract, *An Inquiry into the Legal Mode of Suppressing Riots*. In this he criticized the Riot Acts and felt that the use of military power to suppress riots was unnecessary as the English constitution permits civil power in the form of citizen's militia, 'to repel such rabble'. To prove this point he ransacked English law books and showed that the law allows citizens to take up arms against internal revolts.

He sought Wilkes's help to implement his plans;[3] the old firebrand of sedition had now changed sides and fired at the rioters, who were people of a class similar to those who earlier gathered under the slogan of 'Wilkes and liberty'.[4] Jones also preached his doctrine in the circuits and asked his friend Samuel Parr, a minister, to train his parishioners to use firelocks, 'to defend God and liberty'.[5]

The dual nature of his ideas is further illustrated in his critique of Shelburne's *Plan for National Defence*.[6] In his plan, Shelburne proposed that battalions should be established in each town for the national defence against internal and external enemies. Shelburne wanted the officers of such battalions to be appointed by the king, their ranks to be determined according to the size of the property owned by them. They should be controlled by the army and financed by the government. Jones on the contrary proposed that such battalions be formed voluntarily from among the inhabitants, gentry, yeomanry, and substantial householders. The ranks of the officers were to be determined according to the proportion of their contribution to a common fund which should finance the upkeep of the battalions. Jones's aim was to curtail the influence of the executive and the army, and to put the control of the defence in the hands of men with money, and not necessarily with landed property. He would not give the power to run the militia to people without enough money to contribute to the proposed common fund. So the peasants in the tract are to arm themselves to defend themselves not only against the king and aristocracy but also against those who would defy the law and the sanctity of private property.

So Jones could be described as 'a staunch Whig but very wrong-headed'. He carried the Whig philosophy based on Locke and Cicero's doctrines to the extreme. But he was wrongheaded, as he would not fit in, in Westminster party politics. He was less radical than men like Cartwright, who made a definite departure from the traditional view that the freedom of the individual depended on the ownership of property.[1] Jones adhered to this old view as did the Levellers of the seventeenth century.[2]

It is generally assumed that the withdrawal of Sir William Jones from the Oxford election and the delay he suffered in obtaining the judgeship in Bengal were due to his extreme political views. Thus, according to Cannon,

he decided to stand for Parliament but facing certain defeat because he was outspoken against the slave trade and the continuation of the American war, he withdrew his candidacy. No doubt these same liberal and unpopular views delayed his judgeship.[3]

A similar view is expressed by Arberry[4] though with much caution; this is also shared by most writers old and new.[5]

But his opinions on the slave trade and the American war were not an issue in the election. Jones did not pronounce his indignation against the slave trade until September 1780, at least seven days after the withdrawal from the election,[6] though his dislike of the trade can be traced in his correspondence.[7] Sir William Doblen, who gained the seat in 1780, was a friend of Wilberforce.[8] Here we shall attempt to show that it was largely the lack of political organization which was responsible for his failure to secure sufficient support to stand for the election, though he might have lost a considerable number of votes owing to his political views.

As early as 29 April 1780, when the resignation of Sir Roger Newdigate from the House of Commons was known, Jones expressed his desire to stand as a candidate.[9] But a seat in the House of Commons must have been in his mind for some time. A place in Parliament was an important landmark in the career of the upper-class youth in the eighteenth century in England.[10] Jones's mother also set his mind towards this end; Jones stated that an added reason for standing in the election was his mother's will:

'My mother destined me for the service of my country and her will is sacred.'[1] His frustration in securing a definite answer from the Treasury in connection with the judgeship in Bengal, and the failure to secure a place in high society, intensified his urge to look for a career elsewhere:

On the whole if nothing be determined as to my promotion before the end of this session I shall spend a few weeks in deliberating and consulting my best friends, whether it will not be wiser for me to renounce all idea of the judgeship and to enter boldly on my political career.[2]

The opportunity was opened when Sir Roger, who had sat in the house for Oxford for some years, resigned in Spring 1780.

Jones was a latecomer in the contest. When the resignation of Sir Roger Newdigate was confirmed Sir William Doblen's name was proposed as a candidate for the election. Later some members of convocation approached University College and successfully had Scott nominated by the College.[3] Some time after this 'some young lawyers set up Jones as a man equally qualified for that high post'.[4] Jones was rather hesitant to stand until he was sure of getting an 'honourable nomination', which to him meant at least a support of fifty voters.[5] He wrote to William Adams, the Master of Pembroke College, asking whether he would stand a chance of getting such a nomination.[6] Presumably it was due to Adams's assurances that he allowed his friends to nominate him as a candidate.

Jones was conscious of his shortcomings. He knew he came late in the contest; his political views were unpopular; and his business in the circuit did not allow him much time to acquaint himself with the voters in Oxford. He and his friends decided to put these right. On 5 May an *Address*[7] to the electors was issued anonymously by his friends.

In this, Jones explained that he was not nominated by his college, though he was a fellow there, because his friends presumed that he would receive his post in Bengal in a short time. So his college decided to support Scott, another fellow of the college. But Jones declared that he was then nominated by friends from other colleges.

In the *Address* Jones made some self-advertisement of his virtues, how he would not solicit votes among Masters of Arts, and how he was attached to the interest of the university. To prove his points, passages from his several publications, where he made honourable mention of the university, were added to the *Address*.[1]

To Jones the election at Oxford was a fight between two contesting parties, Tories and Whigs. The Tories being the stronger of the two, he thought that his strategy would be to divide the Tories and unite the Whigs. The Whigs were the only party which stood against the executive and for the people. So in all his correspondence he stressed that the political principles of Scott and Doblen were those of the Tories, and he appealed to the old Whigs to rally around him in support of independence. He mostly concentrated his attacks on Scott; this, he believed, would work both ways—Scott would be exposed as a Tory, and so Tory votes would be divided, and the Whigs would leave Scott for Jones.[2]

To overcome the other difficulty, that he was not a resident in Oxford for long enough to gain the support of the voters, Jones relied mostly on non-residential voters. He sent circular letters to men who had substantial influence on them. In these, Jones gave his reasons for standing for the election; it was to 'answer the purpose of the franchise granted to the academical body, namely to protect as Blackstone says, in the Legislature the rights of the republick of letters'.[3] Such a letter was sent to his Dutch friend Schultens,[4] who had some friends in Oxford. Horace Walpole also received one, and rejected it as 'absurd and pedantic'.[5]

Despite discouragement from some friends,[6] Jones carried on his campaign, made out lists of voters, and sent them to friends, to study them carefully and to make new additions if they were incomplete. He urged his friends to exert their influence on the voters in his favour. Meetings were held in his support.[7] The young radical lawyers, the ladies of the salons, like Mrs Elizabeth Montagu, were among the most enthusiastic supporters of Jones. Mrs Montagu wrote to Weller Pepys urging him to support Jones: 'If the Muses were the electors he would carry the election from every candidate that could offer.'[8] But the Muses were not electors in Oxford. Jones and his friends failed to understand the intricate electoral problems in Oxford. It was not the non-resident voters who decided an election in Oxford of the eighteenth century but the colleges.[9] Jones received no solid support from any college, and he had not much influence among the resident voters. He and his friends showed more enthusiasm and less tact. By advertising his virtues Jones antagonized a good number of voters.[10] Moreover, since 1772 when Lord North, the king's favourite, became Chancellor of the University, the Treasury increased its influence on the voters. To them a writer of an *Ode to Liberty* was a suspicious character. Their worst suspicion was confirmed when Jones gave his plan for suppressing riots, which aimed at curtailing the power of the executive as much as putting down the masses.[1] He also failed to gain support from the old Whig families who were great figures at Westminster, and might have exerted influence in his favour. He could not expect much support from Rockingham, as Burke was against him.[2]

So Jones failed. He was a latecomer, he did not know the real rules of the game, he had no patron or good election manager—and his political ideas alienated a considerable number who would have voted for him otherwise. By 30 August he made up his mind[3] and on 2 September he asked Wheeler[4] to make it known in the university that he had declined the poll.

After the episode of the Oxford election one can trace bitterness in Jones. He failed to make much headway in his law practice, he was kept waiting for the judgeship in Bengal for a long time, and he failed to gain support for a seat in the Commons. He felt that England had no freedom, that the country was corrupted, and that the people with a love for independence and liberty had no place there:

In the great orchestra of politics I find so many musicians out of humour and instruments out of tune, that I am more tormented by such dissonance than the man in Hogarth's print; and I am more desirous than ever of being transported to the distance of five thousand leagues from all this fatal discord.[5]

So he turned his attention more towards India and America. If he received his post in India he would be able to carry on his work on Oriental literature; if he did not he would turn to America where the 'noblest of all men' lived. From the beginning he was against the war and supported the Americans; now he was even willing to migrate to America:[6]

I am very ready (as I need not repeat) to traverse immense seas and burning sands, desiring only that the Chancellor will say yes or no and declaring with perfect coolness that if he will not put me out of suspense, I will put myself out of it and accept a noble offer that has been made me by the noblest of men among whom I may not only plead causes but make laws and write them on the bank of my own river and under my own oak.

He always advised people to go to America,

If young Englishmen had any English spirit, they would finish their education by visiting the United States instead of flitting about Italy and strive rather to learn political wisdom from republicans than to pick up a few superficial notions of the fine arts from the poor thralls of bigotry and despotism.[1]

He was prevented from leaving for America[2] by the Shipley family and also by the hope that he would ultimately get his post in India. This affair of obtaining a judgeship in Bengal is most intriguing, and we shall never know for certain why Jones was kept waiting for four years before he was appointed. From what we now know, it appears that Jones was kept waiting for the post not so much because of his political views as because of his personal relationship with the Lord Chancellor, Thurlow.

In 1778 when a post was vacant in Bengal, Lord Bathurst was the Chancellor. Had Jones had the right qualifications he would have been appointed to the post, as Bathurst was a friend of his.[3] But later in the same year Lord Thurlow became the Lord Chancellor in North's ministry. Jones disliked Thurlow and considered him to be a 'beast'.[4] There was another candidate in F. H. Hargrave, Recorder of Liverpool and a King's Counsel.[5] His name appeared as a successful candidate in the court calendar for two subsequent years and he was friendly with the Chancellor. Why Thurlow was unable to send him to India we do not know. It may be that Thurlow was not interested in Indian affairs. North complained that the Chancellor neglected East India papers sent to him 'always returning them at a great distance of time without any opinion or assistance at all'.[6] There was also a problem of procedure; it was not certain who should recommend a Bengal judge to the king, the First Lord of the Treasury or the Chancellor.[7] If the usual practice at Westminster Hall was followed, then the Chancellor should have nominated the judge, but Thurlow evaded the issue. Moreover, there was the controversy over the future status of the Calcutta Supreme Court in parliament as Jones himself recognized.[8] However, by 1781 the controversy was settled at least for the time being. It may be that Hargrave himself, who was a friend of Jones, did not like to take the post and deprive Jones of it. And on 29 June of the same year Hargrave had accepted a post of King's Counsel,[9] so from then on Jones had no competitor.

It was then entirely up to the Chancellor to decide whether to give him the post or not. Robert Orme and the duchess of Devonshire pleaded for Jones, but Thurlow would not move.[1] When Rockingham came to power in 1782 Jones hoped to gain support. But he was soon discouraged to find Thurlow in the cabinet. He wrote to Burke and Kenyon to persuade the Chancellor at least to give him a definite answer. His last hope was Shelburne. As early as April 1782 Jones approached Shelburne[2] through Dunning (Lord Ashburton), whom he knew intimately from 1775 when they covered the same circuit in Oxford and Wales.[3]

In July 1782 when he was in France he heard that Rockingham had died and Shelburne was chosen as his successor. Jones wrote at once: 'I congratulate the King and people of England on your Lordship's advancement to the helm of government.'[4] He realized that at last he might have a patron in Shelburne. Bathurst, Ashburton and the Spencers had failed to secure a position for him either in India or in Britain; but Shelburne had given shelter to many radicals and he was now the First Lord of the Treasury. Despite all his professed dislike for the monarchy and nobility Jones was now ready to compromise so that he could ascend in his career and gain 'independence': 'My jealousy of regal and aristocratical power is now at an end, and the people will I trust have the happiness of seeing a patriot king and a patriot minister.'[5]

In the autumn, when he was still in Paris, after he had failed to visit America, he hurried back to England as 'Shelburne had written me word that he had nothing more at present than to procure a desirable station for me in Bengal'.[6] He wrote to Shelburne from Margate: 'Your Lordship will permit me to add that I beg to consider you as my sole patron and to place myself wholly under your auspices and protection.'[7] But after waiting for nearly four months Jones grew tired.

I certainly did not love Lord Shelburne nor had I any reason to love him for my own sake, or for that of the publick; but I must have been grateful to him, if he had kept his solemn promises, often repeated verbally and in writing, of placing me on the bench at Calcutta.[8]

In the end it was Lord Ashburton who used his good offices to persuade Shelburne to procure the seat for Jones. In March the King personally intervened; he wrote to Thurlow,

I find from Mr Townshend that Lord Shelburne will think himself unkindly treated if Mr Jones is not sent to the East Indies on the vacancy of Judge which has subsisted some years; I shall take it as a personal compliment to me if you will consent to it. Lord Ashburton answers for his being competent as a lawyer and his knowledge of Eastern languages is a very additional qualification.[1]

Thurlow gave in and Jones got his appointment. He was knighted, he married and in 1783 he left for India.[2]

How did Jones reconcile his political ideas with the Indian situation? In England he maintained that the law is the aggregate will of the people and that the state is made up of the whole community, and the rulers are but servants of the people. But in India he was appointed a judge not by the people there but by their foreign masters. The problem was sarcastically posed by Dean Tucker in his sequel to Jones's *Dialogue*:

I wish to know, whether he himself allows the consequences of his own doctrine, when put into practice against his own interest? Doth he or doth he not permit the poor enslaved Gentoos and plundered Indians to dispute his authority, and disobey his commands, by telling him to his face that they never chose him to be the judge of their country?[3]

Jones was conscious of this problem, which was one which most liberals and social democrats of later times faced when they came to rule a colony,[4] when they were unable to practice the doctrines which they preached at home. Jones wrote to Gibbon in 1781, 'my system is purely speculative, and has no relation to my seat on the bench in India where I should hardly think of instructing the Gentoos with the maxims of the Athenians'. In a later chapter we shall see how Jones reconciled his political ideas with the Indian situation and consequently developed a theory of Indian government and law.

CHAPTER 5

THE BEGINNINGS OF INDOLOGY: THE FOUNDATION OF THE ASIATICK SOCIETY

On 12 April 1783 Jones left Portsmouth on the frigate *Crocodile* for India. At last his dreams were coming true; and he could explore the art and literature of Asia in the continent itself. He had married the lady whom he had known for nearly sixteen years but to whom he was unable to propose until he had sufficient means and a high position in society.[1] He was a judge in Calcutta with a salary of £6,000 a year and had been knighted a few days previously. In India he wanted to stay for six years in order to save as much as £30,000 so that he could retire in England with the independence he desired so much.

I need not add how heartbreaking a thing it will be for me to leave you for six years, nor would I leave you, my dear friend, if I did not consider that at our time of life five or six years make no very material difference and if it should be my good fortune to return to England at the age of seven or eight and thirty years, with thirty thousand pounds in my chest I shall then perhaps be able to concur with you and other friends of liberty and virtue in defending our constitution, amending our laws and encouraging letters.[2]

So he was prepared to lead a frugal life. But saving was only one motive of his self-discipline. He could not waste much time. As he intended to gather as much knowledge of India as he could during his stay in Calcutta, he would have to make stringent economies in whatever leisure time he might have after the discharge of his duty as judge. He started his rather frugal and not very exciting life on board ship, long before he reached India. During the six months' voyage his time was almost equally divided between his wife and his books.

My daily studies are now what they will be for six years to come, Persian and law, and what ever relates to India, my recreation, chess my exercise, walking on deck an hour before dinner, but my great delight is the sweet society and conversation of Anna Maria whose health and spirits are really wonderful in a situation so new to her and by no means pleasing in itself.[1]

A good part of his time was spent in making plans for the future. By 12 July he had made up his mind about what he should do during his stay in Calcutta. The following memorandum[2] gives us some idea of his plans:

The objects of enquiry during my residence in Asia:
1. The laws of the Hindus and Mahomedans.
2. The history of the ancient world.
3. Proofs and illustrations of scripture.
4. Traditions concerning the deluge, etc.
5. Modern politics and geography of Hindustan.
6. Best mode of governing Bengal.
7. Arithmetic and geometry and mixed sciences of Asiaticks.
8. Medicine, chemistry, surgery, and anatomy of the Indians.
9. Natural products of India.
10. Poetry, rhetoric and morality of Asia.
11. Music of the Eastern Nations.
12. The She-King or 300 Chinese odes.
13. The best accounts of Tibet and Kashmir.
14. Trade, manufactures, agriculture and commerce of India.
15. Mughal constitution.
16. Maharatta constitution.

This memorandum covered the map of human knowledge as drawn by Bacon, who had divided it into three main branches, History, Philosophy and Poetry.[3] The sixteen branches of investigation as given in Jones's memorandum may be classified into three parts, History, Science and Arts. Thus the laws, arithmetic, etc., come under the heading of Science where reason reigns (Bacon would call it Philosophy); the scripture, the traditions concerning the deluge, etc., come under History where memory presides; and the poetry, music, trade and commerce come under Arts, where imagination rules. Thus Jones's work in Asia was to be divided.[4] But how to execute it? He had not yet thought of a plan to form a society to investigate into the science, history and arts of Asia. But he knew that he had to gather rare and hitherto unknown manuscripts and seek their explanation from the natives, and this would involve endless discussions with the Asians on religion, history, art and other subjects.

On 28 July the *Crocodile* called for a few days at Johanna, an island off the east coast of Africa *en route* to India. Here for the first time Jones was confronted by non-Europeans in their own country. Though the ruler of the island was an Arab, most inhabitants were of mixed Arab and African descent. Whatever romantic ideas he might have had about the tribal Arabs he had none for these islanders. In fact considering that this was his first meeting with non-Europeans in the East, he was remarkably shrewd in his judgement of the character of the people and the nature of their social and political institutions. There was no unnecessary praise nor undue censure in his description of the islanders. What he detested most was the servile attitude of the people in general and the 'nobility' in particular. He noticed that no 'principle of honour'[1] was instituted by education into the gentry of the island as they often begged presents and were not hesitant to steal even trivial things like Morocco slippers. He found Prince Salim, the eldest son of the ruler of Johanna, a most despicable character. This prince begged for presents and money and harassed Jones by refusing to co-operate in obtaining an audience for him with the king of Johanna. He also begged Jones to obtain confirmation of his silly 'titles' given to him by European visitors. Jones was most annoyed, as not only were such titles silly, but they were not in conformity with their own way of life.

There was more dignity in their own native titles than in those of prince, duke and lord, which had been idly given to them but had no conformity to their manners or the constitution of their government.[2]

Jones disliked their slave trade, which was carried on with African prisoners. He also abhorred their treatment of women:

A rational being would have preferred the condition of a wild beast exposed to the perils and hunger in a forest to the splendid misery of being wife and mistress to Salim.[3]

His search for manuscripts was unsuccessful. Most of those that were shown to him were useless.

On the other hand he was most impressed by the king. Though he thought his ideas of trade with England were ridiculous, as the island had nothing much to offer, yet

it showed an enlargement of mind, a desire of promoting the interest of his people and sense of benefit from trade which could hardly have been expected from a petty African chief and which if he had been sovereign of Yemen might have been expanded into rational projects proportioned to the extent of his dominion.[1]

He found that the Arab form of government for the island 'though bad enough in itself', was apparently 'administered with advantage to the original inhabitants'.[2] The monarchy of Johanna was 'limited' by an 'aristocracy' without whose consent the king could not declare war or conduct a peace treaty with his enemies. The misrule and violence which could be found in the administration of the island were 'probably occasioned by the insolence of an oligarchy naturally hostile to king and people'.[3] By putting the blame on the oligarchy Jones betrayed his dislike for nobility.

Jones was impressed by Prince Hamdullah, who was a *qazi* and a scholar. His only regret was that this prince had not much time to spare for interviews with him. Above all he liked Alavi, a brother of the governor; he was more communicative than the other nobles, as he spoke good English. His knowledge of European affairs surprised Jones, who had long discussions with him on various topics ranging from the slave trade to the divinity of Christ. Here for the first time Jones came out into the open in defending his religion. But the religious dispute ended cordially and Jones promised to help Alavi in some legal matters.

But Jones had no illusions regarding the relationship between the Europeans and the natives. 'In truth our nation is not cordially loved by the inhabitants of Hizuan (Johanna), who, as it commonly happens, form a general opinion from a few instances of violence or breach of faith'.[4] One such violent act had taken place recently, when a woman was badly treated and a man was murdered. The Englishman responsible for this escaped justice. On another occasion, so Jones was told, an English captain cheated Alavi; though he promised to pay him a large sum of money, as Alavi had saved his life, he never paid up.

This visit to the island left a deep imprint in Jones's mind. His future attitude towards Asia was influenced by his experiences in Johanna.

On 25 September 1783 the *Crocodile* reached Calcutta.[5] Jones spent his first few months meeting people and settling down in his new home.[6] His early correspondence from Calcutta shows him in a relaxed mood. Now he was away from England, from political bickering, from Association movements, and from the frustrating years of unsuccessful attempts to gain a place in high society. Now he was in a city which appeared 'large' and 'well-peopled' yet 'airy and commodious', of which the houses were 'in general well built and some often equal to palaces'.[1] Here he would not be disturbed, and he could spend his leisure as he wished. 'Of myself', he wrote, 'I will only say that disliking as I did the politicks and parties of Britain I am very glad to be out of their way and to amuse myself for a few years in this wonderful country.'[2] But soon this rather relaxed mood was at an end, as a very busy and active life was ahead of him.

During this time there was in Bengal a group of young officers who were keenly interested in Asiatic studies. Among them were Charles Wilkins, Nathaniel Halhed (a friend of Jones's since 1768), John Shore, Francis Gladwin, John Carnac, Jonathan Duncan, and William Chambers. Most of these were to be the founding fathers of the Society and to contribute regularly to the Society's journal. However, these people as yet did not form a group in pursuit of their researches, nor were they personal friends, as they belonged to different political factions in the Bengal politics of the period. No doubt Halhed and Wilkins struck up a friendship when they were at Hooghly and together they produced the first Bengal typeface in 1778,[3] but most of them carried out their work individually. Often they produced works of great interest. One such work was Gladwin's *Institutes of the Emperor Akbar*, an abridged version of Abul Fazl's famous work.[4] Charles Wilkins, who came to India in 1770, from 1778 turned his interest to Sanskrit and Persian, following the example of Halhed.[5] In 1776 Halhed, at the age of twenty-three, produced his famous *Gentoo Laws*, which two years later was followed by his *A Grammar of the Bengal Languages*. These people worked against great odds; there was a lack of books and manuscripts and they were short of time. They had no way of putting the results of their research before the learned people of Europe.[6] In 1781 Wilkins brought out a translation of an inscription written in Sanskrit but in characters which had fallen out of use. This was the Monghyr Inscription of Devapāla written in *Kuṭila* characters.[7] It was the first attempt at deciphering old Indian characters, but no notice of such a revolutionary move was taken until the translation was republished in the first volume of the

Asiatick Researches.[1] We have no knowledge of the methods Wilkins used in deciphering these characters, which later helped him to read the *Gupta Brāhmī*.[2] The position of Oriental Studies in Bengal, prior to Jones's arrival there, is best summed up in John Shore's letter to Ford, an Oriental scholar at Oxford,

Some books have lately been published in Bengal but the expense of printing them is so enormous and the reputation derived from the labours of translating so little that few attempts more will be made.[3]

He complained that there were not enough Arabic books,

amongst the variety of Arabic authors quoted or mentioned by Mr Jones in his commentaries, I do not, the Koran excepted, recollect one that is found here.[4]

However, they carried on their work bravely. Wilkins was labouring hard in translating the *Mahābhārata*. Halhed collected numerous Persian manuscripts.[5] Shore himself had done the same;

I have in my possession Persian translations of many valuable Sanskrit books of Religion and Morality; and these are acquired within six months only. A Brahmin is also ready to attend me whenever I want him; and from him I find I can depend on my Persian versions.[6]

He made an attempt to assess the nature of Hinduism,

in fact it is pure Deism and has a wonderful resemblance to the doctrines of Plato. I doubt if any of his writings are more metaphysically abstract than some of the Hindoos.[7]

This was the conclusion that Holwell[8] and Dow[9] had already arrived at and that Jones was to arrive at later. However, Shore's letter shows that Oriental Studies in Calcutta was in danger of disintegrating unless some new life was put into it. This was what Sir William Jones did. Robert Orme, who was a well-wisher of Jones and had lent a hand in his obtaining the judgeship in Bengal, thought that no one before Jones had just ideas 'previously acquired' about the life and manners of the Indians. So his hours of leisure, spent on Asiatic studies, would be most rewarding to the Orientalists.[10] Jones's fame had already reached Bengal long before his arrival there and Shore and others were pleased to have him among them:

If Mr Jones should as we are taught to expect, arrive in Bengal, I may venture to pronounce that notwithstanding the disadvantages he will labour under from the want of pronunciation, he will possess more real knowledge of the Persian and Arabic languages than any person here Native or European.[1]

The only man to encourage the young officers who were thus pioneering the field of Indology was Warren Hastings, who had been ruler of Bengal since 1772. A history of Oriental Studies is incomplete without a mention of Hastings. He came to India at an early age and a long stay in this country had made him an admirer of Indian manners and customs. He mastered the Persian language, gathered Indian paintings and manuscripts, and in his letters to his wife he used to quote from the *Gītā*, which he found a source of inspiration.[2] It was only natural that he should patronize Oriental learning. He encouraged most of the pioneer Indologists in their work, fought for them in the Supreme Council[3] and held long discussions with them on their subjects.[4] They acknowledged their debt to this man. In 1781 Wilkins dedicated his first work to Hastings.

As it was by your immediate counsel I undertook to translate this very curious relick of Hindu antiquity, I think it my duty thus publicly to acknowledge such a distinguishing mark in your favour.[5]

Similar sentiments were expressed by Shore and Halhed in their letters and works.[6]

Hastings's encouragement of Oriental Studies had a practical side. He had his own ideas of how India should be ruled. He was ready to assert British sovereignty. The so-called 'dual government' was to go, and the Company was to take the management of the whole of Bengal into its own hands. But this did not mean the introduction of English laws and English ways in India. His idea was to rule the conquered in their own way. This was how the Romans maintained their empire, this was how he could elevate 'the British name'.[7] He founded the Calcutta Madrasa and provided money for it to 'soften the prejudices' which he said were 'excited by the rapid growth of the British dominion'.[8] Thus he wanted to reconcile British rule with Indian institutions. This meant a further investigation into the manners and customs of the country, and more studies in the literature and the laws of the Indians. The *Gentoo Laws* of Halhed was one realization of his schemes. Halhed echoed Hastings's ideas:

The importance of the commerce of India and the advantages of a territorial establishment in Bengal have at length awakened the attention of the British legislature to every circumstance that may conciliate the affections of the natives or ensure stability to the acquisition. Nothing can so favourably conduce to these two points as a well timed toleration in matters of religion and adoption of such original institutes of the country, as do not immediately clash with the laws or interests of the conquerors.[1]

Recently[2] it has been suggested that the *Gentoo Laws* was a reaction against North's Regulation Act of 1773. But there is nothing in this act which would prevent Hastings from ruling India according to Indian laws.[3] Even his enemy Philip Francis had similar ideas.[4] Later Cornwallis was to abolish Hastings's personal form of government and replace it by an impersonal 'system', but neither he nor any other Governor-General had any intention of attacking the Indian way of life. Jones worked with Cornwallis for eight years and the Asiatick Society flourished. In this way the marquis was as much a patron of Oriental Studies as Hastings had been, and its pragmatic value was well realized by the Company's colonial government. Cornwallis attended most annual meetings of the society; Shore, the marquis of Hastings and Lord Hardinge were its presidents and all the Governor-Generals throughout the period of British rule were its patrons.[5] Later rulers had less sympathy for India and less eagerness to learn about Indian culture, but they all realized that to rule a conquered country the conquerors must have a sound knowledge of the conquered. Just as the scientific revolution of the seventeenth century was stimulated by the needs of navigation,[6] so Oriental Studies was stimulated by the birth of colonial rule. Jones predicted this prospect in 1771,

since a variety of causes which need not be mentioned here give the English nation a most extensive power in that kingdom [India]...the languages of Asia will now perhaps be studied with uncommon ardour; the valuable manuscripts that enrich the publick libraries will be in a few years elegantly printed; the manners and sentiments of the eastern nations will be perfectly known; and the limits of our knowledge no less extended than the bounds of our empire.[7]

As we have seen already,[8] until this time Oriental research had been chiefly the work of individuals—travellers, missionaries and theologians of the universities—who worked independently of one another. Their methods were far from scientific. Their knowledge of the languages was insufficient, their conclusions were hastily drawn and coloured with prejudices, and most of their works were written to feed the European appetite for the exotic. Two forces brought an end to this: one was the establishment of European rule in Asia, and the other the changing methods in the study of what are now called the humanities. In France the *Académie des Inscriptions et des Belles Lettres*, originally instituted to record the progress of Louis XIV's ambitions, had extended its scope in 1718 to inquiries into the antiquities of France and the other kingdoms.[1] In England the Society of Antiquaries received its charter in 1751 and by 1780 the Royal Society ceased to be a rival organization for antiquarian research.[2] In 1768 Sir Joshua Reynolds established the Royal Academy for the purpose of studying the arts. This method of organized study was now to be extended to Oriental Studies. The Batavian Society[3] established by the Dutch in the East Indies in 1778 in its early years chiefly contributed to the study of the natural sciences, though the study of the humanities was not left out.

Before the end of the year 1783 Jones must have come to the conclusion that his plans for Asiatic studies could not be realized by a single man or by men working independently. He 'considered with pain that in this fluctuating imperfect and limited condition of life such enquiries and improvements could only be made by the united efforts of many'.[4] In January 1784 he sent out a circular letter, the text of which is now missing, putting forward a plan to establish a society to encourage Oriental Studies in Calcutta.[5] This circular was apparently addressed to all those who showed interest. Thirty gentlemen responded to the letter and on 15 January 1784 they gathered in the Grand Jury Room of the Supreme Court of Calcutta. Here Sir Robert Chambers, the Chief Justice, an old fellow of University College, Oxford, presided at the first meeting and Jones delivered his first famous discourse.[6] Here he gave his plans for the Society. He stressed the pragmatic value of Oriental Studies. Asia was the 'nurse of sciences', the 'inventress of delightful and useful arts'. Europeans could profitably spend their leisure time in inquiring into the laws, religion, forms of government of the Asiatics and the natural wonders of Asia.[7] This would at least help to improve the mode of ruling the new empire.

According to Jones the objects of the inquiries of the Society should be Man and Nature, and 'whatever is performed by the one and produced by the other' in Asia. By Asia, Jones meant Asian civilization, for the researches were to be carried out beyond the geographical limits of the continent:

Since Egypt had unquestionably an old connection with this country, if not with China, since the language and literature of the Abyssinians bear a manifest affinity to those of Asia, since Arabian arms prevailed along the African coast of the Mediterranean, and even erected a powerful dynasty on the continent of Europe, you may not be displeased occasionally to follow the streams of Asiatick learning a little beyond its natural boundary.[1]

This was the reason why Jones preferred the term 'Asiatick' to 'Oriental', which was in truth 'a word merely relative'. There was of course an additional reason: the man who as a boy had composed verses imitating Sophocles and who took Cicero as his model preferred 'Asiatick' because it appeared 'classical and proper'.[2]

In this discourse Jones drew the map of human knowledge according to the plan he had already made during his journey from England. Like Bacon he recognized three faculties of mind—memory, reason, and imagination, and so the three main branches of learning were History, Science and the Arts. History 'comprehends either an account of natural productions or the genuine records of empires and states'; science 'enhances the whole circle of pure and mixed mathematics together with ethicks and law as far as they depend on the reasoning faculty'; and arts 'includes all the beauties of imagery and the charms of invention'.[3] His discourses were to cover this map of knowledge. While the first two dealt with the plan and methods of research the subsequent eight discourses were on what Jones called History, and the eleventh dealt with Science. The discourse on Arts was never written.

Jones stressed that there should be no formalities or rigid rules for the members of the Society; he wished 'to establish but one rule namely to have no rules at all'. He hoped to hold weekly meetings in the Grand Jury Room where original papers should be read and discussed.[4] No translations except of those papers written by Indian authors would be allowed. If there was sufficient material towards the end of each year then 'let us present our Asiatick miscellany to the literary world'.[5] Jones recommended the Society, on no account to admit a new member who has not expressed a voluntary desire to become so; and in that case you will not require I suppose any qualification than a love of knowledge and a zeal for the promotion of it.[1]

He did not recommend that Indians should be allowed to become members of the Society; it was left to the others to decide whether they would enrol as members 'any numbers of learned natives'.[2] It was not until 1829 that Indians were admitted as members of the Society.[3] But some Indian scholars contributed to its *Journal* regularly from the very first number.

After they had heard Jones's discourse, the gentlemen gathered at the Grand Jury Room thanked him, agreed with its contents, and called themselves the Asiatick Society.[4]

The birth of the Asiatick Society is a milestone in the history of Oriental Studies. By establishing it Jones helped to usher in the age of scientific specialization, by forming a society which would study the Asians at close quarters and draw conclusions about their social, political and economic institutions from the observations of its members. Thus Bacon's methods were extended to Oriental Studies. The Society was to contribute to the comparative study of law, and society. This was one realization of Ferguson's idea of the graphic study of man. As early as 1763 Ferguson regretted that, while human knowledge of the material system of the world 'consists in a collection of facts or at most in general tenets derived from particular observations and experiments', human knowledge of man himself was still based on 'hypothesis'.[5] Such sentiments were echoed by Monboddo[6] and Herder,[7] who demanded that there should be an objective study of man and his culture. In 1786 Jones was studying Ferguson's work for the second time.[8] He must have known about the idea of graphic study of man through his friend Monboddo.[9] Jones consciously modelled the Society on the Royal Society in England. Since the King was the patron of the Royal Society it was decided that the Governor-General and his Council should be asked to become patrons of the new Society. Accordingly on 22 January two letters were sent, one to the Governor-General and the other to the Supreme Council. The first invited Warren Hastings to become the first president of the Society and the other requested the Council to 'honour us with accepting the title of our patrons'.[10] The Council readily agreed, 'We very much approve and applaud your endeavours to promote the extension of know-

ledge in a degree perhaps exceeding those of any part of the globe'.[1]
Thus the Society received official blessing from the very beginning.
However, Hastings declined the invitation;

from an early conviction of the utility of the institution it was my
anxious wish that I might be by whatever means instrumental in promoting the success of it; but not in the mode which you have here
proposed which I fear would rather prove if of any effect an incon-
venience on it.

He suggested that the post should be given to the gentleman
'whose genius planned the institution and is most capable of
conducting it to the attainment of the great and splendid purposes
of its function'.[2] This letter from Warren Hastings was read to the
Society on 5 February. Meanwhile on 24 January David Anderson
had proposed William Jones as the Vice-President and G. H. Barlow as the Secretary of the Society.[3] These two posts were formally
balloted for and Jones and Barlow were elected at the third
meeting of the Society held on 29 January.[4] However, on 5 February
the Society passed a resolution which thanked Warren Hastings
and requested Jones to 'reaccept' the offer of President of the
Society.[5] The term 'reaccept' is rather odd, as there is no indication
that Jones had been previously requested to become President or
that he had accepted such a request before 5 February. It may be
that the writer was carried away by his pen.

During the first ten years of its life the president had to struggle
hard to keep the Society alive. He advised that the members
should follow a middle course between 'languid remissness and an
over zealous activity',[6] to ensure permanence and success. But it
was no easy task to avoid 'languid remissness' in Calcutta, where
life was uncertain and light entertainment easily available. If the
Calcutta Gazette[7] is any indication of their interests, most Anglo-
Indians (in the old sense of the term) took little notice of the
activities of the Society. Their chief interests were the latest news
of the war with Tipoo, masquerades in Calcutta, new fashions in
furniture and dress, and recapturing runaway slaves. However,
there was a small number who were keenly interested in Asiatic
Studies. Almost all of these were high Company officials busy at
their respective tasks and often posted to places far away from the
capital. So though membership increased from 30 in 1784 to 110
in 1792 the attendance at an ordinary meeting was never more

than fifteen, and usually the figure was as low as seven or eight. For the first month the Society met once a week as was originally resolved. But soon there was no such regularity and it met once a fortnight or even at longer intervals. In the first ten years the Society met little more than 100 times.[1]

Though the attendance was poor and there was little enthusiasm for the proceedings of the Society among the Anglo-Indians, official support was always given. The annual meetings, which used to attract as many as thirty people, were attended by the Governor-General, the members of the Supreme Council, high Company officials and the Judges of the Supreme Court. Here Jones used to deliver his anniversary discourses. The government was also ready to supply useful information to the Society.[2] On 8 April 1784 the Governor-General sent Samuel Turner's description of Tibet to be read by the Society. Macpherson, who came to govern Bengal after the departure of Hastings, gave the Society some official status. He requested them to elect a member 'conversant in the Mohamedan law and customs' as a visitor to the Calcutta Madrasa, who would refer to the Society 'the state of the colleges and the progress of the students'.[3] William Chambers was elected to this post. The Company also lent its press for the publication of *Asiatick Researches* in 1788.

But official encouragement alone could not make the new organization a going concern. It needed sufficient papers to be read and discussed at the meetings. For this more information had to be collected from manuscripts, and from Brahmin and Muslim scholars. Many places of importance like Benares had to be visited to collect data. Then there was the problem of publicity; the Society's activities must be made known in Europe. All these tasks fell on Jones. No doubt there was a secretary,[4] who used to keep the manuscripts and books of the Asiatick Society at his own home, and men like Wilkins, Chapman and Chambers supplied numerous papers, but by 1787 most of the Society's papers were written by Jones and he replied to most of the correspondence of the Society. He corrected papers written by others and read them to the Society in their absence.

The author of *Nader Shah*, 'Persian Song' and the *Law of Bailments* had collected an odd combination of friends in varied circles throughout Europe. This was fully utilized for the publicity of his and the Society's works. 'I have answered fifty very long letters from Europe and a multitude of short ones.' This was his 'annuity of European letters'[1] which he paid every autumn from Krishnagar, where he purchased a house in 1785. The letters were meant to be circulated among friends.

The annexed discourse will show you how I pass my hours of leisure and you shall know when I am able to inform you fully how my business is conducted. The Bishop of St Asaph will I trust send you a copy of my speech to the Grand Jury, which contains the outline of my system in administering justice here.[2]

Similarly a copy of his 'Oriental epistle on silver paper scented with oils of roses' was sent to the duchess of Devonshire, who was supposed to pass it around.[3] The fame of the Society spread farther when Jones published his first discourse, together with his *First Charges to the Grand Jury* and a *Hymn to Camdoo* (Kāmadeva, the Hindu love-god), in 1784.[4] This was favourably received by the *Monthly Review*.[5]

The same elegant taste and the same ardent spirit which we have so frequently admired in the writings of this extraordinary genius glow with equal lustre in the Discourse, the Charge and the Hymn.

This view was shared by most readers in Europe. Letters started coming in with queries and congratulations. William Marsden, the author of the *History of Sumatra*, later son-in-law of Charles Wilkins, was most impressed by the discourse:

I have learned with a degree of pleasure, which none but those who have laboured in the field of ancient knowledge can experience of the institution of your Society, and flatter myself with the well founded hope of seeing it attended with all those effects no less splendid in themselves than interesting to the literary world.[6]

He applied for membership of the Society, which was granted. Dr Robert Watson, bishop of Llandaff, who, as Professor of Divinity in Cambridge, had suggested that an Oriental Institute should be formed in the university, was another to welcome the birth of the Society.[7] His interest in the Society was of course mainly theological.[8] He was concerned to find confirmation of the biblical tradition in Hindu literature, and asked whether there were 'any marks of Judaism among any of the casts' or 'any reason to believe that Indians are not derived from the same Noaic stock with ourselves'.[9] Sir George Younger, a correspondent of Jones, put a series of questions before the Society concerning the history, antiquities, religion and philosophy of the 'original people of Hindustan'. He also urged the Society

to endeavour to trace whether in the worship of water, some allusion may not be preserved with regard to the destruction of mankind by a general deluge, and the fresh origin of mankind, by certain divine persons, who were saved on a mountain from destruction.[1]

All these and other letters came from Europe as a result of Jones's own correspondence and his first publication from India.

Soon it was realized that a magazine solely devoted to Asia would be most fruitful. Francis Gladwin, a member of the Society, who had had experience as an author and a journalist,[2] brought out a magazine *Asiatick Miscellany*[3] in 1785. This contained mainly translations from eastern literature, extracts from old works, poems on Oriental subjects and a few original papers. The title was taken from the first discourse of the president, who readily provided the magazine with some contributions. But Jones did not approve of the plan for publication: 'The Asiatick Miscellany to which you allude is not the publication of our Society, who mean to print no scraps, nor any more translations.'[4] Jones had his own plan for a magazine of the Society, which should be a collection of original papers. On 6 July 1787 the president put forward a proposal to the members 'for having their transactions printed by the superintendents of the Honorable Company's press'. This was agreed and it was decided that each member should purchase a copy of the magazine for Rs. 20 to help towards the cost of printing.[5] It was also agreed

that the *Treatise on Orthography* communicated by the President on the 19th February 1784 be printed first as an introductory paper to the transactions and that the astronomical observations communicated by Col. Pearce on the 30th June 1785 stand second.[6]

The rest of the contents were to be decided by the president. The publication put a few more tasks on the already overworked Jones. He had to choose the contents carefully as there was a great deal to choose from. He had to read through the proof, correct mistakes and standardize the Sanskrit spellings. Then there was the additional task of reminding the contributors to send their papers in time; Daniel had to be reminded to make an etching of Samuel Davis's drawings of the ruins of Mavalipuram, Beatridge to be chided for not sending his drawings of the Roman coins from Nellore.[1] When it came to the proof-reading of the second volume Jones was already tired: 'My eyes are weak and my time always occupied, I must have assistance.'[2] The press, though available for the Society, was heavily booked for official papers so the progress in printing was slow. He complained of the slowness of the official press and declared that, months after submitting the copy of the first volume of *Asiatick Researches*, only eight sheets had been printed though he already had material for two further volumes.[3] At last the first volume came out in January 1789. Earlier Jones had cautioned his friend George John not to raise too high his 'expectation of entertainment or instruction from the transactions of our Society', for

it is not here as in Europe where many scholars and philosophers are professedly without any other pursuit; here every member of our Society is a man of business occupied in his respective line of revenue, commerce, law, medicine, military affairs and so forth; his leisure must be allowed in great part to the care of his health even if pleasure engage no share of it, what part of it remains then for literature.[4]

So Jones pleaded that Europe should appreciate these shortcomings instead of being surprised that so little had been done. 'The world if they are candid', he wrote, 'will wonder that we have done so much.'[5]

But Jones's apprehension was unnecessary. The standard of the *Asiatick Researches* was as high as that of any other magazine of the period. It produced numerous original papers which would readily appeal to the readers of *Archaeologia* or *Philosophical Transactions*. The contents were carefully chosen to satisfy men with varied tastes; there were articles on ancient land grants, a Sikh college in Patna, a journey to Tibet, on the manners, religion and languages of the Hindus, on Indian literature, trial by ordeal, and a number of other articles on natural sciences. This was the first European journal to publish papers written by at least four Indian scholars.[6] In fact it created a stir in the European literary world. The *Monthly Review*[7] praised it without censure; and the first volume of the *Asiatick Researches* was reviewed in four instalments. The *Gentleman's Magazine*[8] was more restrained, but it acclaimed the outcome in no lesser terms. Soon all the copies were sold and to satisfy the popular appetite a pirate edition was brought out from London.[9]

This was followed by translations of this and other volumes in various European languages. Soon the Society's fame spread across the Atlantic. The President of Yale College wrote a 148-page letter to the President of the Asiatick Society, chiefly contesting Jones's chronology of the Hindus.[1] The Massachusetts Historical Society elected Sir William Jones as a corresponding member. This was done not only to honour him but also to establish contact and carry on correspondence with the Asiatick Society:

As the correspondence of literary and philosophical societies established in different nations is an intercourse of true philanthropy and has a manifest tendency to increase their friendship and to support that harmony in the great family of mankind on which the happiness of the world so much depends it can never solicit your aid without success.[2]

Jones's contribution to the Society was not restricted to publicity, proof-reading and organizing regular meetings. From 1787 onwards he wrote most of the papers himself and gave all the annual discourses until his death. For all this he had to gather information from manuscripts and from conversations with Muslim and Brahmin scholars. His day started well before sunrise. His daily routine included the study of Sanskrit and law, and an hour in the evening when he used to read Italian with Anna Maria.[3] His holidays in Krishnagar and elsewhere were spent mostly in the search for materials for papers to submit to the Society.

In July 1784 he left for Benares by boat. He wrote to his friend:

In July and during the rainy season I shall live in a floating house on the Ganges as I have resolved to pass my long vacation in a pinnace on the great river seeing all the principal towns as far as I can proceed and then I shall be able not only to fill volumes for you but even to dictate to Anna Maria a translation of a beautiful Persian tale called the four Dervises for Lady Althorp.[4]

But in this trip he did more than write volumes for his friends. He established contacts with British officers in Benares, Bhagalpur and Malda and persuaded them to write for the Society.[5]

On his way to Benares, in Bhagalpur, he saw Hastings, who was on his way back to Calcutta,[6] and they discussed Indian literature. Jones received his first taste of the *Gītā* from Hastings. In Benares he met Aly Ibrahim Khan and Brahmin pandits, with whom he spent his mornings.[7] On his way back he met Charles Grant at Malda and visited the ruins at Gaur with him.[8] The same curiosity, the urge to collect manuscripts and gems of eastern wisdom from the pandits and maulavis persisted throughout the rest of his life. In Krishnagar he met and discussed regularly every autumn with the pandits from Navadvip, which he called his third university.[1] He corresponded regularly with Aly Ibrahim Khan, an Indian scholar-administrator who was appointed the chief magistrate of Benares in 1782, wrote a work on Hindustani poets[2] and an article on the 'Trial by Ordeal' for the *Asiatick Researches*. He also became a good friend of Ghulam Hussein, the famous historian, Pandit Ramlochan, his Sanskrit teacher, Radhakanta Sharman, the pandit who worked with Hastings and John Shore, and Jagganatha Tarkapanchanan, the 'Great Sage,[3] who edited Jones's *Digest of Hindu Law*. These were the Alavis and Hamdullas of India, scholarly, deeply convinced in their own faith, but tolerant and communicative.

But this whole range of activities, which made the Society almost solely his concern, was not always carried on without complaints and moods of depression.

I have written four papers for our expiring Society on very curious subjects and have prepared materials for a discourse on the Chinese, the Society is a puny rickety child and must be fed with pap; nor shall it die by my fault; but die it must for I cannot alone support it.[4]

But by 1792 he had regained his confidence:

I cannot persuade [myself] that a dissolution of our Asiatick Society will be a consequence of my departure, while you are constantly making discoveries in astronomy, Wilford in geography and others in different branches of natural history.

He looked forward to seeing the 'fourth volume printed before I leave India and the fourteenth at least before I leave this world'.[5] He died when the fourth volume was still in press. On 3 April, twenty-four days before his death, Jones presided over the meeting of the Society for the last time, when a young man read a paper on the duties of a Hindu wife. This was Henry Colebrooke, who, like Jones, was a lawyer and an Orientalist.[6] It was he, more than anyone else, who carried out the incomplete task of the pioneer under the patronage of Sir John Shore, the Evangelical Governor-General, who succeeded his friend as the President of the Society.[7]

CHAPTER 6

THE BEGINNINGS OF INDOLOGY: THE 'GREAT DISCOVERIES'

The beginnings of Indology are generally associated with the birth of the Asiatick Society and Jones is often described as 'the Father of Indology'. In the textbooks he is particularly credited for three outstanding achievements, the discovery of the common origin of what came to be known as the family of Indo-European languages; the identification of Sandrocottas of the classical sources with Candragupta Maurya of the Indian sources; and the translation of *Śakuntalā*, and the introduction of Sanskrit literature into Europe. Here we attempt to find out how far these claims are true; how far Jones succeeded in using the critical methods which he prescribed for others in his own researches and how far his discoveries helped to shape the science of Indology.

Ever since the days of King Psammetichus[1] of Egypt and perhaps before then men in the West searched for the origins of languages and the reason for their similarities and diversities. In the ancient world the Greeks and Romans had little interest in the languages of others, who were considered barbarians. Neither did they reach very far in the pursuit of etymological studies; they were centuries behind the Indians in this science. In the medieval period the situation did not change very much. The biblical tradition of the Tower of Babel was easily understood, and satisfied the curiosity of men whose knowledge of languages was very limited. There was a tendency to put all languages in chronological order with the holy language, Hebrew, as the starting point. Any new language discovered was fitted into the pattern.[2]

But not all men were satisfied with classical linguistics and the biblical tradition. As early as 1194 a Welshman, Giraldus Cambrensis, in his *Description of Wales* noticed the similarities between Welsh and Greek and Latin. Rodericus Ximenez de Rada, a Spanish archbishop, recognized that there were various groups of languages in Europe and his groupings were substantially correct. Dante also recognized such a classification of the languages of

Europe, though his division of languages into three groups was less correct than that of Rodericus. With the discovery of printing, books in various European languages crossed national borders easily and reached a wider public than ever before. There was then a possibility of a more comprehensive survey and the recognition of kinship among languages. We find in Germany that J. J. Scaliger, in his work *Diatribe on the Languages of the Europeans* written in 1599 and published in 1610, divided the languages of Europe into eleven groups. He further subdivided them into four major and seven minor classes. His classification was largely correct, but he decided that the eleven matrices were completely independent of each other.

Meanwhile the Germans had discovered the resemblance between Greek and German, and Franciscus Raphelengius discovered that Persian was very similar to German. It was then thought that Greek, Persian and German were all Germanic languages. Thus by the end of the seventeenth century there were many who recognized the interrelationship of European languages, but they did not attempt to discover the reason for the resemblances and differences. Some, like Scaliger, were satisfied with the theory of independent development, while others tried to explain the resemblances as due to trade or invasions, or suggested that Persian was derived from German, or Latin from Greek and so on. They did not yet postulate that most European languages and Persian came from some extinct language. Nor had they, without Pāṇini, the tool to investigate the roots of words.

Marcus Zeurius Boxhorn, a Dutch scholar, was the first to postulate a theory of common origin of the Indo-European languages. He did not publish his work; but through his friend George Horn his ideas were made known to Europe in the latter half of the seventeenth century. He observed that innumerable words are common in the languages of the Greeks and other nations throughout Europe. He conjectured 'that the resemblance started from a common source, that is from the common origin of all these peoples'.[1] So he postulated some sort of common language which he called Scythian, as the mother of the Greek, the Latin, the German and the Persian from which 'like dialects would start'. No lesser man than Leibniz added his authority to this theory of the 'Scythian' origin of the peoples and the languages of Europe. In the first volume of the Memoirs of the Berlin Academy (*Miscellanea Berolinensia*) Leibniz attacked the old Hebraic hypothesis, but he did not support Scaliger's theory of independent development. He put forward a theory which was very similar to that of Boxhorn and he clearly distinguished the Indo-European from the Semitic and the Finno-Ugrian groups, though he failed to add Persian to the other 'Scythian' languages.

Meanwhile Job Lidoff, who made a complete study of the Semitic languages as they were known in his time, in 1702 discovered the significance of inflectional forms in the study of languages. His methods were recognized by Heras of Spain. The Hungarian scholar Gyernathi probably learnt these methods from them as he used similar tools in his study of the Finno-Ugrian languages in 1789. Under Catherine II's patronage there appeared in 1786–7 a survey of two hundred languages of Europe and Asia edited by P. S. Pallas, a German scientist and traveller. In France, Fréret, working on the origin of the nations, came to the conclusion in 1743 that by differences and conformity of languages he could distinguish and recognize nations which have a common origin.[1] Though he recognized the significance of resemblance in grammatical structures in the study of languages, he took a step backwards from Leibniz and Boxhorn by thinking that European languages developed independently of one another.

Thus studies in linguistics reached the threshold of the scientific era by the end of the eighteenth century. By then this science had finally departed from classical and medieval linguistics. There are two factors in this development. Europeans had expanded their horizon, they now knew more languages than ever before, and secondly they had already evolved some scientific methods of the study of language.

Jones was well aware of these developments. He wrote to his Polish Orientalist friend, Prince Adam Czartoryski:

How so many European words crept into the Persian language I know not with certainty. Procopius, I think, mentions the great intercourse both in war and peace between the Persians and the nations in the north of Europe and Asia whom the ancients knew by the general name of Scythians. Many learned investigators of antiquity are fully persuaded that a very old and almost primaeval language was in use among these northern nations from which not only the Celtic dialects but even the Greek and Latin are derived.[2]

But Jones had little or no interest in the study of languages *per se*. Admittedly in 1770 in his *Plan of an Essay on Education* he recognized the importance of learning the languages of other nations, but these were of 'those people who have been in any period of the world distinguished for their superior knowledge'. In Johanna, when a manuscript containing a hymn written in an African language and in Arabic script was presented to Captain Williamson of the *Crocodile*, Jones declined to examine it as he thought that the study of language had 'little intrinsic value' and was 'only useful as the instrument of real knowledge which we can scarce expect from the poets of Mozambique'.[1] A similar view was expressed in his first discourse to the Society.[2] So, although he acquired a mastery of many languages both classical and modern within a short span of time, he was in his own admission no scientific linguist. He wrote his *Persian Grammar* which was at least a good guide to the study of 'Shiraz literary dialect'[3] as known from the eighteenth-century Persian manuscripts in Europe. But this was not a part of a project of research in languages; it was chiefly meant to help the Englishman in the East. The famous letter to Duperron, as we have seen, was a misadventure in the study of linguistics and it was brought out mainly to defend Oxford;[4] moreover, his chief arguments against Duperron were historical.[5]

When he came to India he had no plans to study Sanskrit. He left that field to Wilkins:

Happy should I be to follow you in the same track; but life is too short and my necessary business too long for me to think at my age of acquiring a new language...All my hopes therefore of being acquainted with the poetry, philosophy and arts of the Hindus are grounded on the expectation of living to see the fruits of your learned labour.[6]

But the study of Indian laws which his profession required of him and the possibilities of Wilkins's early return to England induced Jones to learn Sanskrit.[7] By 1 March 1785 he received a copy of a *Dharma Śāstra* from Benares. Jones decided to make a thorough study of the subject, and he asked Wilkins to send a better version of the work.[8] His interest in the subject was further stimulated by practical judicial difficulties; he had to find out the Indian ways of punishing criminals for perjury. He knew that the 'beginning of the eighth chapter of Minoo (Manu) has some rules on the form of oaths'. He wanted Wilkins to explain them to him.[9] He regretted that he could not spell in Sanskrit properly.[10] But he had to wait until September of that year, when he came to Krishnagar, to learn Sanskrit. At this time the Brahmins were away from the town.

Some are gone to the Rany Bhavany, others to other votaries of Durga from whom they receive presents at this season: but I have found a pleasant old man of the medical cast who teaches me all he knows of the grammar; and I hope to read the Hitapades or some other story book with him. My great object is the Dharmasastra to which I shall arrive by degrees.[1]

By then he had already gathered most material for his paper on the Hindus, through the *Bhāgavata Purāṇa*, the *Yogavāsiṣṭha* and the *Saṅgīta Darpana* in their Persian translations.[2]

On 2 February, less than four months after he had started learning Sanskrit seriously, he read his famous paper on the Hindus; this contained the often quoted passage which is supposed to have sparked off the research which ultimately led to the discovery of comparative and historical philology.[3]

The Sanskrit language, whatever be its antiquity, is of a wonderful structure; more perfect than the Greek, more copious than the Latin, and more exquisitely refined than either, yet bearing to both of them a stronger affinity, both in the roots of verbs and in the forms of grammar, than could possibly have been produced by accident; so strong indeed, that no philologer could examine them all three without believing them to have sprung from some common source, which, perhaps, no longer exists.

It is easy to read too much into this passage when taken out of context. Before we explain its significance, it should be remembered that philology, as we have seen, had already made considerable progress, and that Jones was not the first to discover the resemblance between Sanskrit and Latin and Greek. The affinity was noticed as early as the sixteenth century; Thomas Stevens,[4] an English Jesuit in India, in 1583 and Fillipo Sasseti,[5] an Italian merchant in Goa, in 1585 discovered independently the affinity between Sanskrit and European classical languages. In respect of the reason for this affinity, Jones was not the pioneer in the field. He only added to Boxhorn's 'Scythian' family of languages. Again, Cœurdoux, a Jesuit missionary of Pondicherry, made a remarkable observation nearly twenty years before Jones's famous philologer's passage. In 1768 he thought that 'this resemblance of terms cannot be attributed it seems but to one of six causes:

commerce, sciences, vicinity of the countries, religion, domination and common origin or to all these causes together'.[1] After long consideration he decided that common origin would be the most likely explanation of the resemblance. Being true to his faith, the Jesuit fitted the discovery into old biblical tradition.

The languages were mixed up at the Babel tower. But was this confusion so complete that a few common words did not remain in all new languages?...Many common terms remained in the new languages; others have been so disfigured with the lapse of time that they are no longer recognizable. A few have been saved from the shipwreck to serve as an eternal memorial to mankind of their common origin and ancient brotherhood...Japhet the eldest son of Noah left the places of Sennar taking with him one third of the human race, to the West. His seven children must have been without doubt chiefs of many great families each speaking one of the new original languages like Latin, Greek and Slavonic etc. Let me be permitted to add the Sanskrit.[2]

The missionary made a clear distinction between all the human languages which were of common origin before the episode of the Tower of Babel and the languages of the family of Japhet. To prove the similarities between Sanskrit and the classical languages Cœurdoux gave a long list of words and verbal roots. He would have received recognition for adding Sanskrit to the Boxhorn family of languages had he published his letter of 1768.[3]

Jones must be credited with independently discovering the resemblance between Sanskrit and Latin and Greek and with postulating the possibility of a common mother language. He had, no doubt, that uncommon talent for grasping the problems of linguistics without going into details. He should also be credited for making his theory public at a time when the European mind was moving away from the neo-classicism of the eighteenth century.[4] This movement is often described as a revolt against the Age of Reason and is known under the general term of Romanticism. The idea that the Europeans migrated from a distant and unknown land soon fired the imagination of the Romantic mind.[5] Significantly it was a high priest of the Romantic movement, Friedrich Schlegel, who coined the term 'comparative grammar'.

This fascination for the distant past was generally neglected by the historians of the Enlightenment. Jones, as we have already noticed, was firmly grounded in the eighteenth century, with its Whig philosophy, classical education and the cult of Reason. His historical ideas were similar to those of the *philosophes* of the Enlightenment.[1] A first indication of a new trend in Jones's historical ideas is to be found in the memorandum which he wrote during his journey to India. Here for the first time he showed his interest in such problems as the confirmation of the tradition of the Deluge and the early history of India.[2] Perhaps the study of the *Gentoo Laws*, which starts with the Hindu idea of creation, stimulated his interest in comparing the Hindu mythology with the biblical tradition.

Though Bacon had shown that fallen man may improve his lot through scientific research, and Newton had finally replaced Aristotle in natural sciences, the Creator still had a great role to play in the Newtonian universe.[3] The accepted chronology still started at 4004 B.C. Some thought that the history of the human race started before that date, and that the Creation occurred at an earlier age; but they had no geological or historical evidence to support their theory.[4] Such fossils as were found were conveniently ascribed to the antediluvian period. While Jones was reading his annual discourses James Hutton was already working on geology, but was yet to bring out the results of his research.[5]

With this limited knowledge of the world and its history, and within a short space of time, Jones set about to write a short comprehensive history of 'the ancient world'. This was to be a critique of J. Bryant's monumental work on *The Analysis of Ancient Mythology*.[6] Bryant wrote this book in 1775. In it he aimed at proving the universality of the Deluge and the migration of the human race. He made some derisive comments on Asian languages, for which he was heavily censured by Richardson, a friend of Jones.[7] In 1777 Jones had read Bryant's work but then he was less interested in 'fables' and 'mythologies':

There is an infinite profusion of learning in his book, but I cannot help thinking his system very uncertain. I see no occasion to hunt for explanations of old fables, many of which had no foundation at all except in the poet's imagination.[8]

But now he was interested in explaining the fables. His discourse ' On the Hindus' was part of a series of short dissertations 'unconnected in their titles and subjects, but all tending to a common point of no small importance in the pursuit of interesting truths'.[9] These 'interesting truths' were the Creation, the Deluge and the migration of human races. He rejected Bryant's methods, which put too much emphasis on etymology in the study of 'ancient history'.[1] He decided to judge the affinities and diversities among the human races according to their 'languages and letters; philosophy and religion; remains of old sculptures and architecture and memoirs of their sciences and arts'.[2] So language was but one method of making a comparative study of the human race. Thus the famous philologer's passage was an integral part of Jones's master plan to write a history of mankind. The Greeks not only spoke a similar language but they also worshipped the same gods,[3] their philosophy had much in common with that of the Hindus[4] and their alphabet sprang from the same origin.[5] Jones held that at the time of Muhammad there were five nations in Asia, the Hindus, the Arabs, the Persians, the Tartars and the Chinese. He wrote five dissertations, each dealing with one of those nations. His eighth discourse was on the 'borderers, mountaineers and islanders of Asia'[6] With a very superficial knowledge of the Chinese, early Persia and the Egyptians, and a definite faith in the Book of Genesis, Jones made a bold attempt to draw conclusions from his researches in his discourse, 'on the origin and families of nations'. He maintained that some of his conclusions are certain: (a) 'The first race of Persians and Indians, to whom we may add the Romans and Greeks, the Goths and the old Egyptians or the Ethiops originally spoke the same language and professed the same popular faith', and (b) 'the Jews and Arabs, the Assyrians or second Persian race, the people who spoke Syriack and a numerous tribe of Abyssinians use one primitive dialect wholly distinct from the idiom just mentioned'.[7] He thought that it was no more than highly probable that the 'settlers in China and Japan had a common origin with the Hindus' and that 'all the Tartars as they are inaccurately called were primarily of a third separate branch totally differing from the two others in language, manners and features'.[8]

Once he had reduced the number of original races he had to find out their original home. He agreed with Linnaeus, the most advanced botanist of the age, that in the beginning God created one pair of humans only. He found that one pair was sufficient to populate the whole earth as the numbers increased in geometrical progression.[9] The story of the Flood was true, confirmation of the historicity of Moses was to be found in the Purāṇas and the Vedas 'which stand next in antiquity to the five books of Moses'.[10] After the Flood the language of Noah was lost irretrievably and his family settled in Iran, whence they migrated in all directions. The sons of Ham were the ancestors of the Hindus (by which Jones meant Indo-Europeans); to prove his hypothesis he identified Cush of Moses with Kuśa of Vālmīki.[1] Thus he found nothing in Hindu mythology which contradicted the Mosaic story.[2]

So Jones had but an indirect influence on the growth of the science of comparative philology. Philology had made definite progress by the end of the eighteenth century and the affinity of Sanskrit with the Greek and Roman languages had already been noticed. Jones arrived at the right theory independently, but he was not the first to do so. He put the idea of common origin in a dramatic and fascinating way, which easily captured the post-Revolutionary European mind and stimulated further research on the subject. Finally Franz Bopp published the first comparative grammar of Indo-European languages in 1816.[3] Jones should also be given credit for rather infectiously spreading an interest in Sanskrit throughout Europe and thus making it easy for Bopp to study Pāṇini, without whose ideas of morphology modern philology would never have been possible.

Perhaps a minor but a very practical contribution to the study of Sanskrit linguistics was his paper on the *Asiatick Orthography*.[4] It may be that his transliteration was made with too many accents and he did not standardize his long vowels; but his principle, to follow the spelling letter for letter, is still being used. As Sir Monier Williams pointed out:

As a result of a kind of natural selection or survival of the fittest the practice of all Oriental scholars so far as Aryan languages are concerned is settling down into an acceptance of Sir William Jones's principle of transliteration.[5]

This is a remarkable achievement if we remember that such a sound observation of Sanskrit phonetics was made before Jones embarked on the difficult task of learning the Language of the Gods.

It is no easy task to reconstruct early Indian history solely from the mass of Indian mythology, with its innumerable gods and heroes, its conception of infinite time and contradictory commentaries on the original works. To this already difficult task Jones added another one. His study of Indian mythology had a purpose other than the mere satisfaction of the curiosity of a few men. Such research might be 'of solid importance in an age when some intelligent and virtuous persons are inclined to doubt the authenticity of the accounts delivered by Moses concerning the primitive world'.[1] Universal history had to be written and Indian mythology explained in order to remove such doubts. So Jones was not making a survey for its own sake but to put Indian mythology in line with biblical tradition. Once his conjectures about the Creation, the Deluge and migration of human races were moulded according to the story of Genesis, Indian history had to be fitted into the framework of chronology based on dating the Creation of the world in 4004 B.C.

From the Renaissance onwards one of the preoccupations of the Europeans was to explain classical mythology and by the seventeenth century Europe had added to the classical pantheon many more Gods from all quarters of the world. Many theologians, both Protestant and Catholic, explained the gods as embodiments of demons or fallen angels and the myths as corruption of sacred history. Bacon thought that most mythology was allegorical, pure metaphysics told in the form of stories. Newton took an Euhemeristic attitude. To him all myths were the results of the deification of the old heroes. There were many works written on mythology and Newton himself tried to reconstruct the ancient chronology of the Greeks, to 'dispell darkness and honour God'.[2]

Jones rejected the pure allegoricism of Bacon and the pure Euhemericism of Newton. He recognized four sources of mythology: (*a*) Historical, 'the truth perverted into fable, ignorance, imagination, flattery or stupidity'. Thus the story of Noah and his flood was known to most ancient peoples, though in a fabulous form. (*b*) Admiration for nature: the wild admiration for nature led to the worship of sun and other constellations and helped the Hindus to invent 'demi-gods and heroes to fill the vacant niches in their extravagant and imaginary periods'. (*c*) The magic of poetry:

Numberless divinities have been created solely by the magick of poetry; whose essential business it is, to personify the most abstract notions, and to place a nymph or a genius in every grove and almost in every flower; hence Hygieia and Jaso, health and remedy, are the poetical daughters of Aesculapius, who was either a distinguished physician, or medical skill personified.

(d) Metaphors: 'Allegories of moralists and metaphysics have been also very fertile in deities.'[1] Thus the Indian Vedantic conception of *Māyā* was personified as the mother of universal nature and of all the inferior gods.

With these four sources in mind, Jones analysed the Hindu pantheon and compared it with the classical one. He came to the conclusion that they all worshipped the same gods under different names. 'We must not be surprised', he said, 'at finding all the pagan deities male and female melt into each other and at least into one or two.'[2] So Gaṇeśa of the Hindus was no other than Janus of the Romans; Ceres, Lakṣmī; and Jupiter, the Hindu triad. This pursuit of 'comparative mythology' led him to discover what he thought the confirmation of 'true history' in a distorted form in the pagan mythologies. He thought that Saturn of the ancient Europeans should be indentified with Noah, for the stories about him are very similar to those of Genesis.[3] Likewise the story about the *Matsya Avatāra* which Jones found in the *Bhāgavata Purāṇa* is evidently 'that of Noah disguised by Asiatick fiction' (to Jones the biblical tradition was neither 'Asiatick' nor fictional). So Manu 'the child of the sun', who was saved by God during the universal Deluge, was Noah of the Bible.[4] So Jones concluded that the Deluge is very important from the point of view of the historians for from this event genuine Hindu chronology begins. He rejected the other deluge mentioned in the *Bhāgavata Purāṇa* as a local one 'intended only to affect the people of Vraja'.[5]

Jones divided the whole of human history into four periods, Diluvian, Patriarchal, Mosaic and Prophetical.[6] The Indian Satya-yuga roughly corresponds with the Diluvian period and the stories of the first three Avatāras or incarnations of God refer to the story of the Flood in allegories. In the fourth and fifth Avatāra God punishes and humiliates presumptuous monarchs. This again probably tells the story of Nimrod and Belus of the Old Testament.[7] He conjectured that the three Rāmas who were incarnations of God should be taken as one person and he was perhaps Rama, son of Cush of the Bible. Rāma in India 'was named Caushalya', as a derivative of 'Cushala', and the name Cush 'is preserved entire in that of his son and successor and shadowed in that of his ancestor Vicuchi'.[8] So Jones concluded 'that government was first established, laws enacted and agriculture encouraged in India by Rama about three thousand eight hundred years ago (2029 B.C.)', and this fact agreed 'with the received account of Noah's death and the previous settlement of his immediate descendants'.[1]

In the reconstruction of Hindu chronology Jones depended largely on the Persian translation of the *Bhāgavata Purāṇa*. John Shore supplied him with another work called *Purāṇārthaprakāśa*.[2]

This latter work was by Pandit Radhakanta, who wrote it for his patron Warren Hastings. In it Radhakanta Sharman summarized the *Paurāṇic* views of history and religion for Western readers. The work is in four parts, (*a*) *Kālasaṅkhyāprakarana*[3]—Brahmanic reckoning of time, etc.; (*b*) *Dharmanirūpanaprakarana*[4]—on all religious texts; (*c*) *Sṛṣtyādinirūpana*[5]—on creation, etc.; and (*d*) *Rājavaṁsa*[6]—on king-lists. It is interesting to note that nearly one hundred and fifty years before Pargiter[7] Pandit Radhakanta tried to bring together all the king-lists from various Purānas. It is surprising to find how often the Bengali Pandit was right. No doubt he believed the Brahmanic reckoning of time rather blindly, but his list of the dynasties of *Kaliyuga* or the modern age (which according to the tradition started in 3102 B.C.) is basically correct[8] and Pargiter's genealogy, which is now widely accepted, follows that of Radhakanta's very closely.

Jones met Radhakanta in the summer of 1787, and held long discussions with him.[9] Govardhana Kaul, a Kashmiri Brahmin, and Pandit Ramlochan, Jones's own teacher, also helped him to reconstruct early Indian history.[10] Jones's chief aim was to reduce the Indian ages to within the limits of his historical period. To do this he had to prove that the *Kaliyuga* started much later than the Hindus would admit.

He found that the Hindu tradition regarding the date of the birth of the Buddha, the ninth incarnation of God, is contradictory. Some said he was born at the beginning of the *Kaliyuga* while others maintained that he appeared at least 1,000 years later. Jones also noticed that although the Brahmins spoke of the Buddha as an incarnation of God they disliked the Buddhas, the followers of the Buddha. To reconcile the contradictions Jones postulated that there were two Buddhas. One was born at the end of the last age and the other 1,000 years after the start of the *Kaliyuga*.[11] The Chinese had left more reliable traditions about the birth of the Buddha. Among the Jesuit accounts of the Fo or Buddha, that of Joseph de Guignes appeared to be most reliable. He put the date of the Buddha in 1027 B.C.[12] Hence Jones held that, even if Fo is identified with the second Buddha, the *Kaliyuga* could not have started much before 2000 B.C. So the Hindus are wrong in assuming that the *Kaliyuga* started as early as 3102 B.C. If the *Kaliyuga* started at a later date, then the Hindus would agree that the other ages were mostly mythological, though they might contain some historical truth in the form of fables. The king-list which ended in 452 B.C. with Candrabhija,[1] who according to Radhakanta was the last king of the Andhras to rule independently in Magadha, was unreliable for it gave 3,150 years to 142 reigns. Taking the date of the Buddha as 1027 B.C. and believing in the statement in *Bhāgavatāmṛta* (a late commentary on the *Bhāgavata Purāṇa*) that the Buddha appeared in Avanti two years after Pradyota's accession to the throne, Jones reconstructed the Indian chronology as follows:

Abhimanyu	2029 B.C.
Pradyota	1029 B.C.
Buddha	1027 B.C.
Nanda	699 B.C.
Balin	149 B.C.
Vikramāditya	56 B.C.
Devapāla	23 B.C.[2]

The last two names were from the Vikrama tradition as it was known to the pandits and from the Monghyr land grant inscription. The date of Devapāla was decided to be 23 B.C. for both Jones and Wilkins took the term *Saṃvat* for Vikrama era. Jones knew that *Saṃvat* could also mean just year.

This date therefore might only mean the thirty third year of the king's reign; but since Vicramaditya was surnamed the foe of Saca, and is praised by that name in a preceding stanza, we may safely infer that the grant was dated thirty three years after the death of that illustrious emperor, whom the king of Gaur, though a sovereign prince, acknowledged as lord paramount of India.[3]

Later he added two more names to the chronology. One was Nārayaṇapāla of the Badal inscription, whose date he fixed at A.D. 67. The other was Śaka, who according to tradition died in A.D. 78.

On 17 June 1790 he read a paper, 'A supplementary essay on Indian chronology'.[4] He had received a copy of *Sūrya Siddhānta* from his friend Samuel Davis. After a tedious effort he was able to read the work with the help of his teacher. From Newton's[1] calculations he found the position of Equinox at the time of the birth of Varāha (i.e. the astronomer Varāhamihira), who according to the tradition lived 1,680 years after Parāśara. So Jones put the date of Parāśara in 1181 B.C. Thus Vāśiṣṭha, the grandfather of Parāśara and preceptor of Rāma, who was mentioned by Manu, could not have lived much before 1300 B.C. So Hindu history started much later than the Hindus would have had him believe. Jones confidently concluded,

Whatever the comparative antiquity of the Hindu scriptures, we may safely conclude that the Mosaick and Indian chronologies are perfectly consistent; that Manu son of Brahma was the Adima, or first created mortal, and consequently our Adam; that Manu, child of the sun, was preserved with seven others, in a bahitra or capacious ark from our universal deluge, and must therefore be our Noah;...and the dawn of true Indian history appears only three or four centuries before the Christian era, the preceding ages are clouded by allegory or fable.[2]

This chronology is no guide to Indian history. Jones used so-called etymology and astronomy in reconstructing the chronology although he censured Newton and Bryant for doing likewise. This led him to fix the dates with unreliable calculations and identify names on their superficial resemblance. He relied solely on *Paurāṇic* sources and ignored the Vedas[3] completely and, in spite of repeated statements to the contrary, he believed in Genesis rather blindly. So naturally his chronology is totally useless. But one cannot help admiring the laborious efforts of Pandit Radhakanta and Jones in bringing together all the king-lists from various sources. Moreover, Jones's efforts shifted the scholarly interest to the 'dark periods' of Indian history, which stimulated further research.

If chronology and geography are two important factors in the study of history of a given country, then neither Genesis nor the *Paurāṇic* tradition without the aid of other sources are any guide to early Indian history. The starting point of Indian chronology and ancient geography would be through the process of synchronism and identification. One could determine the name and date of an Indian prince for certain if he could be identified with someone mentioned in comparatively reliable classical sources about India and if other historical events synchronized with the given date.

In the history of Alexander's invasion of India the classical sources mentioned an Indian prince called Sandrocottas who was an adventurer and who ruled the land of Prasii, whose capital was Palibothra. Many European authors had tried to identify Sandrocottas with one or other Indian prince mentioned in the Indian traditions. Dow in his *History of Hindostan* identified him with Sinsarchund, a Hindu king, who according to Firishta ruled in Kanauj.[1] The garbled version of the late medieval Hindu traditions as preserved by Firishta was no guide to Indian history. But Rennel in 1783 maintained that Palibothra, the capital of Sandrocottas's kingdom, should be identified with Kanauj. Like Palibothra, Kanauj stood at the confluence of two rivers; moreover the latitude of Kanauj was 27°, which is what Ptolemy gave to Palibothra.[2] But contrary to his own conclusion Rennel found that Pliny's itinerary put Palibothra very near the modern city of Patna; as there was no other proof that there was an ancient city near Patna, Rennel preferred Kanauj as the capital of early India.[3] In 1788 however he changed his view. He discovered that the local tradition in Patna maintained that there had been an old city called 'Patelpoother (Pataliputra according to Sir William Jones)', in the same place, 'and that the river Soane whose confluence with the Ganges is now at Moneal 22 miles above Patna once joined it under the walls of Patelpoot-her'.[4]

The French geographer d'Anville who wrote the first ancient geography of India as it could be reconstructed from classical sources identified Palibothra with modern Allahabad, which was known as Prayaga and which stands at the confluence of the Ganges and Jamuna.[5] Robertson, one of the three great British historians of the time, agreed with d'Anville and thought that Rennel was wrong.[6]

In 1769 Maridas Pillai (Poulle), chief interpreter to the Supreme Council of Pondicherry, sent a French translation of the *Bhāgavata Purāṇa* to M. Bertin, minister and secretary of state. In 1772 Joseph de Guignes wrote a note on the work *Bagavadam*.[7] Maridas Pillai must have translated the work very loosely and his transcription of Sanskrit names shows that he pronounced them in the Tamil manner.[8] In the *Paurāṇic* king-list the name of Candragupta appeared as Sandragouten. This helped de Guignes to recognize Sandragouten of the *Bagavadam* as the Sandrocottas of the classical sources.[9] Working from the date of Alexander's invasion, which he took as 328 B.C., de Guignes came to the conclusion that Sandragouten succeeded to the throne in 303 B.C.[10] This date he thought synchronized with the *Paurāṇic* king-list if the date of Paricchiton (Parikṣit) is given as 1051 B.C., which date he reached by working backwards from the Ghaznavid invasion in A.D. 975.[1]

In the ninth annual discourse delivered in 1792 Jones has given his conclusions on universal history and 'the origin and families of nations', and on 28 February of the following year in his tenth annual discourse on 'Asiatick History'[2] he gave his views on the methods and the use of history. He said that in Asia fiction and history are so blended 'as to be scarce distinguishable';[3] so here historians have to work from mythology, tales and even dramas, for they contain some historical events such as the murder of Nanda and the usurpation of Candragupta. But to reconstruct the history from the earliest period to the British conquest one must be competent in Sanskrit, Persian and Arabic and should ask for explanations of the sources from the Brahmin pandits and the Indo-Muslim scholars like Ghulam Hussain.[4] Even after the laborious work of consulting all the sources and scholars a historian could give 'absolute credence to the general outline'[5] only.

Such a general outline he had already given in his other discourses and papers on Hindu chronology and mythology. He had established 'true facts' on Indian history within the long period from Rama (that is the first establishment of an Indian epic) to Candrabhija (who is supposed to be the first Hindu king to rule in Bihar). One of these was the date of Parāśara and so the *Mahābhārata*, which could not have been before the twelfth century B.C., and the other was the date of Vikramāditya in 57 B.C. Now he believed that he could provide a third fact within a certain date.[6] This was the accession of Candragupta to the throne in Pāṭaliputra.

He said that he had already discovered by accident that the river Son had an old name Hiranyabahu (Hiranyavāha) which the Greeks called Eranoboas. At the confluence of this and the Ganges stood the old city of Pāṭaliputra, which was no other than Palibothra of the Greeks.[7] Here he totally ignored Rennel's contribution. We have already noticed that in 1788 Rennel had fixed upon Patna or Pāṭaliputra as the old capital of ancient India, and he cited Jones's authority for it.[8] But we do not know whether Rennel only asked Jones to correct the spelling or received the information about Pāṭaliputra from him. Jones knew in 1788 that Patna was once called Pāṭaliputra and in 1793 he had new evidence to establish this fact.

This led to another discovery;

Chandragupta who was a military adventurer, became like Sandrocottas the sovereign of upper Hindustan, actually fixed the seat of his empire at Pataliputra, where he received ambassadors from foreign princes and was no other than that very Sandrocottas who conducted a treaty with Seleucus Nicator.[1]

Jones already knew from the *Bhāgavata Purāṇa and Purāṇārthaprakāśa*[2] about this adventurer prince of India. But previously his efforts had been devoted to proving that in fact the chronology of Hindu India was much shorter than the Hindus themselves claimed and he paid no attention to the history of Candragupta. But recently Candragupta had again been brought to his notice by two sources, one of which was the well-known *Kathāsaritsāgara* of Somadeva, and the other an eighteenth-century drama *Candrābhīṣekha*[3] by Bāneśvara Bhattacarya; Citrasena, the Maharaja of Burdwan, was the patron of this poet, who had already written a romance called *Citracampu*.[4] The play, which was produced at the Raja's court, was in seven acts and told the old story of the intrigues of Cānakya and Śakaṭāra in overthrowing the Nandas and establishing Candragupta Maurya on the throne. It is quite clear that Bāneśvara drew heavily on the legends especially the Bṛhatkathā tradition as he introduced Śakaṭāra as the chief instigator of the palace revolution.[5] Jones clearly saw that the name had been mispronounced by the Greeks and that the career of this prince fitted in well with the classical accounts of Sandrocottas.

Here again Jones made no mention of de Guignes. He must have been well acquainted with the other works of de Guignes as he had used his date for the birth of the Buddha in reconstructing the Hindu chronology.[6] But there is no evidence that the relevant copy of the journal in which the article appeared was available in Calcutta at that time. Even if Jones had read the article while in England, he would not have been interested enough to remember the details of the article twenty years later. Moreover the whole business of the *Bagavadam* was shrouded in mystery and was not considered to be a reliable source.[7] Joseph de Guignes was recognized only as an expert on China and so his contribution to Indian chronology was neglected not only by Jones but even by the French geographer d'Anville. None of the other authors who dealt with Sandrocottas and Palibothra made any mention of de Guignes.

So it is possible that Jones came to the same conclusion independently.

While his earlier chronology is a useless guide to ancient Indian history, this identification of Sandrocottas and Palibothra was an

important landmark in the history of Indian studies. In the seventeenth and eighteenth centuries many attempts were made by both European and Indo-Muslim scholars to make out a plausible chronology of the numerous dynasties of ancient India which would agree with the 'Mosaic history' sacred to Christians and Muslims alike.[1] Jones had made similar futile attempts. Although he had better Sanskrit manuscripts at his disposal and the best Indian scholars to assist him, he could not bring out a reliable chronology, but now he was able to identify at least one figure from the hundreds and thousands of Indian heroes and gods with a historical character mentioned in Greek sources. No doubt de Guignes had made this discovery in 1772, but his work was ignored by the eighteenth-century scholars. Jones arrived at the same conclusion independently but, what is important, he made his discovery public, as a president of a society which was busy in unveiling the Indian civilization to the learned world. Now it could be utilized fully to reconstruct the history of ancient India. This is the reason why the origins of modern scholarship on Indian studies have to be traced back to Jones and his friends.

Two illustrations from *Asiatick Researches*, vol. I. The inscription was from Gaya, which refers to the Maukharis and is written in the Gupta *Brāhmī* characters (shown opposite), which were deciphered by Wilkins.

At this period Indian archaeology had hardly started. A good number of inscriptions had been discovered; many facsimile copies of such inscriptions were sent to the president from all over the country.[1] They were largely records of land grants to Brahmins and temples, by princes of the many minor dynasties that ruled during the medieval period. These were written in Sanskrit and in *Kuṭila* or early *Devanāgari* characters. Wilkins had already deciphered some of the Pāla inscriptions in 1781.[1] In 1785 some inscriptions from Gaya were sent to him. These were records of the Maukharis, who ruled Gaya during the first half of the sixth century A.D. Wilkins clearly recognized that the characters of these inscriptions were the most ancient that had so far come under his inspection.[2] In fact these were written in Gupta *Brāhmī* characters and he deciphered it. In the same year Radhakanta Sharman read the Delhi–Topra pillar (then known as Firoj Sha's lat) inscription of the Chāhamāna king Visaladeva belonging to the eleventh century A.D. Jones himself was hard at work: 'If I can decypher all the inscriptions on the metal pillar (as I trust I shall) it will be a triumph.'[3] But what puzzled them most was the Aśokan inscription written in old *Brāhmī*: 'The Nagari inscriptions are easy and modern, but all the old ones on the staff of Firoz Shah drive me to despair.' He suggested that they belonged to some foreign conqueror, probably the Ethiopian Sisac who, Jones thought, was known in India as 'the lion of Sac' (Śakya Simha). Jones identified him with his second Buddha who lived one thousand years before Christ.[4] Such wild speculations were made for another fifty years until 1837. In that year James Prinsep successfully deciphered the Aśokan edicts.[5] It is interesting to note that, until much more ground was covered, Indian symbolism understood, Buddhist sources read, Jain scriptures and the Chinese records brought to light, archaeology could not be used in reconstructing ancient Indian history. The history reconstructed from the Roman coins from Nelore,[6] the Gupta coins from Bengal,[7] the ancient ruins in Mavalipuram[8] and the Elephanta caves,[9] the inscriptions, the Paurāṇic sources and the classical references, was misleading. Thus, although Wilkins read the Pāla records, he could not find an exact date for the Pāla princes.[10] Yet a beginning was made. The real contribution of Jones and his colleagues to modern historiography of early India was primarily to draw attention to this early period of history, to Indian historical traditions, and secondly to evolve the foundation of a methodology which was to be improved upon by later scholars. Such methodology included reading *Brāhmī* inscriptions, the study of the ruins and the identification of names and places and persons, like the identification of Palibothra and Sandrocottas. The methodology was summed up by William Chambers: he suggested that Indian history should be reconstructed by 'comparing names and great events recorded by them [Indians] with those interspersed in the memories of other nations and by calling in the assistance of ancient monuments, coins and inscriptions as occasion shall offer.'[1]

James Mill, in his efforts to belittle the achievements of the Hindus, took Jones as his chief antagonist; he tried to show how the Orientalist suffered from illusions about the Hindus and tended to magnify their importance without having any idea of what the term civilization meant.[2] He said that Jones's description of the life of the Arabs and Hindus far surpassed the 'rhapsodies of Rousseau on the happiness and virtue of savage life'.[3] To Mill, Jones was a misguided man, who failed to grasp the problems of India; his reason gave way to the romantic fascination of the East and so in his judgement on India he was uncritical. Ever since the first publication of Mill's famous work in 1817 the history of the British policy in India had been presented as if it were a struggle between Jones and Mill, the romantic versus the rationalist. This theme was developed in a recent conference on Indian historiography.[4] Elsewhere[5] Jones is described as a medievalist. In fact most of these writers presented Jones as James Mill had depicted him even though their sympathies may have been with the Orientalist.

These writers have assumed that the Orientalism of the eighteenth and early nineteenth centuries was closely allied with medievalism and was an offshoot of the Romantic movement. There is no doubt that by the last decades of the eighteenth century the cult of 'rational' China came to an end and it was rapidly replaced by a cult of Brahmanic mysticism.[6] The people who harked back to the Middle Ages also looked to 'spiritual' India. The rationalists like Bentham and Mill had turned their backs on the East. They indeed had an interest in India but that was confined to the improvement of British administration in that country and they had no inclination to learn anything from India. It is also true that most men who rebelled against the eighteenth-century faith in progress and Reason looked to the East for its 'simple' life, its mysticism, and the harmony between man and nature which was supposed to be found there.[7] But Jones could not be fitted into either of these categories. His attitudes towards India and Asia were much too complex to be pigeonholed.[8]

Jones's ideas were similar to those generally held in the eighteenth century. He was brought up in an atmosphere of classical learning and his sympathies were with the men of Reason. To him the real source of human happiness and prosperity was in commerce and labour. Politically he belonged to the extreme group of the Whig radicals, yet in him there was a tendency to dislike 'civilization', to love the 'primitive', and the 'natural'. This led him to admire the Arabs of Yemen where 'true happiness' could still be found.[1] The singular tension between the decorous and stylistic tradition of the eighteenth century and the romantic fascination of uncommon subjects[2] which has been noticed in his poetry may also be traced in his other works, notably in his treatment of history, where the conflict between the historiography of the Enlightenment and that of the Romantic movement is much in evidence. He believed in a concise, periodized and stylistic history yet in India he turned his attention to the 'darker periods', in which he earlier showed little or no interest. His religious views were Deistic and unemotional. He had firm faith in 'Rational' God and he 'proved' to his own satisfaction and to the satisfaction of his Evangelical biographer the Divinity of Christ.[3] His rather unemotional faith in Deity is manifested in his 'Hymn to Narayena' which was, at least in parts, inspired by Milton's 'Paradise Lost'.[4] Yet he was attracted to mysticism and devotional literature like the *Gīta Govinda*. This conflict between what we may call the man of reason and the man of instinct is also manifested in his attitude towards India. Mill and others have only mentioned one trend in Jones's thought.

If the object of his Society was to inquire into everything that is performed by man and produced by nature,[5] then the president himself set about to achieve it. As a young man he studied law, observed with great interest the latest scientific developments,[6] read the account of the voyages of James Cook[7] and attended Hunter's lectures on anatomy.[8] The same encyclopaedic interests continued in India but the primary object of his studies was religious.

In India he developed a passion for botany. He observed numerous Indian plants and tried to classify them according to the Linnaean system. But this study of botany was not merely to satisfy his curiosity but was stimulated by his deep religious feelings,

as to botany, it is my greatest delight in our vacations, partly because it is the most agreeable and interesting branch of natural history but principally because it is the favourite amusement of my darling Anna, who will have the pleasure of showing your ladyship her botanical drawings of Indian plants which we have examined together. Though we have read the works of the learned and eloquent Barrow with many other excellent theological discourses yet we find a more exquisite lecture on the being and attributes of God in every flower, every leaf and every berry than can be produced by the real wisdom and eloquence of man. The sublime doctrine of final causes [is] nowhere so beautifully proved and illustrated as in the plants of the lakes and forests when their different parts and uses of them are minutely and attentively observed.[1]

So nature is to be studied carefully and preserved; the animals brought to Jones for preservation had to be set free in the rocks and woods unless they could be tamed and protected.[2] He preferred to live away from the city and the crowd:

our way of life however is quite pastoral in this retired spot; as my prime favourites among all our pets are two large English sheep which came with us from Spithead and having narrowly escaped the knife are to live as long and as happily with us as they can; they follow us for bread and are perfectly domestic. We are literally lulled to sleep by Persian nightingales and cease to wonder that the Bulbul with a thousand tales makes such a figure in Oriental poetry.[3]

This was how he lived in Alipur five miles away from the city centre. Here he used to spend his evenings reading Italian poetry with Anna Maria and weekends enjoying the life in natural surroundings.[4] He occasionally joined in some of the official functions like the big balls at Government House but he generally kept away from the gay Calcutta society and very rarely entertained friends at home. In autumn he lived at Krishnagar in the heart of nature:

How preferable is this pastoral mansion (though built entirely of vegetable substances without glass, mortar, metal or any mineral except iron nails from its roof to its foundation) to the marble palaces which you have seen in Italy. It is a thatched cottage with an upper story and a covered verome or veranda as they call it here all round well boarded and ten or twelve feet broad. It stands on a dry plain where many a garden flower grows wild.[5]

There he spent most of his time with the Brahmins discussing literature, philosophy and mythology and telling them about the latest scientific discoveries in Europe.[1] His pleasure was the company of these men from Navadvip who called him a 'Hindu of the military tribe'.[2] He composed Sanskrit verses for the children of Krishnagar,[3]

I had made a Sanskrit stanza signifying that as a thirsty antelope runs to a pool of sweet water so I thirst for all kinds of knowledge which is as sweet as nectar. This verse has given me a place among Hindu poets. The Raja copied it, his son got it by heart and the Brahmins entered it among their records.

The life in this cottage was in fact idyllic and must have seemed to Jones like that of the golden age of fable;

I wish your ladyship could see us in our charming cottage; it would bring to your mind what the poets tell us of the golden age; for not to mention our flocks and herds that eat bread out of our hands you might see a kid and a tiger playing together at Anna's feet. The tiger is not so large as a full grown cat though he will be (as he is of the royal breed) as large as an ox, he is suckled by a she-goat and has all the gentleness (except when he is hungry) of his foster mother.[4]

This pastoral life reminds one of the hermitage of Kaṇva, the foster father of Śakuntalā, heroine of Kālidāsa's famous drama. No doubt Jones was charmed by the simplicity of life in Kaṇva's *āśrama* (hermitage) where all living creatures, animals, plants and human beings, lived in peace and harmony.

He first came to know about Śakuntalā in the late summer of 1787. While in Europe he had heard about Indian *Nāṭakas*. Père Pons has described it as Brahminical history mixed with fables.[5] After his inquiries in Calcutta among the Brahmins Jones found out that *Nāṭakas* were not histories mixed with fables but were popular works which 'consisted of conversations in prose and verse held before ancient Rajas in their publick assemblies'.[6] So he concluded that *Nāṭakas* were discourses on music and poetry. However, Pandit Radhakanta told him that the *Nāṭakas* were like the English plays performed in Calcutta during the cool seasons. When Jones asked for the best specimen of such a play he was given *Śakuntalā*.[7] This must have been some time in August 1787 for we find him sending the story of the drama to George John on 4 September of the same year,

I must tell you the subject of a drama in Sanskrit by Calidas (pronounce always as in Italian) the Indian Shakespeare or Metastasio, who was the chief poet at the court of Vicramaditya near two thousand years ago. The dramatick piece, is neither tragedy nor comedy, but like many of Shakespeare's fairy pieces is called Sacontala.[1]

In a year's time he read the Bengali recension of the drama with the help of Ramlochan, his teacher of the Vaidya caste, and on 17 August he completed his translation of the drama first into Latin and then into English.[2] In 1789 the first English translation was published in Calcutta.[3]

This was not the first Sanskrit work to be translated into a European language. In the seventeenth century Abraham Roger had translated Bhartṛhari's proverbs,[4] and Wilkins had already published *Bhagvat Geeta* in 1785 and *Heetopadesa* in 1787. But these works were chiefly intended to convey the Indian religious and secular ideas to Europe, and they were not translated for their literary merit. Neither Hastings nor Wilkins claimed that; in fact Hastings had to make a special plea for *Geeta*, 'I should exclude in estimating the merit of such a production all rules drawn from the ancient and modern literature of Europe'.[5] Jones unlike Hastings did not make any such pleading for Indian literature. To him Kālidāsa could be judged by European standards and he was equal to Shakespeare both as a dramatist and as a poet. He agreed that taste varied but it was from individual to individual and not from one nation to another,

on the characters of the play I shall offer no criticism; because I am convinced that the tastes of men differ as much as their sentiments and passions and that in feeling the beauties of art as in smelling flowers tasting fruits, viewing prospects, and hearing melody, every individual must be guided by his own sensations and the incommunicable associations of his own ideas.[6]

So Jones gave only his individual judgement which might or might not be accepted by others. No doubt the simplicity of Śakuntalā, the love of nature in the play charmed Jones but he ascribed greatness to it more for its style and decorum. Such style was the result of a highly complex and cultivated civilization,

Whatever the age when drama was first introduced in India, it was carried to great perfection in its kind, when Vicramaditya, who reigned in the first century before Christ gave encouragement to poets, philosophers, and mathematicians at a time when Britons were as unlettered and unpolished as the army of Hanumat:[7] nine men of genius commonly called the nine gems attended his court and were splendidly supported by his bounty, and Calidas is unanimously allowed to have been the brightest of them.[1]

The drama, with its complex use of mythology in allegorical form,[2] was produced at a time when the 'Indian empire' was in its full vigour and 'the national vanity must have been highly flattered by the magnificent introduction of those kings and heroes in whom the Hindus gloried'.[3] If Jones had been merely fascinated by primitiveness, he would have preferred the 'unlettered Britons' to Kālidāsa of Vikramāditya's court. He was charmed by the simplicity of Śakuntalā, the peacefulness of Kaṇva's *āśrama*, yet he used the drama to prove that the Hindus had a civilization in its own way equal to that of the Greeks. This is the reason why he purposely avoided passages like the one describing the swelling breasts of Śakuntalā. The sense of decency which earlier made him change the sex of the subject in his *Persian Song* manifested itself here.[4] He admitted that he had excluded from his translation passages of *Gīta Govinda* which he considered to be 'too bold' or 'too luxuriant'.[5] All this was to prove that the achievements of the Hindus were not much different from those of ancient Europe;

To what shall I compare my literary pursuits in India? Suppose Greek literature to be known in modern Greece only and there to be in the hands of priests and philosophers; and suppose them to be still worshippers of Jupiter and Apollo; suppose Greece to have been conquered successively by Goths, Huns, Vandals, Tartars and lastly by the English; then suppose a court of judicature to be established by the British parliament in Athens and an inquisitive Englishman to be one of the judges; suppose him to learn Greek there, which none of the countrymen knew and to read Homer, Pindar, Plato, which no other Europeans had ever heard of. Such am I in this country; substituting Sanscrit for Greek and the Brahmins for the priests of Jupiter and Valimic, Vyasa and Calidasa for Homer, Plato and Pindar.[6]

This complex personality, the product of romanticism on the one hand and a classical training on the other, found in India an echo of his own being—on the one hand simplicity, natural beauty and fascinating strangeness, and on the other a highly complex and well-cultivated civilization.

He had shown that Indians and most Europeans sprang from the same origin; their languages were derived from an original extinct language; and the Hindus, Greeks and all pagans worshipped the same gods under different names. The similarities between early Indian and Greek astronomy was explained in the same vein,

the Indian division of the Zodiack was not borrowed from the Greeks or Arabs, but having been known in this country from time immemorial and being the same in part with that used by other nations of the old Hindu race was probably invented by the first progenitors of that race before their dispersion.[1]

But the Indians also contributed to human civilization after their settlement in India. He supplied new evidence to prove that the game of chess was discovered in India.[2]

The Hindus also developed a complex system of music. Although they were unacquainted with harmony, they could 'like the Greeks' 'distinguished the consonent and dissonent sounds',[3] so their music had attained the same standard.

Even before he could read Indian mythology and the epics in their original language (which he had then read in their Persian versions), he was convinced of the greatness of their religion and literature:

I am in love with Gopia, charmed with Crishen [Kṛiṣṇa], an enthusiastic admirer of Raāma and a devout adorer of Brimha [Brahma], Bishen [Viṣṇu], Mahiser [Maheśvara]; not to mention that Judishteir, Arjen, Corno and other warriors of the M'hab'harat [Mahābhārata] appear greater in my eyes than Agamemnon, Ajax and Achilles appeared when I first read the Iliad.[4]

With the years he grew to admire Indian religion and philosophy. He first read the Persian texts on the subject, like *Dabistān-i-Mazāhib* by Muhsin-fānī, Dara Sikho's translation of the *Upaniṣadas*[5] and the Persian version of the *Dharma Śāstras*. Later he read the Indian texts in their original language with the help of his pandits.[6] He supported the traditional story that Plato and Pythagoras borrowed their philosophical ideas from India with fresh authority. The six philosophical schools of India 'comprise all the metaphysicks of the old Academy'; the fountain source of mysticism was the *Vedāntic* system from which the Persians and Greeks had borrowed, and Pythagoras based part of his philosophy on the *Sāṅkhya* system of India.[7] He felt proud that he could converse with the Brahmins in their own language whereas the ancient Greeks could not communicate with them directly.[8]

The two aspects of Hinduism which attracted Jones most were

the conception of the non-duality of God and the human soul as explained by Śaṅkara in his commentary on the *Vedānta* and the transmigration of the soul. Jones had faith in God and Christ as pictured in the Bible but his views were very similar to those of Dissenters such as Price and Priestley. Of Richard Price's *Sermon* (1787), he said that 'after this publication by good old Price, the Church of England as it is called would inevitably fall and the Religion of the Gospel be substituted in its place'.[1] This sermon if translated into Persian and Sanskrit might convince the Muslims and the Hindus of the superiority of Christianity. In fact the Hindus would have less difficulty 'in admitting the thirty-nine articles; because if those articles were written in Sanskrit they might pass well enough for the composition of a Brahmin'.[2] The Brahmins would not find it difficult to follow the Christian conception of one God. Of the *Vedāntic* system he said,

I have not sufficient evidence on the subject to profess a belief in the doctrine of the Vedanta, which human reason alone could perhaps neither fully demonstrate nor fully disprove; but it is manifest, that nothing can be farther removed from impiety than a system wholly built on purest devotion.[3]

He agreed with Voltaire[4] that the multitude of the Hindus were superstitious. They practised a false religion under the guidance of a dishonest priestcraft although Hinduism contains the knowledge of the true philosophy:

With all my admiration of the truly learned Brahmins I abhor the sordid priestcraft of Durga's minister but such fraud no more affects the sound religion of the Hindus than the Lady of Loreto and the Romish impositions affect our own rational faith.[5]

He warned the missionaries:

Our divine religion, the truth of which (if any history is true) is abundantly proved by historical evidence, has no need of such aids, as many are willing to give it, by asserting that the wisest men of this world, were ignorant of the two great maxims, that we must act in respect of others, as we would wish them to act in respect of ourselves, and that, instead of returning evil for evil we should confer benefits even on those who wish to injure us.[6]

These maxims were known to the Hindus three centuries before Christ, to the Chinese and to Sadi and Hafiz.

In one respect Jones thought Hinduism was superior to Christianity. He could not believe in the Christian doctrine of punishment and eternity of pain.[1] He found that the Hindu idea of transmigration of soul 'more rational' than the Christian idea of the future state.

I am no Hindu but I hold the doctrine of the Hindus concerning a future state to be incomparably more rational, more pious and more likely to deter men from vice than the horrid opinions inculcated by the Christians on punishment without end.[2]

He showed that India had excelled in arithmetic, geometry and logic. He thought that it is possible that Aristotle based his system of logic on Brahmanic syllogisms.[3] Hindus can boast of three discoveries, the decimal scale, the game of chess and the science of grammar:

if their numerous works on grammar, logick, rhetorick, musick, all which are extant and accessible, were explained in some language generally known, it would be found that they had yet higher pretensions to praise of a fertile and inventive genius.[4]

In his last discourse to the Asiatick Society he claimed that the whole of the Newtonian theory and part of his philosophy 'may be found in the Vedas and even in the work of the Sufis'. The Vedas abound in allusions 'to a force universally attractive' which they ascribed to the sun, called 'adytya' or 'attractor'.[5]

But, when all this was said about the greatness of the Hindu civilization, its beautiful literature, sublime religion and highly complex metaphysics, Jones did not go so far as to say, as James Mill thought he did, that India was better than Europe. No doubt he maintained that the Indians and the Arabs were more original in literature than the Romans had been, yet they were no better than the Greeks,

As to the works of Greeks I perfectly agree with you and think every line of them to be a gem of exquisite beauty, but I consider the Romans as bright only with borrowed rays and doubt whether Italy would have produced a poet better [than] the Fauns and Sylvens if Greece had not been conquered. The Hindus and Arabs are perfectly original; and to my taste (which can no more be a rule for others than my smell) their compositions are sublime and beautiful in a high degree: but your favourite Virgil would make an indifferent appearance in a verbal translation; and the art of his compositions can only be known to those who like you feel the charm of his original versification.[1]

In fact to Jones Asia flourished in the sphere of imagination only whereas 'reason and taste are the grand prerogatives of European minds'.[2] This made Europeans superior to the Indian and other Asiatics;

though we cannot agree with the sage preceptor of that ambitious Prince (Alexander) that the Asiaticks are born to be slaves, yet the Athenian poet seems perfectly in the right when he represents Europe as a sovereign princess and Asia as her handmaid.[3]

Asia had no conception of freedom. If every reader of history

would open his eyes to some very important conclusions which flow from the whole extent of it, he could not but remark the constant effect of despotism in benumbing and destroying all those faculties which distinguish men from the herd that grazes; and to that cause he would impute the decided inferiority of most Asiatick nations, ancient and modern to those in Europe who are blest with happier governments.[4]

This was the reason why Indian natural sciences were inferior to those of Europe. He noticed that *Āyurveda*, supposed to be the work of a celestial physician, 'is almost entirely lost',

unfortunately for the curious European, but happily for the patient Hindu; since a revealed science precludes improvement from experience, to which that of medicine ought, above all others, be left perpetually open.[5]

Earlier he had warned his audience not to expect 'from the chymists of Asia those beautiful examples of analysis which have but lately been displayed in the laboratories of Europe'.[6]

To Jones the greatest achievements of human wisdom were embodied in the British constitution. Significantly in the second plan of his proposed epic poem, *Britain Discovered*, which was to be written in praise of the British constitution, gods and heroes from India came to pay homage at the nuptials of Britan (Royalty) and Albion (Liberty).[7] The union of Royalty and Liberty could only be found in the British constitution which made Britain far superior to any other nation in the world. This love for the British constitution and a sense of the superiority of Europe in the field of science and law, were dominant emotions in Jones's mind, as was the romantic fascination which the exotic had for him.

The 'Great Discoveries'

We cannot judge Jones's contribution to the development of Indology by adding up various isolated 'discoveries' supposed to have been made by him. Some of these discoveries were already known at least to some of the French scholars. Others like that on orthography were of very small importance. His real contribution to Indology lies in the foundation of the Asiatick Society which eventually unveiled India to the intellectual world, with the active help of the Indians, especially since 1829 when they were allowed to join as full members of the Society. He presented his theories about Indian civilization in a dramatic way which infectiously spread the romantic fascination of India and her culture throughout Europe. He and his Society evolved a methodology for the study of Indian history. His publication of *Śakuntalā* and the *Gīta Govinda* put Indian literature on the world map. After this no one could deny its merits. Walpole[1] might have disliked it, but even Mill[2] had to admit that parts of the drama were beautiful.

CHAPTER 7

THE LEGACY OF JONES

In the autumn of 1793 Jones took Anna Maria to Bandel, a town near Calcutta. He had to cancel his annual trip to Krishnagar, for Anna Maria was suffering from a chronic stomach complaint because of the climate; this was causing anxiety to her doctors, and Jones was advised not to go very far from Calcutta. Since 1786[1] he had been persuading her to return to England, because of her ill health, and in 1793 she had at last agreed. He had almost completed compiling the Digest, so he thought his days in Calcutta were coming to an end. On 25 September he looked back upon his ten years in India:

This day ten years ago, my dear Lord, we landed at Calcutta, and if it had not been for the incessant ill health of my beloved Anna, they would have been the ten happiest years of a life always happy because always independent; her sufferings from this climate and consequently mine (though the climate has not affected me personally) [are] approaching I trust their termination.[2]

Anna Maria would leave on 28 November and he would follow her as soon as he could complete his task of translating the Digest of Hindu and Muslim laws. He prepared to leave with some regret:

Having nothing to fear from India and much to enjoy in it, I shall make a great sacrifice whenever I leave it. I shall leave a country where we have no royal court, no House of Lords, no clergy with wealth or power, no taxes, no fear of robbers or fire, no snow and hard frost followed by comfortless thaws and no ice except what is made by art to supply our desserts, add to this, that I have twice as much money as I want, and am conscious of doing very great and extensive good to many millions of native Indians who look up to me not as their judge only, but as their legislator.[3]

This picture of his life in India was not realistic. He had many anxious moments when Anna Maria was ill; his own health was not as good as he made out. He had a serious attack of sunstroke in 1784 which reduced him to a skeleton, and from which he never quite recovered.[4] If Devis's picture is any guide, then the young

122

Sir William Jones by A. W. Devis

man whom Sir Joshua Reynolds painted in 1769 had certainly lost his youth and was much emaciated. Ever since his illness, he followed Hastings's advice and avoided the Indian sun.[1]

There were other moments of doubt, when he was overworked at the Asiatick Society, or as in 1786 when the Judges of the Supreme Court were left unpaid for some time, and he was compelled to borrow money.[2] But, in spite of these anxious moments and doubts, the years in India were the happiest of Jones's life. He had all the material comforts he could ask for, a large salary, a garden house in Alipur, an estate in Krishnagar, and an entourage of servants and slaves. He had saved already more than £30,000 (though not quite in five or six years, as he originally thought he would),[3] the capital which was necessary to purchase a 'Sabine farm' and live independently in England. He had his other pleasures, in exploring Oriental literature and organizing the Asiatick Society. But he received the greatest satisfaction from compiling the laws of India:

I speak the language of the Gods, as the Brahmins call it, with great fluency, and am engaged in superintending a Digest of Indian Law for the benefit of twenty four millions of black British subjects in these provinces. The work is difficult and engages all my leisure, every morning between my breakfast and the sitting of the Court. The natives are charmed with the work, and the idea of making their slavery lighter, by giving them their own laws, is more flattering to me than the thanks of the King, which have been transmitted to me.[4]

To be the legislator of the Indians was his greatest desire in the last years of his life. This, he thought, would be his 'legacy to India'. In October 1793 it looked as though this were going to be the case.

In Bengal Jones steered clear of politics (meaning faction feuds among the British officers). He had decided that as a judge he should have no politics. When he heard that Burke had charged him for siding with Hastings, he wrote to his friend:

he ought to know that as a judge I side with no man, that I have indeed an equity side and a common law side, an ecclesiastical side and an admiralty side but I am quadrilateral by act of Parliament and no power on earth while I continue in my present station shall give me a political side. What have I to do with politicks? It is my sole duty to convey law or what I believe to be law...if I am ignorant let me be disgraced, if corrupt, let me be hanged: but let me not be menaced by every fiery fool, who may happen to measure my principles and conduct by his own.[1]

However he realized that, although the judges should be independent of the government, the court of justice should not obstruct the work of the Supreme Council:

I always thought before I left England that a regard for the public good requires the most cordial union between the executive and judicial powers in this country; and I lamented the mischief occasioned by former divisions. Since I have no view of happiness on this side of the grave, but in a faithful discharge of my duty, I shall spare no pains to preserve that cordiality which subsists, I trust and will subsist between the government and the judges.[2]

It was to Jones's own credit that he remained an independent and honest judge, yet friendly towards the members of the Supreme Council in Calcutta. Even the cynical Hickey had to admire Jones for his scholarship and independence.[3] Jones was a particular friend of Warren Hastings, and shared with him an admiration for Asian literature and the Indian institutions. Soon after his arrival, the two families were drawn closer together; as the Governor-General was staying at Alipore, Jones decided to purchase a house there in preference to one at Kasipur, the purchase of which was almost arranged.[4] Later, after his return to England, Hastings used to visit the Shipley family.[5] When Hastings was threatened with impeachment Jones wrote: 'This letter will find you covered with laurels and in full triumph over rancours of your enviers.'[6] However, he was also friendly with the other Governor-Generals, Macpherson, Cornwallis and Shore, although he did not always support all their policies.[7] Cornwallis admired him, attended many of his Annual Discourses to the Society and sought his advice on many judicial and administrative reforms.[8] Jones on his part admired Cornwallis and found much in common with the Whig principles of the marquis. He had the same faith in the 'rule of law', 'the separation of powers', 'the sanctity of private property' and the 'mild government'. He praised both Cornwallis and John Shore: 'In my opinion this country was never so justly and so mildly governed as it now is by Lord Cornwallis and Mr Shore, the first of whom has the best intentions, and the second, not them only, but every talent that a man of his station ought to possess together with [an] accurate knowledge of the revenues.'[9]

So, although Jones was not involved in faction feuds, as a judge of the Supreme Court, Calcutta (where he had also to function as a Justice of the Peace for the settlement), he had to be concerned with the big questions related to the law and government of Bengal; the authority of the Supreme Court, the interrelationship between the Supreme Court and the Supreme Council, the administration of criminal justice, the nature of Indian law and the interrelationship between Indian courts of justice which the British had inherited from the old régime and the Supreme Court. Although Jones was primarily concerned with the administration of justice in Bengal, his suggestions for reform touched upon all aspects of the British administration in India and were derived from a definite theory of politics. Jones had always been interested in the great principles of politics and he could not act as a judge without any reference to them.[1] In all his charges to the Grand Jury he came back to them again and again. Jones had also to find a *raison d'être* for his position in Calcutta. According to his own radical theory, in a civil society 'the collected will of the people' is the ultimate authority and the officers are chosen by the whole community, but, in India, Jones was made a judge not by the Indians but by their foreign masters and here the British government functioned authoritatively and without the consent of the Indian people. He had to work out a theory for the British government in India which would reconcile his political principles with the Indian situation.[2]

In England, before he had even obtained the judgeship, he had decided that the 'Gentoos' should not be ruled according to the maxims of the 'Athenians'.[3] When he had obtained the judgeship he told Ashburton: 'As to the doctrines in the tract, though I shall certainly not preach them to the Indians who must and will be *governed by absolute power*, yet I shall go through life with a persuasion that they are just and rational.'[4] His researches on Indian history and culture had convinced him that India, with other Asian nations, had flourished in many aspects of human civilization, especially in literature and philosophy, but had failed to produce a satisfactory system of government. The people had never experienced political freedom and had been ruled under absolute power: 'the religious manners and laws of the natives precluded even the idea of political freedom.'[5] Here 'millions are so wedded to inveterate prejudices and habits, if liberty could be forced upon them by Britain, it would make them as miserable as the cruelest despotism'.[1] His experience in Johanna must have strengthened his views on the authoritarian form of government in Asia and Africa. He thought that in Johanna the enlightened king could administer the island well, if he could rule according to the 'constitution' and with the help of the scholar-governors like Alavi and Hamddullah, and provided that his authority had not been curtailed by the 'nobility'. Hence, in Asia and Africa where the 'nobility' is not virtuous (for 'virtue is the only source of public and private felicity')[2] and where millions are wedded to inveterate prejudices, absolute rule is essential for the benefit of the people.

But Jones's absolutism was a legal and enlightened one. He had never supported the theory of Oriental Despotism as developed by Bernier, Montesquieu and Dow. He still shared Voltaire's enthusiasm for Asian civilization and Eastern wisdom and believed that the Asians could not have flourished if they were ruled according to the whims of their monarchs and had no experience of private property. The Indian princes had never been above the control of law: 'I answer firmly that Indian princes never had, nor pretended to have an unlimited legislative authority, but were always under the control of laws believed to be divine, with which they never claimed any power of dispensing.'[3] This was true both for the Hindus and for the Muslims. It would be unworthy of the British government to impose their system on the Indians for 'a system forced upon the people invincibly attached to opposite habits would in truth be a system of cruel tyranny'.[4] So the British should follow the example of the Indian princes, and the Indians should be allowed to live according to their customs and laws under the protection of a mild but absolute ruler.

To Jones the Indian customary laws, like the English common laws, were 'the collected will of the people', in the sense that they were 'the collected wisdom of many centuries, having been used and approved by successive generations'. But in India, where millions are 'superstitious' and 'ritual ridden', they consider their laws as sanctions from Heaven. In the ultimate analysis good Indian laws were based on natural reason, as he had asserted earlier. But ordinary Indians did not understand that this was so; here it would be impossible to impose new regulations which have not the sanction of the Indian customary laws:

It is a maxim in the science of legislation and government that laws are of no avail without manners, or to explain the sentence more fully, that the best intended legislative provisions would have no beneficial effect even at first and none at all in a short course of time, unless they were congenial to the disposition and habits, to the religious prejudices, and approved immemorial usages of the people for whom they were enacted.[1]

Hence in India the British should exercise absolute power but allow the natives to live under their 'immemorial usages'. This he thought was the decided policy of the British government at least since 1773:

The object then of the court, thus continued with ample powers, though wisely circumscribed in its jurisdiction, is plainly this: That, in every age, the British subjects resident in India are protected, yet governed by British laws; and that the natives of these important provinces be indulged in their own prejudices, civil and religious and suffered to enjoy their own customs unmolested.[2]

In a way Jones was right; the British government had decided not to change the Indian civil laws and to administer justice outside Calcutta according to the Indian customs and through the Indian courts. During the pre-British periods the *suba* of Bengal, Bihar and Orissa was governed by the Muslim law. However, the Muslim rulers recognized the authority of the Hindu *śāstric* laws, only in civil cases between the Hindu litigants. If the litigants brought a case before the court of law, the case would then be referred to a Brahmin jurist who was a scholar in the *Dharma śāstras* and would be attached to the court; the judges used to give their decision on such cases according to the interpretations of the Brahmin pandits. In criminal cases and in other civil cases Muslim law prevailed.

The Indian courts did not follow any strict system which defined the limits of the jurisdiction of the court and the persons involved, or followed precedents. There was sufficient vagueness about the nature of law, and the limits of the authority of the court, which allowed the magistrates to use their personal discretion in each case. Since 1765 the East India Company was the Diwan of Bengal and in that capacity they not only were responsible for the collection of revenue, but were also in charge of the administration of civil justice in that province. The British retained the old law and the old institutions; even after 1772 when Hastings had assumed full sovereignty in Bengal, all his reforms aimed at retaining 'the ancient constitution as far as it was practicable'.[1] However, in Calcutta the Mayor's Court, which was established in 1726, administered justice according to the English common law. But it became customary that in civil cases where both the litigants were Indian, Indian laws were the final authority.[2]

In 1773, North's Regulation Act established a King's Court in Calcutta—the Supreme Court. The Regulation did not clearly define the exact authority of the court, but it was clear from the beginning that the Supreme Court should administer justice according to English law among the inhabitants of Calcutta and the servants of the company. The jurisdiction of the court was revised by an Act of Parliament in 1781. This act recognised the customs and usages of Hindus and Muslims as the law applicable to Hindus and Muslims respectively in 'inheritance and succession to land rent and goods and all matters of contract and dealing between party and party'.[3] However, this had been the practice since the establishment of the Mayor's Court. Already, there were pandits and maulavis attached to the Supreme Court to interpret Indian laws to the judges, as there were in the company's courts. But this act gave the old practice a new authority and the Indian laws were recognized by parliament; the British government now wanted to decide cases in Indian laws as if they had been cases in English law.

Jones's advice was sought when this particular act was passed.[4] He wanted to follow the principles behind the act rather strictly. This was the reason why he wanted to know the Indian laws thoroughly and had learnt Sanskrit.[5] In fact he wanted to know India 'better than any other European ever knew it', largely because he could be useful in supplying the legislature with just and accurate intelligence for the reformation of 'this imperfect judicature'.[6] Every time there was a case to be judged according to the Indian laws, Jones would ask many questions on inheritance, *Stri Dhana* (female property), joint family, of the pandits and maulavis. Some of these queries and answers are recorded in a notebook which is now preserved in the National Library of Wales, Aberystwyth.[7] He wanted to know for certain where the Indian laws stood on such matters.

But soon he began to suspect the pandits and maulavis, feeling that they might deceive the judges if they had some financial interest in the case concerned; moreover, they were not always consistent: 'I can no longer bear to be at the mercy of our Pundits, who deal out Hindu law as they please and make it at reasonable rates, when they cannot find it ready made.'[1] Soon he mastered the language and was able to detect deception: 'I have the delight of knowing that my studies go hand in hand with my duty, since I now read both Sanscrit and Arabick with so much ease that the native lawyers can never impose upon court in which I sit. I converse fluently in Arabick with Maulavis and in Sanscrit with Pundits and in Persian with nobles of the country.'[2] Jones tried to reach decisions on Indian personal laws himself without aid from the pandits and maulavis. There is at least one entry in the National Library of Wales notebook which records Jones's own decision on inheritance among the Hindus, in cases where a person dies without a son.[3] If cases in Indian laws had to be treated as if they are cases in English law, then Indian law must have the certainty and consistency of the English law. As Derrett has pointed out, Jones wanted to find a 'fixed form'.[4] This he soon realized could not be done unless the Indian laws were codified.

If the Indians were to be ruled according to their own laws, then their laws should be codified in a manner which would make it easy for the European judges to understand them. The codification of Indian laws and the reform of the British court of justice in India had been in his mind for some time. He discussed this with his friends in England,[5] and in 1782 he was prompted to translate 'the Mahomedan law of succession to the property of intestates', from the Arabic original, 'to help English judges of Calcutta Supreme Court, the provincial councils and council general in India or the Great Court of Appeal in Britain while dealing with civil cases between two Muslim contestants'.[6] This work was neither accurate nor very useful. However, in 1786 he made out a definite draft plan for the codification of Indian laws.

But my great object at which I have long been labouring, is to give our country a complete digest of Hindu and Musulman law. I have enabled myself by excessive care to read the oldest Sanscrit law books with the help of a loose Persian paraphrase; and I have begun a translation of Menu into English; the best Arabic law tract I translated last year. What I can possibly perform alone I will by God's blessing perform; and I would write on the subject to the Minister, Chancellor, the Board of Control, and the Directors.[7]

But Jones did not write to the Minister or other officials; instead he intimated his plans to his friend John Rous, a Member of

Parliament. Rous was to use his influence with Pitt and Dundas to support Jones's plan.[1] In his letter to Rous he gave some detailed information on the material he wanted to use for his Digest:

The materials would be these: six or seven law books believed to be Divine with a commentary on each of nearly equal authority; these are analogous to our Littleton and Coke. Next Jimutbuhun [Jimutavāhana], the book on inheritance and above all a digest of Hindu law in twenty-seven volumes (which was compiled about four centuries ago by Raghunenden [Raghunandana], the Comyns[2] of India. For the Muham-medan laws, besides Hedaya, the Cammdkayik and other excellent works, I have a noble copy in five folio volumes of the decisions collected by order of Aalemgir [Alamgir], which are of high authority in all Muslim countries, and are called in Arabia the Indian decisions.[3]

From these materials Jones wanted to compile a digest in Justinianian fashion.

This idea was further developed in a letter to Cornwallis. In this Jones said that the British principles in India were to uphold the private laws of the inhabitants and 'these laws should not be superseded by a new system of which they could have no know-ledge and which they must have considered intolerant'.[4] But there were many and considerable difficulties in putting this principle into practice. The laws were written in Arabic and Sanskrit and most Europeans could not be expected to learn the languages and they should not rely on Indian interpreters:

We can never be sure that we have not been deceived by them. It would be absurd and unjust to pass an indiscriminate censure on a considerable body of men; but my experience justifies me in declaring that I could not with an easy conscience concur in a decision, merely on the written opinion of native lawyers, in any case, in which, they could have the remotest interest in misleading the court.[5]

The remedy was to compile the native laws in the way Justinian wrote his Digest, that is by collecting the law tracts and their commentaries together, and then translating them in the form of a new digest of Indian law. 'The copies of the work should be deposited in the proper offices of Sedr Diwani Adalet and of the Supreme Court',[6] so that the judges and the lawyers can consult them when required. This was a great task and the British govern-ment in India ought to perform it; 'It would not be unworthy of a British government to give the natives of these Indian provinces a permanent security for the due administration of justice among them, similar to that which Justinian gave to his Greek and Roman subjects'.[1] He proposed to employ two pandits, one from Bengal representing the eastern school of Hindu jurisprudence, another from Bihar or Benares representing the western school; two maulavis, one from each of the two known Muslim sects, Sunni and Shia; and two writers. He calculated that the total cost would be about one thousand Sicca Rupees per month and that it would take three years to complete the work. Jones volunteered himself to spend some time each day in guiding the compilation and in translating it without pay. The Governor-General and the Council intimated Jones's project to the Court of Directors.[2] The Council had already approved his plan and promised to provide the cost:

We therefore with the highest pleasure accept of your offer to direct and translate this work and we shall entirely rely upon your knowledge and judgment to select and appoint as many of the most respectable Maulavis and Pundits of this country as you may think necessary to give you effectual assistance.[3]

It is significant to note that, although Jones modified his Whig philosophy to suit the Indian situation, the central theme of his ideas, that is the protection of the individual, his person, property and freedom, was still valid. In India an ordinary Indian was denied political freedom, but he should have the freedom to enjoy the fruits of his industry—'descendable property'[4] and his religious beliefs. So the purpose of the British government in India would be best served by 'promoting the security of the right of property to the natives, who by their cheerful industry will enrich their benefactors and whose firm attachment will secure the permanence of our Dominion'.[5] Jones had reached the conclusion that the future of British prosperity was tied to the prosperity of India, 'the well directed industry' of the natives 'would largely add to the wealth of Britain'.[6] This was not possible without the security of the individual, his person and property. The right of private property was not a new right to be imposed by the British upon the Indians. To Jones's way of thinking it was fundamentally impossible to benefit a country 'under the ideas of the assumption of landed property by government'.[7] India could not have been happy and prosperous and produce such a complex civilization unless the ordinary Indians were allowed to enjoy the fruits of their own industry. Hence the Indians had enjoyed private property throughout history:

Unless I am greatly deceived, the work now presented to the public, decides the question which has started, whether, by the Mugul constitution, the sovereign be not the sole proprietor of all the land in his empire, which he or his predecessors have not granted to a subject and his heirs; for nothing can be more certain, than that land, rents and goods are in the language of the Mohammedan Lawyers, property alike alienationable and inheritable...No Musalman prince in any age or country would have harboured a thought of controverting these authorities.[1]

As to the Hindus, 'they most assuredly were absolute proprietors of their land, though they called their sovereigns lords of the earth'.[2] Jones's theory on ownership of land and the fragmentation of political authority in pre-British India could be noticed in his translation of *Manu* books VII, VIII and IX.[3] So Jones thought that Bernier was wrong:

Aurangzib himself the bloodiest of assassins and the most avaricious of men, could not have adopted and proclaimed such an opinion whatever his courtiers and slaves might have said in their zeal to aggrandize their master, to a foreign physician and philosopher who too hastily believed them and ascribed to such a system all the desolation of which he had been a witness.[4]

Jones felt that much mischief was done, because the British officers questioned the validity of this theory that India had experienced fragmentation of authority, the rule of law and private property:

Our nation in the name of the king has twenty-three million black subjects in these two provinces, but nine-tenths of their property are taken from them and it has even been publickly insisted that they have no landed property at all: if my Digest of Indian law should give stability to their property, real and personal, all security to their person it will be the greatest benefit they ever received from us.[5]

So he was in favour of making a permanent settlement with the landholders and in a way his work was complementary to Cornwallis's *zemindary* settlement. 'It is now settled here that the natives are proprietors of their land and that it shall descend by their own laws. I am engaged in superintending a complete system of Indian law.'[6]

Jones's antipathy towards the slave system should also be understood in relation to his political doctrines. The slave system was unacceptable to Jones's political ideas both in Britain and in India. The slave system forced a man to sell his person to another. The man who is sold loses his freedom completely, including the freedom to enjoy the fruits of his industry. To Jones this is against the natural law. A man cannot claim a property in rational beings, 'since our creator had given our species a dominion to be moderately exercised over the beasts of the field and the fowls of the air but not to man over man'.[1] The slave system does not only prevent the slaves from enjoying the fruits of their industry, it also encourages the traders to laziness, who might well have made use of their labour. As an economic system this cannot be supported either:

I pass with haste by the coast of Africa whence my mind turns with indignation at the abominable traffick in the human species, from which a part of our countrymen dare to derive most inauspicious wealth. Sugar, it has been said would be dear if it were not worked by Blacks in the Western islands; as if the most laborious, the most dangerous works, were not carried on in every country, but chiefly in England by freemen; in fact they are so carried on with infinitely more advantage, for *there is an alacrity in a consciousness of freedom*, and *a gloomy sullen indolence in a consciousness of slavery*.[2]

So slavery must be condemned not only because it violates 'the primary law of nature' but also because the system is economically unsound. No leniency towards the slaves gives the system a legal status.

On 10 June 1785 when a case of murder of a slave girl by a European master called Osborne was brought before the Supreme Court, Jones took the opportunity to condemn the slave trade and the slave system. 'Many of you, I presume, have seen large boats filled with children coming down the river for open sale at Calcutta; nor can you be ignorant, that most of them were stolen from their parents, or bought, perhaps for a measure of rice in a time of scarcity.'[3] Such trade must be stopped and the merchants severely punished and 'one great example of a just punishment, not capital, will conduce more to the prevention of similar cruelties, than the strongest admonition or severest verbal reproof'.[4] There were many reasons why he supported the Americans in their struggle for independence but perhaps the chief reason was that they held similar ideas on freedom and the slave system. He was assured by his friends in America that they would 'emancipate their slaves' as soon as 'times and circumstances shall permit' them to do so.[1]

Slavery is indefensible, but so long as the system persists and if one has to employ slaves one should treat them as servants under contract.

It is needless to expatiate on the law (if it be law) of private slavery; but I make no scruple to declare my own opinion, that absolute unconditional slavery, by which one human creature becomes the property of another, like a horse or an ox, is happily unknown to the laws of England and that no human law could give it a just sanction; yet though I hate the word, the continuance of it, properly explained can produce little mischief. I consider slaves as servants under contract, expressed or implied, and made either by themselves, or by such persons as are authorized by nature or law to contract for them, until they attain a due age to cancel or confirm any compact that may be disadvantageous to them. I have slaves whom I rescued from death or misery but consider them as other servants and shall certainly tell them so, when they are old enough to comprehend the difference of the terms.[2]

Locke would have approved of this.[3] A similar view was expressed when one of Jones's friends, Morris, purchased a slave in St Vincent in the West Indies: 'They intend to employ him as a shepherd which indulgence (while the detestable traffick in creatures subsists) may be better for the poor man than his liberty as he would be in danger of losing it again and being sold to a bad master.'[4] If one has to lose freedom it is better to have a good master than a bad one.

It would be a mistake to think that Jones's antipathy towards slavery was stimulated by purely humanitarian motives, out of a real concern for the depressed class. In fact he had no faith in an egalitarian society. He treated his slaves as his servants and this did not mean that he treated them as his equals; on the contrary he defended the traditional view that the master has a right to 'correct' his servants if need be, by corporal punishment.

On 16 June 1785 a man called Humphrey Stewart was brought for trial before the Judges of the Supreme Court. He was charged with the murder of his munshy by beating him with a stick. In this case John Hyde, another Judge of the Supreme Court, summed up the evidence for the jury and he explained to them the various types of homicide. In this he was helped by Jones, 'I made considerable use of the annexed analysis of this case which brother Jones took the trouble to draw up for me'.[1] This analysis in the form of a diagram is now in the National Library of Wales notebook.[2] In this analysis Jones fully supported the traditional view on the relationship between the master and the servant. He argued that the beating would be an illegal act if the deceased was not a servant of the accused. Then the latter could be charged with murder if he was beating him deliberately to kill, or with manslaughter if the action was not deliberate but the use of the stick was 'immoderate'. If, however, the munshy was a servant by contract and the accused used the stick with 'moderation' then the act was lawful and he should be acquitted. But if the accused used the stick immoderately then he would be charged with manslaughter, if he was under provocation, or with murder if he was beating the deceased in 'cold blood'.[3]

If in his correspondence during the Gordon riots one could detect his distrust of the ordinary people[4] he was equally distrusting towards the Indian masses. It was the Brahmins, the Muslim scholars and the propertied upper class, men like Radhakanta, Ramlochan, Aly Ibrahim Khan and the Maharaja of Krishnagar whom he treated as his equals. He had very little sympathy for the ordinary Indians:

Excessive luxury, with which the Asiaticks are too indiscriminately reproached in Europe, exists indeed in our settlements, but not where it is usually supposed: not in the higher, but in the lowest condition of men; in our servants, in the common seamen frequenting our port, in the petty workmen and shopkeepers of our streets and markets, there live the men, who to use the phrase of an old statute, sleep by day and work by night, for the purposes of gaming, debauchery and intoxication.[5]

British subjects both black and white have to be protected from these men and the Court of Justice should inflict severe punishment on such men to deter them from crime. He did not hesitate to recommend corporal punishment by 'having both ears nailed to the pillory'[6] for perjury. He was charmed by Manu's concept of *Daṇḍa* which he thought the British government should follow in administering justice in Bengal, that is it should inflict severe punishment on the guilty one.[7]

But, being true to his Whig doctrines, he could not allow too much concentration of power in one branch of the government. He envisaged an authoritarian form of government, which should follow strict rule of law and whose power should be checked by a strong and well-organized judiciary. Without an independent and vigilant Court of Justice a good government cannot function. Hence the court should keep an eye on the executive. This was the reason why he was against summary jurisdiction and for trial by jury. Jones suggested that there were three great advantages which the sacred law had conferred upon the people of England. The first was a share of the legislative power, the next was the right and duty of men to arm and to protect property and life against internal and external aggression and third was the right to be tried by jury. If they lost the other two rights 'the trial by jury would be the only anchor left that, could preserve our constitution from total ship-wreck'.[1] He was against retaining the Superintendent of Police in Calcutta—'an officer unknown to our system' whose power was 'dark and unlimited'. Instead of giving the Superintendent of Police undue power, Jones suggested that the government should employ six to twelve gentlemen as Justices of the Peace to maintain law and order in Calcutta.[2] He was against forcible entry to a person's house by the police, putting irons on prisoners under trial[3] and he took up the cause of the imprisoned debtor who suffered in the prisons in Calcutta. British subjects, black or white, had to be protected against any encroachment upon their person, property and freedom from the lower orders and from the powerful officials who might misuse their position:

The progress of arbitrary power is commonly slow at first and imperceptible to all but the vigilant, like the creeping of a tiger at night in a brake; and it behoves us by all decent and legal remains to guard posterity against that ultimate spring from which nothing less than doubtful horrours of civil war might be able to protect them.[4]

Thus Jones wanted to see in India a British government true to the Whig principles, the separation of powers, the rule of law, protection of the individual, yet authoritarian and ruling according to the Indian laws. He read back many Whig principles in the Indian law and history except the principle of political freedom. All English officers, whatever their political belief, agreed that the Indians are incapable of enjoying political freedom. Cornwallis, despite his Whig idea of the separation of powers, refused to accept the Governor-Generalship until an act was passed, in 1786, which enabled Cornwallis to override the opinions of the Councillors, who had previously given Hastings considerable trouble. The marquis was also against Indian participation in the British India government: 'Although we hope to render our subjects the happiest people in India, I should by no means propose to admit the natives to any participation in framing Regulations.'[1]

However, Jones was not consistent. He did not hesitate to support Joseph Emin. Joseph Emin was an Armenian from Calcutta. He was inspired by the idea of freedom and went to Europe to seek support to raise an army to drive the Turks out of Armenia and establish a constitutional government there. Having failed in his task, he came back to live in Calcutta and wrote his autobiography. Jones supported him: 'If your design was to transplant our constitution to Armenia I heartily lament your disappointment.'[2] The transplantation of the English constitution to Armenia was desirable although, according to Jones, the Armenians were Asians.[3] But he could not agree to the transplantation of the English system to India, another Asian country. It would seem that there was some truth in the complaint that was made by Anquetil Duperron, that the concept of despotism (authoritarian government as Jones saw it) was devised by the Europeans to justify their oppressive rule in Asia.[4]

Once the project of his Digest was accepted by the government, Jones proceeded to appoint Indian scholars in whom he had 'perfect confidence'. He appointed Radhakanta Sharman, for the eastern school of Hindu jurisprudence: 'A Brahmen of distinguished abilities and highly revered by the Hindus in Bengal for his erudition and virtue.'[5] Sarvoru Trivedi was appointed to represent the western school of Hindu jurisprudence. For Shia and Sunni laws he recommended Sirajul Haq and Muhammad Kasim respectively. The nominations were confirmed on 14 April 1788 and Jones worked, as he had promised, regularly, every day, for nearly six years. The task took much longer than he had originally expected and he had to change his first plan. Originally he had intended to have two digests of Hindu law representing the two schools, *Mitākṣarā* and *Dāyabhāga*. Accordingly, Sarvoru Trivedi in 1789 compiled a work called *Vivāda-sārāṇava*.[6] This work was neither translated nor published and, as far as we know, was never sent to the Supreme Council, for already in August 1788 Jones had approached Jagannatha Tarkapanchanan, the great pandit, 'whose learning and ability were held in the highest veneration'[1] throughout northern India, to compile a new digest. It was hoped that in the new digest the conflicting interpretations would be brought together and explained by Jagannatha, who was well versed in the two schools of Hindu jurisprudence. The Council approved of this and agreed to pay Rupees three hundred per month for the pandit and Rupees one hundred for his assistant to help 'Sir William Jones in compiling the Digest of Hindu and Muhammadan law'. Jones and his maulavis and pandits were hard at work bringing together all the texts and commentaries.[2] By November 1792 he presented the government with 'the first fruits of my enquiries in India concerning the laws of the Musalmans and Hindus'.[3] This was *Al Sirajiyyah*, which was also translated and published later in that year. He was then confident that he would complete the translation of the *Dharma śāstras* by the next summer vacation, and all the scholars were discharged except Sarvoru and Radhakanta: 'whose assistance I still find necessary.'[4] By June 1793 he completed the translation of Manu which was printed by the Company's press and sent to the Judges of the Diwani Courts in the provinces.[5] But he died before the Digest was complete.

He had been planning to travel to China and America before he finally returned to England, to retire to the 'Sabine farm' which he wanted to purchase in Middlesex. He probably gave up his original plan when he realized that the compilation of the *Digest* would take longer than he expected, for he arranged with Harford Jones, an English agent in Baghdad, to travel to England through Persia and Turkey.[6] But by 1 March 1794 he had decided to travel by boat when the Digest was complete and to translate it during the voyage.[7]

But none of his last plans was fulfilled. His health was as precarious as his wife's, although he never admitted it. In 1793 he was twice taken ill. Perhaps since Anna Maria's departure on 28 November he had not been as careful as he should have been.[8] In early April he had not been well and on the 20th he was taken ill again. On the morning of 27 April John Shore, now the Governor-General and a neighbour of Jones, was aroused by Sir William's servants and asked to attend their master in order to hear his last words. When Shore reached him it was too late, and Jones had breathed his last.[9]

The funeral was held on the next day with all the ceremony that was to be expected on such occasions in eighteenth-century Calcutta. There was a procession headed by the European troops of the garrison with arms reversed and drums muffled, marching to the accompaniment of sacred tunes played by the artillery band. The gentlemen of the settlement followed in their carriages and palanquins while guns were fired from the ramparts of Fort William.[1]

The news of her husband's death reached Anna Maria late in 1794. In January 1795 she was still filled with grief, consoling herself with Barrow's sermons, especially the one on the submission to Divine Will, which her husband had selected for her in 1789 when he received the news of her father's death. She thanked her God for being able to live with such a friend as her husband. 'Few can glory in like happiness or consequently lament the like loss',[2] she wrote to Charles Grant.

There were many others who lamented his death both in India and in Britain. John Shore described how, in his Durbar on 1 May 1794, 'the professors of Hindu law' 'burst out into unrestrained tears'[3] as they spoke of Jones. Their feelings were understandable. The pandits and the Muslim scholars had lost a great friend by his death. Men like Radhakanta, Ramlochan, Govardhana Kaul, Aly Ibrahim Khan and Ghulam Hussain were all indebted to him. He had loved them and had been proud of their friendship.[4] When Pandit Radhakanta was in trouble with his estate Jones persuaded Shore to help him.[5] Again it was largely through Jones's persuasion that Jagannatha received a pension of 300 sicca rupees a month on his retirement.[6] Similarly, Jones had pleaded with John Rous to reward Ghulam Hussain by enlarging his *jagir* in Hussainabad.[7]

What is the legacy of Jones? Jones himself had thought that the Digest would be 'a noble legacy from me to three and twenty millions of black British subjects'.[8] But the work was unfinished when he died and when it was at last completed and translated it was of very little practical value. The new middle classes had no doubt benefited from the British law courts but Jones's Digest helped very little in protecting their persons and property, for the work was not used as frequently as Jones had expected.[9]

Jones's Digest was heavily criticized by the Utilitarians. Mill described it as 'a disorderly compilation of loose, vague, stupid and unintelligible quotations and maxims'.[10] Bentham also had no praise for Jones: 'He was an industrious man with no sort of genius', who 'sent spinning cobwebs out of his own brain and winding them round the common law'.[1]

This was unfair to Jones, for he wanted, as much as the Utilitarians, to have a comprehensive code of law collected for ready reference and intelligible to everyone concerned. But Jones was wrong in assuming that it was possible to draw a definite line between the customary and modern law and retain the former. He failed to see that the Indian views on law and customs were changing, as the society around them was taking an entirely new shape. The old pandits were not immune from the impact of the changing society. Although Jones wanted Jagannatha Tarkapanchanan to compile a digest in which all the important texts and their commentaries would be put together and the conflicting interpretations explained, the great pandit wrote an entirely new work. It was not without some foundation that Colebrooke complained that the pandit's commentaries were 'frivolous' and often self-contradictory.[2] In fact, this great pandit of Bengal was only trying to understand the extracts from the Indian classics in terms of the circumstances he knew well. His comments on the ownership of land, the slave system and contract show that Jagannatha was well aware of the conflicting views among the British officers on administrative policy, particularly in connection with the revenue administration. He explained the question on the ownership of land in terms of the conflicting views of the British officers.[3] Hence it was not possible to retain 'the ancient constitution' and the customary laws, as the society which upheld them, was changing. Moreover, Jagannatha used a method which was unintelligible to the British judges not trained in *Nyāya* logic and *Mimaṃsā* philosophy.[4] So the Digest could not be used as a work for ready reference. Jagannath's *Vivādabhaṅgārṇava*, although a great work, could not be more useful than Halhed's *Gentoo Laws*.[5]

The greatest contribution of Jones to India was the foundation of the Asiatick Society. Through this Society enthusiasm for Indian studies spread throughout Europe and India. From 1829 onwards the Indians played a full part in the activities of the Society. No doubt modern Indian nationalism is a result of the growth of a new social order which was indirectly helped by the British, but India could hardly have withstood the cultural challenge of the west without drawing heavily on her past glory. It was Jones and his Society which he founded who discovered that India had produced a civilization equal to any other in the ancient world. The dignity and pride this discovery gave to the Indians is an undeniable factor in the growth of Indian nationalism. Jones's *Śakuntalā* gave them a Shakespeare in Kālidāsa and other works inspired them. When Raja Rammohan Roy spoke of the unitarian concept of God in the *Vedānta*, he was enlarging upon Jones's ideas[1] and, when Vivekananda talked about the *Vedānta* as the 'fountain source of all religions',[2] he was using a similar argument used by Jones a hundred years earlier. In fact, Jones gave India a weapon with which to hit back whenever the European administrator-scholars had attempted to belittle the Indian civilization.[3]

He made very little impact on European thought. No doubt Goethe borrowed a device of dramaturgy from Kālidāsa which is to be found in the prologue of *Faust*. Perhaps his final chorus of the second part of that work was inspired by Indian thought.[4] If Hegel was influenced by Indian thought it was largely through Anquetil Duperron's work and not through Jones's.

His impact on the Romantic poets was negligible.[5] The Romantic statesmen in India had shared his admiration for the Indian institutions, but their administrative philosophy was based on very different premises.[6] But he was undoubtedly a precursor of the authoritarian liberal statesmen in India. Like them he preached liberalism at home, but upheld the authoritarian rule in India.[7]

Jones left behind him an attitude of mind, a profound reverence for men irrespective of their race and their different cultural backgrounds. This attitude is valid for all time, and Jones's support of it was an inspiration to many men of later generations who had dealings with India. This and his admiration for human endeavour as a means to virtue and happiness is best illustrated in a Persian couplet which he translated:

> Crush not yon ant who stores the golden grain:
> He lives with pleasures and dies with pain:
> Learn from him rather to secure the spoil
> Of patient cares and pursuit of toil.

He loved this because it upheld, first, the maxim of the love of all creatures, 'one great article of primitive religion delivered by God to man', and secondly 'the necessity of labour if we wish to be virtuous and happy'.[8]

'THOUGHTS ON A SYSTEM OF JUDICATURE FOR INDIA'

The following plan for the British administration of justice in India was written by Jones for Burke. We do not know the exact date when this was written, but it must have been before 13 April 1784, for soon after that Jones quarrelled with Burke over his friendship with Hastings.[1] This is perhaps another example of how Jones compromised his Whig conception of the balance of power with the British Indian system. His proposed system was to follow the old Mughal customs, yet it should be worked out in such a way that there would be reciprocal checks and balances of power for the security of the natives and Europeans.

'The best practical system of judicature for India:

1. A system forced upon a people invincibly attached to opposite habits would in truth be a system of cruel tyranny.

2. Any system of judicature affecting the natives in Bengal and not having for its basis the old Mogul constitution would be dangerous and impracticable.

3. All original jurisdiction against natives without the Mahratta ditch except that exercised by the Courts *Dewanei adalet* according to the forms used and approved will produce confusion and misery.

4. The native suitors in the *Dewanei* Courts should be enabled to obtain justice as formerly, with the least possible expense and delay.

5. The criminal jurisdiction must be left to the courts of *Foujdaree adalet* and on appeal to the Nizamet; while the revenue jurisdiction remains wholly with the Governor and Council as *Dewan* of the provinces.

6. An effective appellate jurisdiction or *Sedr Dewanei adalet* is essential to the complete dispensation of justice in disputes among the natives.

7. The court of appeal should consist of the Governor and Council as Dewan with one assistant judge or president of the *Sedr Adalet*.

8. Digests of Hindu and Mohamedan laws should be compiled by chosen *Canongos*, *Mulavis* and *Pandits* and copies of them reposited in the Treasuries of the several *Dewanei adalets*.

9. Native interpreters of the respective laws must be duly selected and appointed with such subjects as will entitle them to respect and raise them above temptation.

10. The laws of the natives must be preserved inviolate; but the learning and vigilance of the English judge must be a check upon the native interpretors.

11. The decrees in the *Sadr adalet* must be conformable to Hindu and Mahomedan law as the parties of defendants shall be Hindus or Mahomedans.

12. The natives must have an effective tribunal for their protection against the English or the country will soon be rendered worse than useless to Britain.

13. An effective original jurisdiction over all the English (except the Governor and Council) and against the natives within the Mahratta ditch is essential to the peace and preservation of Bengal.

14. The English Court should consist of four, six and any even number of aldermen assisted by the knowledge and sagacity of a judge or president.

15. The climate would make it necessary to appoint a deputy judge in each court to relieve the president in case of illness.

18. The aldermen must be restrained by frequent elections from influence or cabal, and the judges in both courts secured from want of dignity and danger by liberal not extravagant salaries.

17. No suit must be continued in Bengal on any particular suggestion whatever against the Governor and Council.

18. The English court should be compelled to receive and record evidence if any be offered against the Governor and Council and transmit it, if required to England.

19. Pleas to the jurisdiction would involve all the mischiefs incident to an original jurisdiction over the natives in general.

20. If wrongs are committed by the native agents of Europeans, actions may be commenced and process must issue against the principals.

21. A circuit would be ruinous in point of expense beyond all calculation here, and beyond the produce of any tax upon the proceedings.

22. The provincial *adalets* should be impowered to take depositions or such evidence as the several religions, casts, and sexes of the witness will allow and the evidence so taken should be admissible in the court at Calcutta.

23. A system like this consisting of reciprocal checks and balances of power would give satisfaction and security to the natives, the government and the English subjects in India.'[1]

A LETTER TO
LORD CORNWALLIS

Melville papers N.L.S. 3386, f. 207

The following letter is perhaps an example of close co-operation between Jones and Cornwallis.

Court House 20 Nov. 1790.

My Lord,

The adjournment of the Court having given me a whole day of leisure I have spent the morning in reading with great attention your Lordship's Minute on the administration of criminal justice in the provinces, and in perusing the papers which accompany it. I read them all with my pen in my hand, intending to write without reserve all objections that may occur to me: but I found nothing to which I could object, and did not meet with a single paragraph to which, if I were a member of the Council I would not heartily express my assent. The power of pardoning which (in par. 44) is reserved to the Court should be always exercised, I think, by the Governor in Council in his executive, not his judicial, capacity, and in par. 61 the words 'which is always to be received with circumspection and tenderness' are applied to the accusation, though, I presume, they were intended for the prisoner's confession. These are trifling remarks, but I cannot start one serious objection; and think the whole minute unexceptionably just wise and benevolent.

I am with great respect
Your Lordship's
ever faithful Servant
[Signed] W. JONES

NOTES

PAGE 1

1 Stokes, E. *The English Utilitarians and India*, pp. xii–xiii.
2 See *ibid.* and K. Ballhatchet, *Social Policy and Social Change in Western India.*
3 For my criticism of modern British scholarship on Indian history see S. N. Mukherjee, *South Asian Affairs*, no. 2 (St Antony's Papers, no. 18), pp. 9–18.
4 Namier, *The Structure of Politics at the Accession of George III*, p. 2.

PAGE 2

1 For a short history of the discovery of ancient India see A. L. Basham, *The Wonder that was India*, pp. 4–8.

PAGE 3

1 Burke Notes, 9c, Burke papers, Wentworth Muniments. Cf. N.L.S. 3386, f. 207.

PAGE 4

1 Walpole, *Memoirs of George II*, vol. II, p. 278.
2 Sir Harold Nicolson, *The Age of Reason (1700–1789)*, p. xix.
3 Butterfield, *Origins of Modern Science*, pp. 166–74. Cf. Bernal, *Science in History*, p. 253.
4 Butterfield, *op. cit.* p. 166.
5 Pope, *Minor poems*, p. 145.

PAGE 5

1 Venturi, 'Oriental Despotism', *Journal of the History of Ideas*, XXIV (1963), 135.
2 Shackleton has shown that the doctrine of 'mixed state' is quite different from the Theory of the Separation of Powers. However, a large number of political commentators in the eighteenth century had confused the two doctrines, especially since advocates of both doctrines used the English constitution as their model. Shackleton, *Montesquieu— a Critical Biography*, pp. 298–9.
3 Locke, *Second Treatise*, § 124.
4 *Ibid.*

PAGE 6

1 Schwab has suggested that Duperron's translation of the *Zend Avesta* in 1771 was unique and revolutionary in the intellectual history of Europe, as the contents of this work were unconnected with the biblical and classical traditions. But translations from the Chinese classics appeared during the second half of the seventeenth century and Ignatius da Costa's

work on Confucius was the new Bible for the eighteenth-century Enlightenment. Abraham Roger published his book on Bhartṛhari's proverbs more than a century before the publication of the *Zend Avesta*. Surely all these works were unconnected with the biblical and classical traditions. See Schwab, *La renaissance orientale*, pp. 16, 18 and 25.

2 Reichwein, *China and Europe*, p. 77.

3 Lach, *Asia and Europe*, vol. I, bk I, pp. xii–xiii.

4 Reichwein, *op. cit.* pp. 90–1.

5 Aronson, *Europe looks at India, a Study in Cultural Relations*, p. 9.

6 Stokes, *The English Utilitarians and India*, pp. 8–25.

7 Aronson, *op. cit.* Cf. Mukherjee, 'Sir William Jones and the British attitudes towards India', *J.R.A.S.* parts I and 2 (1964), p. 37.

PAGE 7

1 Voltaire, *Fragments sur l'Inde*, pp. 46–7.

2 Purchas, *Pilgrimage*, p. 477.

3 Weber, *Metrical Romances*, vol. I, pp. 199–247.

4 Slessarev, *Prester John*, p. 4.

5 *Ibid.* p. 33.

6 Purchas, *op. cit.* p. 481.

PAGE 8

1 Whiteway, *The Rise of the Portuguese Power in India*, p. 80. Cf. Davies, *A Historical Atlas of the Indian Peninsula*, p. 40.

2 Ralph Fitch was an English traveller who visited India during the reign of Akbar. See Foster, *Early Travels in India*, p. 19.

3 *Ibid.* p. 308.

4 *Ibid.* p. 218.

5 Thomas Coryat, a rather eccentric and romantic seventeenth-century English adventurer in India, wrote to Lawrence Whitekar, 'I have been in a citie in this country called Delee where Alexander joyned battle with Porus K(ing) of India and conquered him; and in token of his victory erected a brasse pillar which remained to this day.' Foster, *Early Travels in India*, p. 248. Cf. *idem*, *The Embassy of Sir Thomas Roe*, p. 82.

6 Khan (ed.), *John Marshall in India*, p. 8.

PAGE 9

1 Referring to an event in which Thomas Coryat was involved in a religious dispute with a Muslim, Terry wrote 'here every man hath liberties to profess his own religion freely'. As quoted in Foster, *Early Travels in India*, p. 315.

2 *Ibid.* pp. 303–4.

3 Foster, *The Embassy of Sir Thomas Roe*, p. ix.

4 *Ibid.* p. 104.

5 *Ibid.* p. 89.

6 Evennett, 'New Orders', *N.C.M.H.* vol. II, p. 289.

PAGE 10

1 Cronin, *A Pearl to India*, p. 185.
2 Winternitz, *A History of Indian Literature*, vol. I, p. 9.
3 Cronin, *op. cit.* p. 74.
4 Khan, *op. cit.* p. 181.

PAGE 11

1 Bernier, *Travels*, p. xx.
2 Harrison, 'Europe and Asia', *N.C.M.H.* vol. V, pp. 213–15.
3 Bernier, *op. cit.* pp. 342–3.
4 *Ibid.* p. 355.

PAGE 12

1 Bernier, *op. cit.* p. 212.
2 *Ibid.* p. 227.
3 *Ibid.* p. 234.
4 Habib, I. 'An examination of Wittfogel's theory of Oriental Despotism', *Enquiry*, no. 6, p. 69.
5 Macpherson, *The Political Theory of Possessive Individualism*, pp. 203–21.

PAGE 13

1 Bernier, *op. cit.* p. 238.
2 Montesquieu, *The Spirit of Laws* II. Cf. Shackleton, *Montesquieu—a Critical Biography*, p. 268.
3 Montesquieu, *op. cit.* V, 13, 14 and 15.
4 *Ibid.* III, 8, 9 and 10, V, 14. Cf. Shackleton, *op. cit.* pp. 269–72.
5 Montesquieu, *op. cit.* XIV, 3, 4, 5 and 10 and XXX, 1. Cf. Marc Bloch, *Feudal Society*, vol. 2, p. 441.
6 Boulanger, *The Origin and Progress of Despotism in the Orient and other Empires*, etc. (see title-page).
7 *Ibid.* p. 13.
8 Dow, *The History of Hindostan*, vol. III, p. vii.

PAGE 14

1 *Ibid.* pp. vii–ix.
2 Dow, *op. cit.* vol. III, p. xiii.
3 *Ibid.* p. cxxviii.
4 *Ibid.* pp. xxviii–xxix and xliii–li.
5 Venturi, *op. cit.* p. 130.
6 Koebner, 'Despot and Despotism: vicissitudes of a political term', *Journal of the Warburg and Courtauld Institute*, vol. XIV, nos. 3–4, p. 276.
7 *Ibid.* p. 278.

PAGE 15

1 Voltaire, *op. cit.* pp. 10–11.
2 *Ibid.*
3 *Ibid.*
4 Scrafton, *Reflections on the Government of Indostan*, pp. 24–5.
5 Voltaire, *op. cit.* pp. 42–3.

6 Daniel, *Islam and the West*, p. 290.
7 Scrafton, *op. cit.* p. 3. Cf. Holwell, *Original Principles*, p. 50, and Dow, *op. cit.* vol. I, pp. lxxiv–lxxvi.
8 Holwell, *op. cit.* p. 25.

PAGE 16

1 *Ibid.* p. 5.
2 Clive to the Court, 30 Sept. 1765. *Fort William–India House Correspondence*, vol. IV, pp. 337–8.
3 *C.H.B.E.* vol. IV, p. 151.
4 John Shore to Dr Ford, 17 Sept. 1783, as quoted in C. Teignmouth, *Memoirs*, vol. I, p. 106.
5 Lewis, *British Contributions to Arabic Studies*, p. 12.

PAGE 17

1 In the eighteenth-century social pyramid, the position of the yeomanry was much lower than that of the 'great proprietors' and the country gentry. See Briggs, *The Age of Improvement*, pp. 10–11.
2 Shore, *Memoirs*, p. 1.
3 Letter to George John Spencer, the second earl, 20 Sept. 1775, Spencer Papers (which include all quoted correspondence between Jones and the Spencer family unless otherwise stated).
4 W.J. to G.J.S., 14 April 1775.
5 *Ibid.* 28 Sept. 1781.
6 *Ibid.* 11 Feb. 1782.
7 Letter to L. Morris, 30 Oct. 1790, as published in Shore, *op. cit.* pp. 343–4.
8 Marsh, 'Sir William Jones', *University College Records* (1954–5), p. 82.
9 Shore, *op. cit.* p. 4.

PAGE 18

1 Shore, *op. cit.* pp. 4–7.
2 Kenyon, *John Locke's Directions Concerning Education*, pp. 1–27.
3 Bayne-Powell, *The English Child in the Eighteenth Century*, pp. 6–8.
4 Locke, *Some thoughts concerning education*, p. 74.
5 Shore, *op. cit.* p. 13.

PAGE 19

1 *Ibid.* p. 17.
2 Letter to George Hardynge, 24 Sept. 1788, as published in Shore, *op. cit.* p. 320.
3 This anecdote was given by Rev. David Roderick to John Johnstone. See *The Works of Samuel Parr*, vol. I, p. 15.
4 *A.B.* vol. I, pp. 447–8.
5 W.J. to G.J.S., 11 Nov. 1768.
6 *Ibid.* 9 July 1771.
7 Maurice, *Memoirs*, pp. 85–6.
8 Letter to Lady Georgiana, 5 May 1780.

PAGE 20

1 'The boys to this day hold that master in abhorrence, who placed him in the shell in the quondam companions of the fourth form; and punished him while there for stupidity because he had not kept pace with them while confined to sick bed from and after their remove.' *A.B.* vol. I, pp. 447–8.

2 Shore, *op. cit.* p. 17.

3 W.J. to G.J.S., 20 Nov. 1771.

4 Shore, *op. cit.* p. 21.

5 Letter to C. Reviczki, n.d., as published in Shore, *op. cit.* p. 44.

6 W.J. to G.J.S., 23 April 1773.

7 See *The Works of Samuel Parr*, vol. I, pp. 12–14.

PAGE 21

1 He also wrote other dramas together with Parr and Bennet; one such play, in which turbans and flowing robes were worn by the characters, was staged in the parlour of Parr's father's home. *Ibid.* vol. I, p. 19.

2 Shore, *op. cit.* p. 21.

3 *Ibid.*

4 *Ibid.* p. 28.

5 *Ibid.* p. 23.

6 Letter to S. Parr, n.d., as published in *The Works of Samuel Parr*, vol. VII, p. 210. He was consistent in this attitude. On the death of Dr Sumner, the headmaster of Harrow, he told William Bennet: 'You will think more highly of my sincerity than my gratitude when I tell you that I was not so deeply affected with the loss of Sumner as you seem to be. My confidence in him had been considerably decreased for the last three years, and I began to take less pleasure in his company than ever. As for himself he had too many misfortunes to make life any longer desirable.' Letter to W. Bennet, 10 Nov. 1777, as published in *The Works of Samuel Parr*, vol. I, p. 54.

PAGE 22

1 Letter to Lady Georgiana, 28 Feb. 1774.

2 Letter to William Pitt, 5 Feb. 1785. Joseph Smith's papers. H.M.C. 12 R, pt. 9, pp. 344–5.

3 Letter to Lady Georgiana, 2 May 1774.

4 Shore, *op. cit.* pp. 26–7.

5 Mallet, *A History of the University of Oxford*, vol. III, p. 2.

6 *Ibid.* p. 123.

7 Gibbon, *Memoirs of My Life*, p. 150.

8 Mallet, *op. cit.* p. 2.

9 Shore, *op. cit.* p. 32. This complaint must have been made in the second year at the University for, according to Laudian Statutes, ethics and logic were taught in the second year. Goldley, *Oxford in the Eighteenth Century*, p. 3.

PAGE 23

1 Mallet, *op. cit.* vol. II, p. 130, and vol. III, p. 126.
2 Gibbon, *op. cit.* pp. 61–2.
3 Shore, *op. cit.* p. 33.
4 *Ibid.* It is interesting to note that at this time Jones had no idea of linguistic groupings as then known in Europe. See pp. 91–3 above.
5 Shore, *op. cit.* p. 33.
6 Letter to Lady Georgiana, 3 Sept. 1768. Cf. Milton, *Of Education*, pp. 3–6.
7 W.J. to G.J.S., 11 Nov. 1768.
8 *Ibid.* 23 July 1773.

PAGE 24

1 Letter to C. Reviczki, Dec. 1771, as published in Shore, *op. cit.* p. 101.
2 Maurice, *op. cit.* pt. 2, p. 148.
3 Letter to E. Burke, 17 March 1782. Burke papers, Wentworth Muniments, Sheffield.
4 See p. 67 above.
5 Shore, *op. cit.* p. 35.
6 Letter from Lady Georgiana, 22 July 1764.
7 Letter to Lady Georgiana, 3 Sept. 1768.

PAGE 25

1 W.J. to G.J.S., 24 June 1774.
2 *Ibid.* 20 Sept. 1775.
3 *Ibid.* 1 Jan. 1774.
4 *Ibid.* 26 Dec. 1774.
5 *Ibid.*
6 *Ibid.* 6 Sept. 1774.
7 *Ibid.* 23 April 1774.
8 *Ibid.*
9 Letter to Lady Georgiana, 26 Feb. 1773.

PAGE 26

1 W.J. to G.J.S., 2 Nov. 1773.
2 *Ibid.* 8 March 1774.
3 *Ibid.* 15 Sept. 1776.
4 *Ibid.* 4 Nov. 1776.
5 *Ibid.*
6 Letter to Samuel Parr, 19 July 1779, as published in *The Works of Samuel Parr*, vol. I, p. 110.
7 W.J. to G.J.S., 8 April 1774.

PAGE 27

1 Letter to Lady Georgiana, 6 Oct. 1791.
2 Shore, *op. cit.* p. 36.

3 *Ibid.* p. 40.
4 Charles Reviczki (1737–93), an Orientalist. *A Treatise on Turkey* (1769) and the *Fragments from Persian Literature* were his best-known works.
5 Macartney to 'my dearest friend', 12 Oct. 1783, as published in Davies, *The Private Correspondence of Lord Macartney*, p. 223.
6 Letter to Lady Georgiana, 23 Nov. 1782. Cf. Shore, *op. cit.* p. 37.
7 W.J. to G.J.S., 27 Oct. 1782.

PAGE 28

1 *Ibid.* 26 Dec. 1774.
2 *Ibid.* (26 Jan.) 1771.
3 Letter to Lady Georgiana, 27 Aug. 1768. When Jones heard that this was how Lady Spencer had described him to a common friend, he wrote to say that had he known his behaviour had caused her uneasiness he would have bidden farewell to his studies.
4 Letter to C. Reviczki, March 1771, as published in Shore, *op. cit.* p. 93.
5 Horace Walpole to Lady Ossory, 14 Jan. 1781, *Correspondence*, vol. 29, p. 36 n.
6 W.J. to G.J.S., 6 Sept. 1774. No doubt he took part in rather frivolous and uninhibited drinking parties in Wales, given by his lawyer friends, where 'Welsh damsels' used to be present; but he was not very enthusiastic about such parties: 'They let me drink as little as I please; and very little I please to drink.' W.J. to G.J.S., 28 Sept. 1781.

PAGE 29

1 Letter to Lady Georgiana, 7 Sept. 1769, as published in Shore, *op. cit.* p. 69.
2 W.J. to G.J.S., 17 Aug. 1769.
3 Letter to N. Halhed, 1 March 1770, as published in Shore, *op. cit.* p. 74.
4 Letter to Reviczki, (April/May) 1770, as published in Shore, *op. cit.* pp. 75–8.
5 Letter to Lady Georgiana, 10 Oct. 1770.
6 *Ibid.*

PAGE 30

1 Letter to John, the first Earl Spencer, 22 Oct. 1770.
2 On 28 September Jones suddenly left Wimbledon leaving the following note for Lady Georgiana which sparked off the quarrel, 'Lord Althorp's education is not settled as much as his health, at present he is as much to be pitied as he is amiable'. Letter to Lady Georgiana, 28 Sept. 1770.
3 Horace Walpole to William Mason, 19 May 1786, *Correspondence*, vol. 29, p. 36.
4 W.J. to G.J.S., 18 Aug. 1772.
5 Letter to William Bennet as published in *The Works of Samuel Parr*, vol. I, p. 55.

PAGE 31

1 W.J. to G.J.S., (Feb.) 1775.
2 *Ibid.* 23 Feb. 1776.
3 Maurice, *op. cit.* p. 153.
4 Shore, *op. cit.* p. 110.
5 *Annals of the Club*, pp. 8–10.
6 W.J. to G.J.S., 16 Feb. 1769.
7 Leslie and Taylor, *Life and Times of Sir Joshua Reynolds*, vol. I, p. 312.
8 *Ibid.* p. 319.
9 Letter from E. Burke, 12 March 1779, as in Shore, *op. cit.* p. 157.
10 Johnson to Warren Hastings, 30 March 1774, as published in *Boswell's Life of Johnson* (ed. G. B. Hill), vol. IV, p. 69.
11 Gibbon, *The Decline and Fall of the Roman Empire* (ed. J. B. Bury), vol. IV, p. 296.
12 *Annals of the Club*, plate III.

PAGE 32

1 W.J. to G.J.S., 30 Nov. 1778.
2 *Ibid.* (Feb.) 1775.
3 *Ibid.* 15 Sept. (1776).
4 On 23 November 1782 he gave a summary of his financial state. His average annual income for the last five or six years had been £600 including his income from the Fellowship of University College, Oxford. Letter to Lady Georgiana, 23 Nov. 1782.
5 'Lord Eldon and the chances of the Bar' (review of Twiss's 3 vol. work), *E.R.* vol. 81, p. 154.
6 Roscoe, *Lives of Eminent British Lawyers*, pp. 306–28.
7 *Ibid.* p. 327.
8 *The Speeches of Isaeus* etc., p. vii.

PAGE 33

1 Holdsworth, *A History of English Law*, vol. XII, pp. 393–4.
2 *An Essay on the Law of Bailments*, p. 3.
3 *Ibid.* p. 4.
4 *Ibid.* pp. 123–4.
5 *Ibid.*
6 W.J. to G.J.S., 23 July (1773).
7 Maurice, *op. cit.* pt. II, p. 139.

PAGE 34

1 Letter to the Duchess of Devonshire, 24 Oct. 1782, as published in *Anglo-Saxon Review*, Sept. 1899, p. 63.
2 Letter to Lady Georgiana, 28 Feb. 1775.
3 *Ibid.*
4 *Ibid.* 17 May 1775.
5 He had to pay fines for not attending the club dinners regularly. *Annals of the Club*, p. 9.

6 Letter to Samuel Parr, n.d. (1774), as published in *The Works of Samuel Parr*, vol. VII, p. 286.
7 W.J. to G.J.S., 13 Oct. 1778
8 *Ibid.* 6 April 1782.
9 Letter to Lady Georgiana, 24 May 1778.

PAGE 35

1 See p. 73 above.
2 Letter to Count Reviczki, Dec. 1771, as published in Shore, *op. cit.* pp. 101–2.
3 1. *Histoire de Nader Chah.* 2. *A Grammar of the Persian language.* 3. *Dissertation sur la littérature Orientale.* 4. *Lettre à Monsieur A... du P....* 5. *Poems consisting chiefly of translations from the Asiatic languages.* 6. *The history of the life of Nader Shah.* 7. *Poeseos Asiaticae Commentariorum.* 8. *The Muhammadan Law of Succession.* 9. *Moallakat or seven Arabian Poems.* In *The Law of Bailments* Jones made a comparative study of the laws of Bailments in various countries including those of the East.

PAGE 36

1 Letter to H. A. Shultens, Oct. 1774, as published in Shore, *op. cit.* p. 122.
2 See pp. 30–1 above.
3 *Works*, vol. 12, pp. 321–2.
4 *Ibid.* p. 323.
5 *Ibid.* p. 328.
6 *Ibid.* p. 325.
7 *Ibid.*
8 *Ibid.* p. 327.

PAGE 37

1 *Ibid.* pp. 328–31.
2 W.J. to G.J.S., 23 Feb. (1776).
3 *Works*, vol. 12, p. 342.
4 These two tracts were first published together with his *History of the Life of Nader Shah* in 1773. Cf. Shore, *op. cit.* pp. 491–513. The *Prefatory Discourse* was printed but the History was never published.
5 *Works*, vol. 12, pp. 346–8. The plan of Atticus is to be found in Cicero's *On Oration.*
6 *Works*, vol. 12, pp. 347–8.
7 *Ibid.* vol. 5, p. 410.
8 Collingwood, *The Idea of History*, pp. 76–8.
9 *Works*, vol. 12, p. 434.

PAGE 38

1 Shore, *op. cit.* p. 512.
2 *Ibid.* p. 491.

3 *Lettre à Monsieur A . . du P . . . .*
4 E. Browne, *A Literary History of Persia*, vol. I, pp. 49–56. Cf. Arthur Waley's 'Anquetil Duperron and Sir William Jones', *History Today*, vol. 2, pp. 23–33. All these writers have somewhat neglected Jones's attack on Anquetil Duperron in his *History of the Persian Language*.
5 *Works*, vol. 5, p. 416.
6 *Ibid.* p. 415.

PAGE 39

1 *Ibid.* vol. 12, p. 314.
2 See p. 21 above.
3 He was of the twelfth dynasty of Egypt, and reigned between 1950 and 1935 B.C.
4 *Works*, vol. 12, p. 315.
5 Lockhart, *Nadir Shah*, p. 296.
6 Shore, *op. cit.* p. 40.
7 He wrote to Count Reviczki in July 1770 that the translation of the Life of Nadir Shah was a 'most disagreeable task'. Shore, *op. cit.* p. 81.
8 *Histoire de Nader Shah*. The letters concerning the French translation were not added to this edition as Cannon seems to believe (see Cannon, *Bibliography*, pp. 14–15) but were published with the *History*.

PAGE 40

1 *Works*, vol. 12, p. 316.
2 Lockhart, *op. cit.* p. 1.
3 See pp. 10–13 above.
4 *Works*, vol. 12, pp. 389–90.
5 'The Tenth Discourse', *As.R.* vol. IV, pp. 7–9.
6 *An Essay on the Law of Bailments*, p. 114.
7 See p. 33 above.

PAGE 41

1 *The History of the Life of Nader Shah*, p. 104.
2 *Ibid.* pp. 38 and 92–3.
3 *Ibid.* p. 11.
4 J. P. de Bougainville put this idea in his *Parallèle de l'Expédition d'Alexandre dans les Indes avec la conquête des mêmes contrées par Tahmas Kouli Khan* in 1752 which was based on Fraser, Harvey, and others' works. See Lockhart, *op. cit.* p. 266.
5 A. L. Basham, 'Modern Historians on Ancient India', in *Historians of India*, pp. 266–74.
6 *History of the Life of Nader Shah*, p. 107.
7 *Ibid.* p. 113.
8 *Ibid.* p. 115. The last sentence was from Voltaire's *History of Charles XII*.
9 *History of the life of Nader Shah*, p. 120.

PAGE 42

1 *The Catalogue of the Library of Sir William Jones*, no. 364.
2 Letter to Lady Georgiana, 4 June 1770, as published in Shore, *op. cit.* p. 78.
3 *A Grammar of the Persian language*, p. v.
4 Tritton, 'The student of Arabic', *B.S.O.A.S.* XI (1946), 695–8.
5 *Moallakat or seven Arabian poems. Works*, vol. 10, p. 8.
6 Letter to E. Cartwright, 12 Nov. 1780, as published in *Memoirs of the life etc. of Edmond Cartwright*, p. 329.
7 See p. 6 above.
8 W.J. to G.J.S., 10 May 1772.
9 Gibbon, *The Decline and Fall of the Roman Empire*, vol. V, pp. 319–25.

PAGE 43

1 Lovejoy, 'The supposed primitivism of Rousseau: Discourse on inequality', *M.P.* vol. XXI, pp. 15–86.
2 Burke, *Philosophical inquiry into the origin of our ideas of the sublime*, pp. 330–1, 332, as quoted in Wellek, *History of Criticism*, vol. I, p. 112.
3 'On the arts commonly called imitative', *Poems*, p. 202.
4 Wellek, *op. cit.* p. 123.

PAGE 44

1 Cannon, *Oriental Jones*, p. 29.
2 *Poems*, p. vi.
3 Bryant, *Burke and His Literary Friends* (Washington University Studies, no. 9), p. 12.
4 'On the poetry of the Eastern nations', *Poems*, p. 174.
5 *Poems*, p. v.
6 'On the arts commonly called imitative', *Poems*, pp. 202–3.
7 *Ibid.* pp. 216–17.

PAGE 45

1 'On the poetry of the Eastern nations', *Poems*, p. 174.
2 *Ibid.* p. 188.
3 *Ibid.*
4 *Ibid.* p. 189.
5 *Works*, vol. 12, p. 343.
6 *A Grammar of the Persian language*, pp. vii, viii.
7 *Poems*, p. vii.

PAGE 46

1 *Nader Shah*, pp. 120–1.
2 'A catalogue of the most valuable books in the Persian language', *Works*, vol. 5, pp. 172–3. Cf. B.M. 16, 705 ff., 1–84
3 'Description of Asia', *Works*, vol. 12, p. 391.
4 *Ibid.* p. 389. Cf. Herbelot, *Bibliothèque Orientale*, p. 448.
5 'Description of Asia', *Works*, vol. 12, p. 389.

PAGE 47

1 Letter to R. Griffiths, May 1777, Bodl. (Oxf.) 28460.
2 'On the poetry of the Eastern nations', *Poems*, p. 198.
3 *Ibid.*
4 Letter from Edmund Burke (17 March 1782) as published in Shore, *Memoirs*, pp. 201–2. For the date of the letter see *Checklist of Burke Correspondence*, p. 265.
5 W.J. to G.J.S., 29 June 1781.
6 *Ibid.* 4 Sept. 1780.

PAGE 48

1 Orme collections, 41. 13. This was printed in 1772.
2 Letter to Edmund Burke, 17 March 1782. Burke Papers, Wentworth Muniments.

PAGE 49

1 Arberry, 'New light on Sir William Jones', *B.S.O.A.S.* vol. XI, pp. 677–85.
2 *Ibid.* p. 679.
3 Robbins, *The Eighteenth-century Commonwealthman*, p. 5.
4 Letter to Lord Kenyon, 27 Jan. 1783, H.M.C. Appendix, Part IV, 14 R, pp. 514–15.
5 Horace Walpole to William Mason, May 1780, *Correspondence*, vol. 29, pp. 33–6.
6 Tucker, *A Sequel to Sir William Jones's pamphlet* etc., p. 15.
7 *E.R.* V (1804–5), 340.

PAGE 50

1 Christie, *Wilkes, Wyvill and Reform*, pp. 9–18.
2 Olson, *The Radical Duke*, p. 54.
3 *Ibid.* Cf. Christie, pp. 73–7.
4 Olson, *op. cit.* p. 54. Cf. Plumb, *England in the Eighteenth Century*, pp. 134–5.

PAGE 51

1 Robbins, *op. cit.* p. 261.
2 Letter to E. Gibbon, 30 Aug. 1781, as published in *The Works of Sir William Jones*, vol. I, p. 365.
3 *Oration*, p. 73.
4 *Ibid.*
5 W.J. to G.J.S., 6 Dec. 1779.
6 *Ibid.* 21 Oct. 1782.
7 London S.C.I. *List of Members*, 1782, p. v.
8 He wrote to Thomas Yeates, the Secretary of S.C.I., 'I should indeed long ago have testified my regard for so useful an institution by an offer of my humble service in promoting it, if I had not really despaired in my present situation of being able to attend your meetings as often as I should ardently wish.' Letter to T.Y., 25 April 1782, as published in Shore, *op. cit.* p. 208.

PAGE 52

1 W.J. to G.J.S., July 1777, as published in Shore, *op. cit.* pp. 151–4.
2 Letters to Benjamin Franklin, 28 May 1779 and 5 June (1780). Franklin Papers, A.P.S. Cf. Richard Price to Franklin, 14 Oct. 1779, as published in *The Works of Benjamin Franklin*, vol. VIII, p. 395.
3 W.J. to G.J.S., 5 March 1780.
4 *Ibid.* 16 Sept. 1779.
5 *Ibid.* 28 May 1780.
6 'A Fragment of Polybius' as published in *The Works of B. Franklin*, vol. VIII, pp. 543–7. It was an ingenious plan on the part of Jones to put an end to the American War which he sent to Franklin. Letter to Franklin, 28 May 1779. Franklin Papers, A.P.S.
7 *The Catalogue of the Library of Samuel Parr*, p. 441.

PAGE 53

1 W.J. to G.J.S., 5 Oct. 1782.
2 Tucker, *op. cit.* p. 111.
3 Cartwright, *The Life and Correspondence of Major Cartwright*, vol. II, p. 175.
4 Gurney, *op. cit.* pp. 21–31. Cf. N.L.W. 2598 C.
5 Howell, *State Trials*, vol. XXI, p. 1086.

PAGE 55

1 Robertson, *Select Statutes*, p. 272. Ct. Holdsworth, *op. cit.* vol. 8, p. 374.
2 There were two editions of his political tracts published in 1819 by John Fairburn and E. Wilson.
3 John Cartwright to the Duke of Roxburgh, 4 March 1820, as published in *Life*, vol. II, pp. 175–6.
4 In 1781 Josiah Tucker, dean of Gloucester, wrote a *Treatise concerning civil government* to disprove Locke.

PAGE 56

1 *The Principles of Government* (1782), p. 6.
2 *Ibid.* p. 5.
3 W.J. to G.J.S., 31 March 1781.
4 *Works* (1807), vol. 10, p. 390.

PAGE 57

1 W.J. to G.J.S., 21 Nov. 1779.
2 *Ibid.* 18 Feb. 1780, as published in Shore, *op cit.* p. 212.
3 Above p. 25.
4 W.J. to G.J.S., 13 Jan. 1780.
5 Holdsworth, *op. cit.* vol. XII, pp. 727–37.
6 Blackstone, *Commentaries on the laws of England*, sec. II, subsect. 38.
7 *Ibid.* subsect. 39.
8 Above p. 33.
9 Blackstone, *op. cit.* sect. II, subsect. 44.

PAGE 58

1 *Ibid.* subsects. 43 and 56.
2 W.J. to G.J.S., 5 March 1780.
3 Letter to 'a friend in the Bar', 13 April 1784, as published in Shore, *op. cit.* p. 246.
4 Gurney, *op. cit.* p. 13.
5 *Ibid.* p. 19.

PAGE 59

1 Tucker, *op. cit.* p. 11.
2 As quoted in Aldridge, *Man of Reason*, p. 136.
3 William Burrough to the Earl of Charlemont, 22 Nov. 1791. H.M.C. R.13, Appendix, p. 177.
4 Letter to John Wilmot, 12 Oct. 1790. B.M. 9828, f. 161.
5 Bennet to Parr (1792) as published in *The Works of Samuel Parr*, vol. I, p. 468.

PAGE 60

1 Letter to Thomas Yeates, 7 June 1782, as published in Shore, *op. cit.* p. 212.
2 Above p. 42.
3 Pocock, J. G. A., 'Burke and the ancient constitution', etc., *The Historical Journal*, vol. III, no. 2, pp. 125–43.
4 Holdsworth, *op. cit.* vol. V, p. 47. Cf. Hill, *The Century of Revolution*, p. 67.
5 W.J. to G.J.S., 12 April 1784.
6 *Ibid.* 13 Nov. 1777. Shore published it in the *Memoirs* (pp. 42–3) but suppressed the latter part of it and dated it wrongly as 13 Nov. 1776.
7 *Ibid.*
8 Letter to Count Reviczki (April 1768) as published in Shore, *op. cit.* p. 58. This comment was made in reply to Reviczki's own observation on English politics. 'I confess to you that I never saw anything similar to the mode here pursued of electing members of Parliament.' Letter to William Jones (*op. cit.* p. 55). Shore must have got his dates mixed up here for Reviczki was obviously referring to the incident on 28 March 1768 in London in which he was dragged out of his coach and had his boot soles chalked with the slogan 'no 45'. This was in connection with Wilkes's election, so W.J. wrote this letter in April 1768 and not in April 1766, as Shore believed. Cf. Rudé, *Wilkes and Liberty*, p. 43.

PAGE 61

1 Burke, *Thoughts on the Cause of Present Discontent, Works*, vol. II, pp. 7–8.
2 W.J. to G.J.S., 29 June 1781. The business referred to was a debate on 'Bengal Judicature Bill'.
3 Letter to Thomas Yeates, 25 April 1782, as published in Shore, *op. cit.* p. 209.

4 'Of English politicks, I say nothing because I doubt whether you and I should ever agree on them. I do not mean the narrow politicks of contending parties, but the great principles of government and legislation, the majesty of the whole nation collectively; and consistency of popular rights with legal prerogatives, which ought to be supported in order to repress the oligarchical power.' Letter to John Wilmot, 3 Oct. 1787. B.M. 9828, f. 158.

5 W.J. to G.J.S., 20 Sept. 1775.

PAGE 62

1 *Speech on Reformation, Works* (1807), vol. VIII, p. 506–7. Capell Left found this passage significant enough to publish it in the proceedings of the Society for Constitutional Information. See *Proc. London S.C.I.* 12 Aug. 1782.

2 *Proc. London S.C.I.* 24 May 1782.

3 Hill, 'Norman Yoke' in Saville, *Democracy and the Labour Movement*, p. 12.

4 *Works* vol. 8, pp. 508–9.

5 Above p. 13.

6 Above pp. 14–15.

7 Blackstone, *op. cit.* sect. IV. Cf. Guha, *A rule of property for Bengal*, p. 102.

8 Lehmann, 'John Millar', *B.J.S.* vol. III, pp. 30–46.

PAGE 63

1 *Works*, vol. VIII, p. 509.

2 *Ibid.* p. 511.

3 Macpherson, *The Political Theory of Possessive Individualism*, pp. 263–7.

4 Locke, *The second treatise of civil government*, sec. 27.

5 *Works*, vol. 8, p. 508.

PAGE 64

1 *A letter to a patriot senator*, p. 24.

2 Rudé, 'Gordon Riots', *Trans. Royal Hist. Soc.* vol. VI, p. 111.

3 Letter to Lady Georgiana, 8 June 1780.

4 *Ibid.* 9 June 1780.

5 *Ibid.*

6 *Ibid.* 10 June 1780.

PAGE 65

1 Duke of Portland to William Shipley, 12 Feb. 1796. N.L.W. 2409 C.

2 Letter to C. Reviczki, April 1768, as published in Shore, *op. cit.* p. 59.

3 Letter to John Wilkes, 7 Aug. 1780. B.M. 30, 877, ff. 90–1.

4 Rudé, *Wilkes and Liberty*, p. 192.

5 Letter to Samuel Parr, 21 July 1780, as published in *The Works of Samuel Parr*, vol. I, pp. 116–17.

6 *Works*, vol. 8, pp. 521–4.

PAGE 66

1 Cartwright, *Take Your Choice*, p. 21.
2 Macpherson, *op. cit.* pp. 157–9.
3 Cannon, *Annotated Bibliography*, pp. xiv–xv.
4 Arberry, 'New light on Sir William Jones' *B.S.O.A.S.* vol. XI. p. 673.
5 A. M. A. Parry wrote in her unpublished biography of Jones, 'He had made his opinion known by means of several small tracts he published, which were too advanced for these times and he therefore saw the propriety of withdrawing from the contest'. N.L.W. 5733 D. Cf. Ward, *Georgian Oxford*, pp. 277–8.
6 He wrote to Dr Wheeler at Oxford on 2 September informing him that he had declined the poll and on 9 September he wanted to deliver his speech in which he attacked the slave trade. However, he was unable to deliver it and he published only twenty-five copies of the speech later in the same month. Shore, *op. cit.* p. 179. Cf. *A speech on the nomination of the candidates to represent the county of Middlesex.*
7 W.J. to G.J.S., 8 Jan 1777.
8 Bayley, 'Sir William Jones' (*N. & Q.* July 1910).
9 W.J. to G.J.S., 29 April 1780.
10 Namier, *Structure of Politics*, pp. 1–61.

PAGE 67

1 Letter to Lady Georgiana, 18 May 1780.
2 W.J. to G.J.S., 12 March 1780.
3 Charles Parker to Roger Newdigate, Sat. Morn. (1780), n.d. Newdigate Papers, B 2141, C.R.O. Warwick.
4 *Ibid.*
5 W.J. to G.J.S., 29 April 1780.
6 Letter to William Adams (April) 1780, as published in *N. & Q.* (July 1910), p. 3.
7 *Address to the University of Oxford*, Gough. Bodl. Oxf. 90 (22).

PAGE 68

1 The passages were taken from the following works (*a*) *Lettre à Monsieur A... du P...* 1771; (*b*) *Dedication to Commentaries on Asiatick Poetry; Conclusion of the Preface on the same work*; (*d*) *Preface of the history of the Life of Nader Shah*; and (*e*) *Speech of Oxford Theatre.*
2 W.J. to G.J.S., May 1780.
3 *Ibid.* 29 April 1780.
4 Letter to Schultens, 13 May 1780. BPL. 245 XIII Leiden.
5 Horace Walpole to William Mason, 19 May 1780, *Correspondence*, vol. 29, pp. 35–6.
6 'I own I am much discouraged and think if you are not pretty sure you shall make a tolerable figure, you had better give it up.' Letter from Lady Georgiana, 22 May 1780. Similar views were expressed by others. Letter from Schultens, 2 June 1780, as published in Shore, *op. cit.* p. 178.
7 Letter to Lady Georgiana, 22 May 1780.

8 Mrs Montagu to Weller Pepys, May 1780, as published in Blunt, *Mrs Montagu—Queen of the Blues*, p. 85.
9 Ward, *op. cit.* pp. 277–8.
10 Charles Parker told Sir Roger Newdigate, about the *Address*, 'This is being circulated by his consent, if not desire, seems so like being one's own trumpeter and approving yourself before you are approved of by others, that I think it will do him much more harm than good'. Newdigate Papers, B 2141.

PAGE 69

1 'I have been told that the very ode to which you have been so indulgent lost me near twenty votes.' Letter to E. Cartwright, 8 Sept. 1780, as published in Shore, *op. cit.* p. 184.
2 Jones wrote to Lady Georgiana that all in Turk's Head (where Johnson's Literary Club met) except Burke were his friends. Letter to Lady Georgiana, 26 May 1780.
3 Letter to George John, 30 Aug. 1780.
4 Letter to Dr Wheeler, 3 Sept. 1780, as published in Shore, *op. cit.* p. 179.
5 Letter to Lady Georgiana, 21 Oct. 1782. As published in Shore, *op. cit.* p. 219. He told Franklin. 'All virtue and public spirit are dead in this country: we have the shadow of a free constitution but live in truth under the substance of despotism.' Letter to Benjamin Franklin, 17 Sept. 1781. Franklin Papers.
6 W.J. to G.J.S., 21 Oct. 1782.

PAGE 70

1 Letter to Arthur Lee, 28 Oct. 1788. B.M. Add. 37, 232, ff. 85–7.
2 W.J. to G.J.S., 27 Oct. 1782.
3 Letter to Lady Georgiana, 29 May 1778.
4 Letter to Burke, 25 Feb. 1783. Burke Papers, Wentworth Muniments.
5 *A.B.* vol. I, p. 457.
6 North to Robinson, 3 March 1779, as quoted in Sutherland, *East India Company*, p. 342.
7 Robert Chambers to Philip Francis, 12 Dec. 1785. B.M. Add. 40, 763.
8 W.J. to G.J.S., 12 March 1780.
9 *A.B.* vol. I, pp. 464–5.

PAGE 71

1 Thurlow to the duchess of Devonshire (n.d.) as published in *Anglo-Saxon Review* (Sept. 1890), p. 68.
2 Letter to Shelburne, 22 April 1782. Lacaita–Shelburne Papers, William L. Clements Library.
3 W.J. to G.J.S., 14 April 1775.
4 Letter to Shelburne, 14 July 1782. Lansdowne Papers, Bowood.
5 *Ibid.*
6 Letter to E. Burke, 8 Oct. 1782. Burke Papers, Wentworth Muniments.
7 Letter to Shelburne, 9 Sept. 1782.
8 Letter to E. Burke, 25 Feb. 1782.

PAGE 72

1 George III to Thurlow, March 1783. *Correspondence*, vol. VI, pp. 253–4.
2 He wrote letters thanking Ashburton and Shelburne for their help, but a bitterness against Shelburne continued. When he heard that Shelburne had received a new title, the Marquis of Lansdowne, he described him as a snake 'who changes the skin of his titles only to show in how many forms he can deceive'. Letter to Richard Johnson (March 1793). N.L.W. II, 095 E, f. 13.
3 Tucker, *op. cit.* p. 22.
4 Letter to Gibbon 1781 as published in *Works*, vol. I, p. 387.

PAGE 73

1 Above p. 27.
2 W.J. to G.J.S., 24 April 1778.

PAGE 74

1 W.J. to G.J.S., 22 April 1783.
2 Shore, *op. cit.* p. 228.
3 Collingwood, *op. cit.* pp. 57–8.
4 For a further discussion on Jones's conception of human knowledge see below, p. 82.

PAGE 75

1 Remarks on the island of Hinzuan or Johanna. *As.R.* vol. II, pp. 77–110. This paper was read to the Society on 1 Nov. 1787 (*Transactions*) and was published in the *Asiatick Researches* in 1792. But it must have been written before 11 April 1784 for on that day Jones promised to send a copy of it to Spencer as soon as possible. W.J. to G.J.S., 11 April 1784.
2 *As.R.* vol. II, p. 81.
3 *Ibid.* p. 83.

PAGE 76

1 *Ibid.* pp. 101–2.
2 *Ibid.*
3 *Ibid.* pp. 105–8.
4 *Ibid.* p. 106.
5 Hickey thought that Jones arrived in Calcutta some time at the end of August 1783. *Memoirs*, vol. III, pp. 154–5. But he was wrong as the *Crocodile* reached Balasore on 13 September (see B.M. 16,264, f. 232) and on 25 Sept. 1793 Jones recalled that he arrived in Calcutta ten years before that date. W.J. to G.J.S., 25 Sept. 1793.
6 B.M. 16,264, f. 242, and Hickey, *op. cit.* vol. III, p. 155.

PAGE 77

1 W.J. to G.J.S., 14 Oct. 1783.
2 *Ibid.* 6 Nov. 1783.

3 Halhed, Preface, *A Grammar of the Bengali Language*, pp. xxiii–xxv, and *G.M.* n.s. vol. VI, pp. 97–8.
4 Gladwin, *The Ayine Akbery or the Institutes of the Emperor Akbar*.
5 *D.N.B.*
6 Though Halhed's *Gentoo Laws* received universal attention throughout Europe this was an exception. The works of other English Orientalists did not receive much attention. Halhed's *Grammar* was not reviewed until 1784 (*M.R.* vol. 70, pp. 367–9) and Gladwin's *Institute* received full consideration only in 1788 (*M.R.* vol. 79, pp. 615–36), after Jones had gone to Bengal.
7 Wilkins, *A Translation of a Royal Grant of Land by one of the Ancient Raajas of Hindostan*.

PAGE 78

1 *As.R.* vol. I, pp. 123–30. In 1788, when the first volume of the *Asiatick Researches* came out, Wilkins was made a Fellow of the Royal Society. *G.M.* n.s. vol. VI, pp. 97–8.
2 Wilkins, 'Two inscriptions from the Vindhya mountains', *As.R.* vol. II, pp. 167–9. Cf. *The Classical Age*, p. 67.
3 Teignmouth, *Memoirs*, pp. 103–4.
4 *Ibid.* pp. 101–2.
5 *Ibid.* pp. 107–8.
6 *Ibid.*
7 *Ibid.*
8 Above p. 15.
9 Above pp. 15–16.
10 Letter from R. Orme, 12 March 1784. Orme Collections 202, 253.

PAGE 79

1 Teignmouth, *op. cit.* p. 103.
2 Feiling, *Warren Hastings*, p. 399.
3 H.M.S. 207 (2).
4 Halhed to Hastings, *Gentoo Laws*, p. vi.
5 Wilkins, *A Translation of a Royal Grant of Land*.
6 Halhed, Preface, *Gentoo Laws*. Cf. Shore, *op. cit.* pp. 237–9.
7 Feiling, *op. cit.* p. 236.
8 *Ibid.*

PAGE 80

1 Halhed, *Gentoo Laws*, p. ix.
2 Stokes, *The English Utilitarians and India*, pp. 3–4.
3 Weitzman, *Warren Hastings and Philip Francis*, pp. 15–16.
4 *Ibid.* pp. 49–60.
5 *Centenary Review*, pp. 12–13.
6 Bernal, *op. cit.* pp. 310–17.
7 *A Persian Grammar*, pp. xi–xii.
8 Above, p. 16.

PAGE 81

1 Evans, *A History of the Society of Antiquaries*, pp. 146 n., 176. Cf. 'Free Thinkers', *Encyclopedia of Social Sciences*.

2 Evans, *op. cit.* p. 179.

3 *Het Bataviaensch Genootschap van Kunsten en Wetenschappen Gedurende de Eerste Eeuw van zijn Bestaen*, 1778–1878, p. 27.

4 *As.R.* vol. I, p. x.

5 *Centenary Review*, pp. 1–2.

6 'A discourse on the institution of a society for inquiry into the history, civil and natural, the antiquities, arts, sciences and literature of Asia.' In *As.R.* vol. I, it was stated that Jones delivered his first presidential discourse on 30 Jan. 1784. But 30 January was a Friday and there was no meeting of the Society on that day; and Jones had already delivered his address on 15 Jan. 1784 at the first meeting of the Society where Chambers presided. *Transactions*, 15 Jan. 1784.

7 *As.R.* vol. I, pp. ix–x.

PAGE 82

1 *Ibid.* p. xii.

2 *Ibid.*

3 *Ibid.* p. xiii.

4 *Ibid.* p. xv.

5 *Ibid.* p. xvi.

PAGE 83

1 *Ibid.*

2 *Ibid.* p. xv.

3 *Centenary Review*, p. 8.

4 *Transactions*, 15 Jan. 1784.

5 Ferguson, *History*, pp. 3–4.

6 Lord Monboddo, *Progress of Language*, vol. I, pp. 1–4.

7 Herder, *Philosophy of History*, pp. 161–2.

8 Letter to J. Macpherson, 6 May 1786, as published in Shore, *op. cit.* p. 275. Later in November 1786 he told Macpherson, 'I am correcting proofs of our transactions which will, I hope, satisfy Mr Ferguson' (*op. cit.* p. 287).

9 He knew Monboddo through the bishop of St Asaph, at whose house many eminent men, such as Johnson, dined. W.J. to G.J.S., 29 Sept. 1788. Monboddo corresponded with Jones when the latter was in India. Letter to Monboddo, 24 Aug. 1788, as published in Shore, *op. cit.* pp. 321–2.

10 *Transactions*, 24 Jan. 1784. Also *As.R.* vol. I, p. v.

PAGE 84

1 *Ibid.* p. vi.

2 *Ibid.* pp. vii and viii.

3 *Transactions*, 24 Jan. 1784.

4 *Ibid.* 29 Jan. 1784.
5 *Ibid.* 5 Feb. 1784.
6 *As.R.* vol. I, p. xi.
7 Seton-Karr, *Selections from Calcutta Gazettes*, vols. I and II.

PAGE 85

1 We do not know the exact number of meetings that took place in the first ten years of the Society's life, as the *Proceedings* of the years between 6 Nov. 1788–5 Nov. 1789 are mislaid, except for 8 Jan. 1789. But about 100 meetings are recorded in the *Transactions* now available, so we can assume that there cannot have been more than eleven or twelve meetings in the missing year.
2 *Transactions*, 8 April 1784 and 15 April 1784.
3 *Transactions*, 19 May 1785. Cf. Letter to J. Macpherson, 26 May 1785, as published in Shore, *op. cit.* p. 26.
4 There were three secretaries during Jones's presidency, G. H. Barlow, J. H. Harrington and E. Morris. Most information about the Society is deduced from my study of the manuscript *Proceedings* from 1784–1794.

PAGE 86

1 Letter to John Hyde, 20 Oct. 1789, as published in Shore, *op. cit.* p. 331.
2 Letter to E. Burke, 27 Feb. 1784. Burke Papers, Wentworth Muniments, Sheffield.
3 W.J. to G.J.S. 12 April 1784.
4 *A Charge to the Grand Jury* and a *Hymn to Camdoo translated from the Hindu into Persian and from Persian into English*, London, 1784.
5 *Monthly Review*, vol. 71, pp. 354–7.
6 *Transactions*, 10 Nov. 1785.
7 *A.M.* vol. I, pp. 1–17, and *Transactions*, 10 Nov. 1785.
8 Dr Watson, Professor of Chemistry and Professor of Divinity at Cambridge, was a man of very wide interests. He was most famous for his theological disputes with Gibbon and Paine.
9 *Transactions*, 10 Nov. 1785.

PAGE 87

1 *Ibid.*
2 Francis Gladwin, a member of the Asiatick Society and author of various works, was also the editor of the *Calcutta Gazette*.
3 There was only two volumes of this *Miscellany*. In 1787 Gladwin started another magazine called the *New Asiatick Miscellany* which did not survive after the first issue.
4 Letter to J. C. Walker, 11 Sept. 1787 as published in Shore, *op. cit.* pp. 292–7.
5 *Transactions*, 6 July 1787.
6 Jones told Joseph Banks why such priority was given to Col. Pearce's rather unimpressive article. 'He showed his paper about the prediction of comets and even of earthquakes by the Brahmins and was so offended

by our [in]credulity that we were obliged to print his dull papers merely to keep him in tolerable humour.' Letter to J. Banks, 1 Oct. 1791. *D.T.C.* vol. VII, p. 265–70.

PAGE 88

1 Letters to Samuel Davies, 10 Nov. 1788, 8 Nov. 1789 and 21 Feb. 1790. Davis Papers.
2 Letter to Samuel Davis, 8 Dec. 1789.
3 W.J. to G.J.S., 11 Aug. 1787.
4 *Ibid.*
5 *Ibid.*
6 They were Govardhana Kaul, Pandit Ramlochan, Radhakanta Sharman and Aly Ibrahim Khan.
7 *M.R.* vol. 81, pp. 648–83, and *M.R.* n.s. vol. I, pp. 317–29, 431–45 and 559–68.
8 *G.M.* vol. 59, pt. 2, pp. 1020–1.
9 Such publications were considered as very profitable ventures. In 1793 a collection of Jones's dissertations and hymns was brought out from Dublin and from then onwards until the 1830s almost every other year saw an edition of reprinted papers from the *Asiatick Researches*.

PAGE 89

1 Camb. 00–1–6.
2 Letter from J. Sullivan, 7 Feb. 1795, as published in Shore, *op. cit.* pp. 405–6. This and the letter from the President of Yale College reached Calcutta long after Jones's death.
3 W.J. to G.J.S., 22 July 1788.
4 *Ibid.* 12 April 1784.
5 The 'second discourse', *As.R.* vol. I, p. 406.
6 Feiling, *op. cit.* p. 322.
7 Letter to W. Hastings, 7 Jan. 1785, B.M. 29,167, f. 330.
8 Journal of Charles Grant, 6 Feb. 1785, as published in Morris, *Life of Charles Grant*, pp. 82–3.

PAGE 90

1 He wrote to George John that Navadvip was the 'third university of which I am a member; and there I finish my education'. W.J. to G.J.S., 21 Aug. 1787. Jones was educated in Oxford but in 1774 he received an *ad eundem* degree in Cambridge and was admitted to Emmanuel College. Maurice, *Memoirs*, pt. 1, p. 85.
2 Buckland, *Dictionary of Indian Biography*, p. 10.
3 W.J. to G.J.S., 25 Sept. 1793.
4 Letter to John Hyde, 20 Oct. 1789, as published in Shore, *op. cit.* pp. 331–2.
5 Letter to Samuel Davis, 20 Oct. 1792. Davis Papers.
6 *Transactions*, 3 April 1794.
7 *Ibid.* 1 May 1794.

PAGE 91

1 The story of Psammetichus is to be found in the *Histories* of Herodotus. See Penderson, *Linguistic Science in the Nineteenth Century*, p. 3. For the development of linguistic science before 1800 see Bonfante, 'Ideas on the kinship of the European languages from 1200–1800', *Journal of World History*, vol. 1, pp. 679–99.

2 'The Grammarians carry the older dialect to the family of Heber, the fourth in descent from Noah, and the more modern to Ishmael, the son of Abraham.' Richardson, *A dissertation on the languages, literature and manners of the Eastern nations* (1777), p. 4.

PAGE 92

1 *Scythian origin of the peoples and languages of Europe* as quoted in Bonfante, 'Ideas on the Kinship', etc., p. 691.

PAGE 93

1 Fréret, *Vue générale sur les origines et le mélange des anciennes nations et sur la manière d'en étudier l'histoire. Hist. et Mém. de l'Ac. des I. et B.L.* Tome 9, pp. 1–3. Bréal thought that Fréret 'essaye déjà la méthode et présente quelques unes des modes de découverte de la linguistique moderne'. *Grammaire Comparée*, pp. xvii–xviii n. But Fréret was only re-establishing Scaliger's theory of independent groups and the science had already taken a further step forward with Boxhorn and Leibniz.

2 Letter to Prince Adam Czartoryski, 19 Feb. 1779, as published in Shore, *op. cit.* p. 168.

PAGE 94

1 'Remarks on the island of Hinzuan or Johanna', *As.R.* vol. 2, p. 88.

2 *As.R.* vol. 1, p. xiv.

3 Cannon, 'Sir William Jones's Persian linguistics', *J.A.O.S.* vol. 78, p. 269.

4 Above p. 24.

5 Above p. 38.

6 Letter to Charles Wilkins, 24 April 1784, as published in *J.A.O.S.* vol. 10, pp. 111–12.

7 Letter to Warren Hastings, 23 Oct. 1786, B.M. 29,170, f. 234.

8 Letter to Charles Wilkins, 1 March 1785, *J.A.O.S.* vol. 10, p. 113.

9 Letter to Charles Wilkins, 6 June 1785, *ibid.* p. 114.

10 Letter to Charles Wilkins, 26 July 1785, *ibid.* That his knowledge of Sanskrit was poor is proved from the fact that in writing the Hymns on Hindu gods and goddesses he largely drew on his friends, Johnson and Wilkins. He asked Richard Johnson to write a list of names where 'Camdeo may be supposed to resort'. Letter to R.J. n.d. N.L.W. 1095 E. f. 17. It was Wilkins who corrected the proof of *The Hymn to Camdeo*. Letter to C.W, 6 Jan. 1784, as published in *J.A.O.S.* vol. 10, p. 111.

PAGE 95

1 *Ibid.*

2 *Ibid.*

3 'On the Hindus', *As.R.* vol. I, pp. 422–3. In a recent work the year 1786 is considered as the starting point of modern comparative philology. Hobsbawm, *The Age of Revolution*, p. 236.

4 'Many are the languages of these places. Their pronunciation is not disagreeable and their structure is allied to Greek and Latin.' Fr Thomas Stevens to his father, 24 Oct. 1583, as published in *The Christian Purana of Father Thomas Stephens of the Society of Jesus*, p. xxxvi.

5 'All their sciences are written in a language called Sanscruta which seems well articulated; of which there is no remembrance when it was spoken, for being so ancient they learn it as we do Greek and Latin... and our language of to-day has a lot in common with it because in it we can find many of our nouns especially numbers: the 6, 7, 8, and 9, God, serpent and many others.' Fillipo Sasseti to Bernado Davaurati, n.d. *Lettre de F. Sasseti*, p. 341. Elsewhere Sasetti showed a remarkable insight into Sanskrit phonetics. F.S. to Piero Vettari, 27 Jan. 1585, *op. cit.* p. 283.

PAGE 96

1 *Hist et Mém. de l'Ac. des I. et B.L.* Tome 49, p. 660.

2 *Ibid.* p. 664.

3 It was first published by Anquetil Duperron in 1808. See Bréal, *Grammaire comparée*, pp. xvii–xviii.

4 The news of this discovery, like many others, reached Europe long before the first volume of the *Asiatick Researches* was published. He wrote to his friend, 'I find Sanskrit to be a sister of Latin and even the word Lavinia which is old Hetruscan, signifies in Sanskrit, what if Lady Spencer had not more valuable qualities to boast of would be flattered; but I may whisper to you that it means, with a fine complexion'. W.J. to G.J.S. 29 Sept. 1786. The Irish were fascinated to know that their old language was a sister of Sanskrit and the news spread. J. C. Walker of the Irish Academy wrote to the Earl of Charlemont telling him how Jones wanted to compare the ancient traditions of Irish history with those of India, for Sanskrit had certainly an affinity with the ancient language of Ireland. J.C.W. to the Earl of Charlement, 5 May 1778, H.M.C.R. 13 App. vol. II, p. 75.

5 For the impact of the Romantic movement on historiography and comparative philology see Collingwood, *op. cit.* pp. 87–112, and Neff, *The Poetry of History*, pp. 93–115.

PAGE 97

1 Above p. 37.

2 Above p. 74.

3 Butterfield, *op. cit.* pp. 84–5.

4 Neff, *The Poetry of History*, p. 13.
5 Hutton published his work *Theory of the Earth*, which is considered to be the first scientific work on geology, in 1795. See Gillispie, *Genesis and Geology*, pp. 40–72.
6 'On the Hindus', *As.R.* vol. I, pp. 416–17.
7 Maurice, *Memoirs*, pt. II, pp. 31–44.
8 W.J. to G.J.S., 29 Aug. (1777).
9 'On the Hindus', *As.R.* vol. I, p. 415.

PAGE 98

1 *Ibid.* pp. 416–17.
2 *Ibid.* p. 421.
3 *Ibid.* p. 424.
4 *Ibid.* p. 425.
5 *Ibid.* pp. 423–4.
6 *As.R.* vol. III, pp. 1–16.
7 *Ibid.* p. 479.
8 *Ibid.* p. 480.
9 *Ibid.*
10 *Ibid.* p. 484.

PAGE 99

1 *Ibid.* pp. 485–6, 490–1.
2 We discuss this in further detail later when we review Jones's chronology of the Hindus. See above pp. 102–4. Jones maintained that the sons of Japhet went to Europe first, but they were uncivilized Tartars, who were later overrun by later migrants, the descendants of Ham. *As.R.* vol. III, pp. 490–1.
3 It is interesting to note that it was Alendander Hamilton, a member of the Asiatick Society, who taught Schlegel Sanskrit in Paris, when he was there as a prisoner of war.
4 'A dissertation on the orthography of Asiatick words in Roman letters', *As.R.* vol. I, pp. 1–56. Jones also wrote a paper on the 'Affinity between the Hebrew and Devi Nagry characters', *Transactions*, 19 May 1785. This was never published and the text is missing. It may be that much of what Jones said in this paper was incorporated in his discourse on the Hindus. See *As.R.* vol. I, pp. 423–4.
5 Monier Williams, 'The duty of English speaking orientalists', etc. *J.R.A.S.* (1890), pp. 607–38.

PAGE 100

1 'On the Gods', *As.R.* vol. I, p. 225.
2 Newton, *The chronology of Ancient Kingdoms*, pp. viii–ix. Cf. Manuel, *The Eighteenth Century Confronts the Gods*, pp. 6–9.

PAGE 101

1 *As.R.* vol. I, pp. 222–3.
2 *Ibid.* p. 267.

3 *Ibid.* pp. 228–9.
4 *Ibid.* p. 230.
5 *Ibid.* pp. 234–5.
6 *Ibid.* pp. 236–7.
7 *As.R.* vol. II, pp. 131–2.
8 *Ibid.* p. 132.

PAGE 102

1 *Ibid.*
2 A copy of this is now at the British Museum. See B.M. o.r. 1124.
3 B.M. o.r. 1124, ff. 2–9.
4 *Ibid.* ff. 11–14.
5 *Ibid.* ff. 15–31.
6 *Ibid.* ff. 32–40.
7 Pargitar, *The Purāṇa Text of the Dynasties of the Kali Age.*
8 B.M. o.r. 1124, ff. 36–40.
9 Letters to John Shore, 25 March 1787, 11 May 1787 and 12 May 1787, as published in Shore, *op. cit.* pp. 289–92.
10 *As.R.* vol. II, pp. 121–2 and 124.
11 *Ibid.* pp. 121–2.
12 *Ibid.* p. 125.

PAGE 103

1 He is generally known as Candraśrī Sātakarni, son of Vijaya. See Pargitar, *op. cit.* p. 72.
2 *As.R.* vol. II, p. 144.
3 *Ibid.* vol. I, p. 142.
4 *Transactions*, 17 June 1790. Cf. *As.R.* vol. II, pp. 389–403.

PAGE 104

1 Manuel, *op. cit.* pp. 99–100.
2 *As.R.* vol. II, p. 401.
3 After obtaining the Vedic manuscripts Anthony Polier sent them to Jones. See A.P. to Joseph Banks, 20 May 1789. B.M. 5245, ff. 1–4.

PAGE 105

1 Dow, *op. cit.* vol. I, p. 10.
2 Rennel, *Memoirs of a map of Hindoostan* (1783), pp. 40–1.
3 *Ibid.* p. 40.
4 Rennel, *Memoirs* etc. (1788), p. 54.
5 d'Anville, *Antiquité géographique de l'Inde*, pp. 51–7.
6 Robertson, *An Historical disquisition* etc. pp. 30–1.
7 *Réflections sur un livre Indien*, etc. *Hist. et Mém. de l'Ac. des I. et B.L.* Tome 38, pp. 312–36.
8 I am grateful to Prof. Basham for pointing this out to me.
9 *Hist. et Mém.* etc., Tome 38, pp. 321–2.
10 *Ibid.* p. 323.

PAGE 106

1 *Hist. et Mém. de l'Ac. des I. et B.L.*, p. 323. It is noteworthy that de Guignes's date for the accession of Parikṣit after the Mahābhārata war was different only by 100 years from that of Raychaudhuri, which is widely accepted today. *P.H.A.I.* p. 36.

2 *As.R.* vol. IV, pp. 1–15, and *Transactions*, 28 Feb. 1793.

3 *As.R.* vol. iv, p. 7.

4 *Ibid.*

5 *Ibid.*

6 *Ibid.* p. 6. By now Jones had realized that his early reconstruction of the Hindu chronology was useless. He still believed that the Hindus were well aware of the 'true history'. He particularly mentioned Francis Wilford's 'discovery' of a Purāṇa which mentioned Adam and Noah. Jones failed to detect the trick the Brahmins had played on Wilford (*ibid.* p. 7). Cf. Shore, *op. cit.* pp. xi–xiii.

7 *As.R.* vol. IV, pp. 10–11.

8 Above p. 105.

PAGE 107

1 *As.R.* vol. IV, p. 11.

2 Above p. 102.

3 Jones Collections 52. Cf. Tawney and Thomas, *Cat. of Two Collections*, p. 53.

4 Eggeling, *Cat. of the Sanskrit MSS.* vol. VI, 939 a.

5 Sastri, *The age of Nandas and Mauryas*, p. 147. Cf. Jones Collections, W. 52, ff. 68–82.

6 Above p. 102.

7 *M.R.* vol. 79, p. 593.

PAGE 108

1 Ahmad, *Studies in Islamic Culture in the Indian Environment*, pp. 236–7. Cf. above pp. 97–8.

PAGE 109

1 *As.R.* vol. I, pp. 123–6, 276–87, 357–8 and 379–82; and *As.R.* vol. II, pp. 167–70. Cf. B.M. 8893, 94 and 95.

PAGE 110

1 Above pp. 77–8.

2 *As.R.* vol. I, p. 279.

3 Letter to a friend, 13 Sept. 1789. N.L.S. 5041, f. 164.

4 *Ibid.*

5 *J.A.S.B.* vol. VI, 2 (1837), 566–609.

6 *As.R.* vol. II, pp. 331–2.

7 Allan, *Cat. of the Coins of Gupta Dynasties*, pp. xi–xii.

8 Chambers, 'Some account of the sculptures and ruins of Mavalipuram', *As.R.* vol. I, pp. 157–8.

9 *Archaeologia*, vols. VII and VIII. Cf. Hodges, *Travels in India*, pp. 64–76.

10 Above p. 103.

PAGE 111

1 Chambers, *op. cit.* pp. 157–8.
2 Mill, *History of British India*, vol. II, p. 138.
3 *Ibid.* pp. 139–40.
4 Philips, *Historians of India, Pakistan and Ceylon*, pp. 217–29.
5 Bearce, *British Attitudes towards India 1784–1858*, pp. 20–4.
6 Reichwein, *op. cit.* pp. 151–2.
7 Above p. 6.
8 Above pp. 44–5

PAGE 112

1 Above p. 42.
2 Above pp .43–4. Cf. Benthall, Preface *Sir William Jones's Poems*.
3 Shore, *op. cit.* pp. 65–6.
4 *N. & Q.* (n.s.), I (1954), 527–8.
5 Above p. 82.
6 W.J. to G.J.S., 13 Nov. 1776.
7 *Ibid.* 1 Jan. 1780.
8 *Ibid.* 3 Nov. 1779.

PAGE 113

1 Letter to Lady Georgiana, 24 Oct. 1791.
2 'Discourse On Asiatick history, civil and natural', *As.R.* vol. IV, p. 13.
3 Letter to Charles Chapman, 26 April 1784, as published in Shore, *op. cit.* p. 247.
4 W.J. to G.J.S., 22 July 1787.
5 *Ibid.* 5 Aug. 1787.

PAGE 114

1 Letters to Joseph Banks, 25 Feb. 1788 and 24 Sept. 1788. *D.T.C.* vol. 6, ff. 19–20 and f. 78.
2 W.J. to G.J.S., 12 Aug. 1787.
3 *Ibid.*
4 Letter to Lady Georgiana, 8 Oct. 1787.
5 *Sacontala or the fatal ring*, p.1. Cf. Père Pons to Père Halde, 23 Nov. 1740. *Lettres édifiantes*, p. 72.
6 *Sacontala*, p. 11.
7 *Ibid.* pp. ii–iii.

PAGE 115

1 W.J. to G.J.S., 4 Sept. 1787. The story that Jones sent to George John was a garbled version of the drama. According to Jones's version, Śakuntalā was living with the king in his palace when Durvāsā visited Duṣyanta, the king, and caused the long separation of the couple.
2 Cat. of the Library of Sir William Jones, no. 447.

3 *Sacontala or the fatal ring: an Indian drama by Calidas. Translated from the original Sanskrit and Pracrit*, Calcutta 1789. For the benefit of insolvent debtors.

4 Above p. 10.

5 Wilkins, *The Bhagvat-Geeta*, p. 7.

6 *Sacontala*, pp. ix–x.

7 Hanumān, a mythological figure, a leader of the monkeys who helped Rāma in the rescue of his wife Sītā.

PAGE 116

1 *Ibid.* pp. iii, iv.

2 *Ibid.* p. ix.

3 *Ibid.* p. vii.

4 Pinto, 'Sir William Jones and English literature', *B.S.O.A.S.* vol. XI, p. 687.

5 'On the mystical poetry', *As.R.* vol. III, p. 183.

6 W.J. to G.J.S., 23 Aug. 1787.

PAGE 117

1 'On the antiquity of the Indian zodiack', *As.R.* vol. II, p. 289.

2 'On the Indian game of chess', *op. cit.* p. 159.

3 'On the musical modes of the Hindus', *As.R.* vol. III, p. 85.

4 Letter to Richard Johnson, 14 Aug. 1784. N.L.W. 11095 E, f. 8.

5 Cat. of the Library of Sir William Jones, no. 436.

6 B.M. 14. 767, 768 and 769.

7 'On the Hindus', *As.R.* vol. I, pp. 424–5 and 'On the mystical poetry of the Persians and Hindus', *As.R.* vol. III, p. 165. Cf. *As.R.* vol. IV, pp. 169–70.

8 'Need I say what exquisite pleasure I receive from conversing easily with that class of men who conversed with Pythagoras, Thales and Solon but with this advantage over the Grecian travellers that I had no need of an interpreter.' W.J. to G.J.S., 26 Aug. 1787.

PAGE 118

1 *Ibid.* In this *Sermon* Price stated Christian doctrine of different denominations but upheld the Unitarian view. Price, *Sermons of Christian Doctrines* etc., p. 173.

2 W.J. to G.J.S., 26 Aug. 1787.

3 'On the philosophy of the Asiaticks', *As.R.* vol. IV, p. 172.

4 Above p. 15.

5 Letter to Richard Johnson, 7 Feb. 1790. N.L.W. 11095 E, f. 12.

6 'On the philosophy of the Asiaticks', *As.R.* vol. IV. p. 174.

PAGE 119

1 W.J. to G.J.S., 2 Sept. 1787.

2 *Ibid.* 4 Sept. 1787.

3 'On the philosophy of the Asiaticks', *As.R.* vol. IV, pp. 170–1.

4 'On the Hindus', *As.R.* vol. I, p. 429.
5 'On the philosophy of the Asiaticks', *As.R.* vol. IV, pp. 176–7. He had noticed this in his 'Hymn to Surya'. See *Works*, vol. 13, p. 278.

PAGE 120

1 Letter to Robert Orme, 12 Oct. 1786, N.L.W.C. 14005. This was written in reply to Robert Orme's claim that the Greek literature was superior to that of the Indians. 'I am convinced that the Indian mythology can never furnish ideas of such fine taste as the genius of the Greeks have improved and invented for theirs.' R.O. to W.J. 11 Mar. 1780, Orme collections 214. 5, p. 46.
2 'The second discourse', *As.R.* vol. I, p. 407.
3 *Ibid.* p. 405.
4 'On Asiatick history', *ibid.* vol. iv, pp. 7–8.
5 *Ibid.* p. 167.
6 *Ibid.* p. 13.
7 *Britain Discovered.* Shore, *op. cit.* pp. 416–89.

PAGE 121

1 Horace Walpole to William Robertson, 20 June 1791. *Correspondence*, vol. 15, pp. 211–12.
2 Mill, *op. cit.* vol. II, pp. 56–7.

PAGE 122

1 Letter to Warren Hastings, 23 Oct. 1786. B.M. 29,170, f. 234.
2 W.J. to G.J.S., 25 Sept. 1793.
3 *Ibid.*
4 Letter to Warren Hastings, 7 Jan. 1785. B.M. 29,167, f. 330.

PAGE 123

1 Anna Maria to Warren Hastings, 1 Feb. 1790. B.M. 29,172, f. 26.
2 'I hope none of your friends think of coming hither: our salaries are unpaid and we are forced to borrow money for our daily rice.' Letter to George Milles, 22 Feb. 1786. N.L.W. 6701. Cf. letter to John Macpherson, 5 Feb. 1766, as published in Shore, *op. cit.* p. 269.
3 By 1791 he had saved £27,839, and he then hoped to send another £3,000 in a year's time. W.J. to G.J.S. 20 Feb. 1791. Even by the eighteenth-century standard £30,000 was a large sum of money. It seems that Jones had invested money through the Agency Houses in Calcutta. A.M. to W.H. 1 Feb. 1790. B.M. 29,172, f. 26. It is possible that he purchased his 'Talukdari' in Krishnagar under an assumed name.
4 W.J. to G.J.S., 20 Feb. 1791.

PAGE 124

1 W.J. to G.J.S., 12 Feb. 1784.
2 Letter to Macpherson, 12 March 1785, as published in Shore, *op. cit.* p. 257.

3 Hickey, *Memoirs*, vol. IV, p. 113.
4 Letter to Warren Hastings, 1784. B.M. 29,171.
5 A.M.J. to W.H., 1786. B.M. 29,169, ff. 485–6.
6 Letter to Warren Hastings, 23 Oct. 1786. B.M. 29,170, f. 234.
7 W.J. to G.J.S., 21 Dec. 1791.
8 Aspinall, *Cornwallis in Bengal*, pp. 125–30 and 101.
9 W.J. to G.J.S., 1 Sept. 1787.

PAGE 125

1 Charges to the Grand Jury, 9 June 1792. *Works*, vol. VII, p. 70.
2 Above p. 72.
3 Above p. 72.
4 Letter to Ashburton, 12 April 1783, as published in Shore, *op. cit.* p. 230 (my italics).
5 'On Asiatick history, civil and natural', *As.R.* vol. IV, p. 8.

PAGE 126

1 Letter to 'a friend in the Bar', 13 April 1784, as published in Shore, *op. cit.* p. 246.
2 Letter to Ashburton, 12 April 1783, as published in Shore, *op. cit.* p. 230.
3 *Al Sirajiyyah*, p. xii.
4 Burke Notes, 9*c*. Burke Papers.

PAGE 127

1 *Institute of Hindu Law*, p. iii.
2 Charges to the Grand Jury, 4 Dec. 1783. *Works*, vol. 7, p. 4.

PAGE 128

1 Above p. 79.
2 Derrett, 'Sanskrit Legal Treatise compiled at the instance of the British', In *Z. f. vergleichende Rechtswissenschaft*, Band 63, pp. 78, 79.
3 *Ibid.* p. 82.
4 Above p. 47.
5 Above p. 94.
6 W.J. to G.J.S., 14 Oct. 1783 and 17 Aug. 1787.
7 N.L.W. 5476 D.

PAGE 129

1 Letter to Chapman, 28 Sept. 1785, as published in Shore, *op. cit.* p. 264.
2 W.J. to G.J.S., 22 July 1787.
3 'A copy of a paper in the handwriting of Sir William Jones', N.L.W. 5476 D. Cf. letter to Warren Hastings, 23 Oct. 1786. B.M. 29,170, f. 234.
4 Derrett, *op. cit.* p. 82.
5 Letter to Edmund Burke, 27 Feb. 1784. Burke Papers.
6 *The Mohamedan Law of Succession*, Preface.
7 Letter to Macpherson, 6 May 1786, as published in Shore, *op. cit.* p. 276.

PAGE 130

1 Letter to Rous, 24 Oct. 1786. Camb. Add. 6958.
2 Sir John Comyns (d. 1740). Judge, author of *A Digest of the Laws of England.*
3 Letter to Rous, 24 Oct. 1786. Camb. Add. 6958.
4 Letter to Cornwallis, 19 March 1788. B.M. 29,171, f. 161.
5 Letter to Cornwallis, 19 March 1788. B.M. 29,171, f. 163.
6 Letter to Cornwallis, 19 March 1788. B.M. 29,171, f. 164.

PAGE 131

1 *Ibid.*
2 Bengal Public Letter, 6 Nov. 1788.
3 Bengal Public Consultations (original), 19 March 1788. N.A.I.
4 Letter to William Shipley, 5 Oct. 1786, as published in Shore, *op. cit.* p. 285.
5 *Al Sirajiyyah*, p. xiii.
6 *Ibid.*
7 Letter from Robert Kyd, 8 April 1791. M.S. Eur. F. 95/1.

PAGE 132

1 *Al Sirajiyyah*, pp. ix–xi.
2 *Al Sirajiyyah*, p. xiii.
3 James Mill was quick to detect the tendentious nature of the translation. In his effort to prove that the Hindus had no idea of private property and considered their kings the supreme lords of the soil, Mill used Jones's translation of Manu VIII, 39. However, to suit his theory Mill rearranged the relevant passage on the ownership of land: 'I have substituted the word supreme for the word paramount used by Sir William Jones (which has but) as it relates to the *feudal institutions of Europe and is calculated to convey erroneous ideas*' (my italics). See Mill, *The History of British India*, vol. I, p. 260n.
4 *Al Sirajiyyah*, p. xi.
5 Letter to Lady Georgiana, 24 Oct. 1791.
6 Letter to William Shipley, 11 Oct. 1790, as published in Shore, *op. cit.* p. 341.

PAGE 133

1 'Remarks on the island of Hinzuan or Johanna', *As.R.* vol. II, pp. 88–92.
2 *A speech on the nomination of candidates to represent the county of Middlesex*, p. 5 (my italics).
3 Charges to the Grand Jury, 10 June 1785. *Works*, vol. VII, p. 16.
4 *Ibid.* p. 17.

PAGE 134

1 *A speech on the nomination of candidates*, p. 5.
2 Charges to the Grand Jury, 10 June 1785. *Works*, vol. VII, pp. 14–15.
3 Larkin, *Property in the Eighteenth Century*, pp. 75–6.
4 W.J. to G.J.S., 8 June 1777.

PAGE 135

1 Hyde Papers, 16 June 1785. Bar Library, Calcutta.
2 N.L.W. 5476 D. Cf. above p. 128.
3 'An analysis of a trial for murder', N.L.W. 5476 D.
4 Letters to Lady Georgina, 8 June 1780 and 9 June 1780. Cf. above pp. 64–5.
5 Charges to the Grand Jury, 10 June 1787. *Works*, vol. VII, p. 25.
6 *Ibid.* 4 Dec. 1788. *Works*, vol. VII, p. 34.
7 *Ibid.* 10 June 1788. *Works* vol. VII, p. 20. Cf. Ghosal, *A History of Indian Political Ideas*, pp. 167–71.

PAGE 136

1 Charges to the Grand Jury, 9 June 1792. *Works*, vol. 7, p. 68.
2 Letters to John Shore, 7 Feb. 1788, as published in Shore, *op. cit.* pp. 316–17.
3 Charges to the Grand Jury, 4 Dec. 1788. *Works*, vol. 7, p. 45.
4 *Ibid.* 9 June 1792. *Works*, vol. 7, p. 70.

PAGE 137

1 Minutes, 11 Feb. 1793, as quoted in Aspinall, *op. cit.* p. 172.
2 Letter to Emin, 10 Aug. 1788, as published in the *Life and Adventures of Emin*, by Joseph Emin, p. xx.
3 *Ibid.*
4 Venturi, 'Oriental Despotism', *J.H.I.* vol. XXIV, pp. 138–9.
5 Letter to the Supreme Council, 13 April 1788. Public Consultations (original), 14 April 1788. N.A.I.
6 Derrett, *op. cit.* p. 91.

PAGE 138

1 Minute of the Governor-General, 22 Aug. 1788, Consultations N.A.I.
2 Some of the pandits went to Benares to obtain rare books. See Home Dept. Consultations, 19 Dec. 1790. N.A.I.
3 Letter to E. Hay, 6 Nov. 1792. Public Consultations (original), 9 Nov. 1792. N.A.I.
4 *Ibid.*
5 Public Consultations (original), 11 June 1793, 7 Feb. 1794 and 5 May 1794. N.A.I.
6 Letter from Harford Jones, 12 June 1793. N.L.W. 4904 F.
7 Letter to Henry Dundas, 1 March 1794, as published in *Works*, vol. 8, pp. 157–8.
8 Blechynden, *Calcutta Past and Present*, pp. 157–8.
9 John Shore to his wife, 27 April 1794, as published in Shore, *op. cit.* p. 286.

PAGE 139

1 *Calcutta Gazette*, 1 May 1794. *Selections*, vol. II, p. 387.
2 Anna Maria to Charles Grant, 29 Jan. 1795, as published in Morris, *William Jones*, p. 25.

3 Journal of John Shore, 1 May 1794, as published in Shore, *op. cit.* p. 289.

4 'On Asiatick history, civil and natural', *As.R.* vol. IV, p. 7.

5 Letter to John Shore, 16 Aug. 1787, as published in Shore, *op. cit.* pp. 294–5.

6 W.J. to G.J.S., 25 Sept. 1793. Cf. Despatches to Bengal, vol. XXVIII.

7 Letter to John Rous, 24 Oct. 1786. Camb. 6958, f. 224.

8 W.J. to G.J.S., 19 Oct. 1791.

9 Derrett, *op. cit.* pp. 109–12.

10 Mill, *op. cit.* vol. V, p. 513.

PAGE 140

1 As quoted in Holdsworth, vol. XII, p. 393.

2 Colebrooke, *A digest of Hindu Law*, vol. I, pp. xi–xii.

3 *Ibid.* pp. 460–1.

4 Derrett, *op. cit.* pp. 91–2.

5 *Ibid.* pp. 83–95.

PAGE 141

1 Roy, *Works*, pt. II, pp. 41–9.

2 Vivekananda, *Complete Works*, vol. I, pp. 386–91.

3 Voigt, 'Nationalist interpretations of Arthasastra in Indian Historical Writing', in Mukherjee (ed.), *South Asian Affairs*, no. 2, pp. 46–66.

4 Basham, *The Wonder that was India*, p. 487.

5 Above pp. 42–4.

6 Above p. 6. Cf. Stokes, *The English Utilitarians and India*, pp. 8–25.

7 *Ibid.* pp. 281–7.

8 W.J. to G.J.S., 20 Aug. 1787.

PAGE 142

1 Letters to Edmund Burke, 27 Feb. 1784 and 15 April 1784.

PAGE 143

1 Burke Notes 9c. Wentworth Muniments.

BIBLIOGRAPHY

I. MANUSCRIPTS AND RECORDS

British Museum [Cited as B.M.]

Hastings MSS. Additional MSS 29,167; 29,169; 29,170; 29,171; 29,172; 35655; 355656; 6583; 6584; 39,871; 39,898; 40,763.
Impey MSS. Add. MSS 16, 264.
Wilmot MSS. Add. MSS 9828.
Wilkes MSS. Add. MSS 30,877.
Myvyrian MSS. Add. MSS 14,968.
Francis Place MSS. Add. MSS 27,814; 27,849; 27,888.
Miscellaneous MSS. Add. MSS 14,767; 14,768; 14,769; 53.46; 8885; 8889; 8893; 8895; 8896; 13,877; 16,705; 37,232; and o.r. 1124.

Natural History Museum [Cited as D.T.C.]

The collection of copies of the correspondence of Sir Joseph Banks made for Dawson Turner. Vols. 6 and 7.

Royal Asiatic Society [Cit. Davis Papers]

Samuel Davis Correspondence.
Miscellaneous MSS. File no. XVII. C. E.

Commonwealth Relations Office, India Office Library

Records
Despatches to Bengal, vols. 5, 8, 17, 28, 31, 32 and 33 [Cit. Desp. to Bengal].
Letters from Bengal [Cit. Public Letters].
Home Miscellaneous Series [Cit. H.M.S.]
   207 (2); 418 (1); 456.
Public consultations [Cit. Public Consultations].

Manuscripts [Cit. MSS Eur.]
B. 15; F. 95/1; D. 491; Photo Eur. 21 A and Sir Robert Abercrombey papers, microfilm copy from Cleveland Public Library, Ohio. Reel no. 759.

Orme Collections [Cit. Orme Collections]
41.13; 214.50; 202.253; 168.4 and 5; 293.44; 147.2. (2).

Jones Collections [Cit. Jones Collections]
Sanskrit Manuscripts of Sir William Jones.

Bibliography

Marquis of Lansdowne's Library, Bowood, Wiltshire [Cit. Lansdowne Papers]

Seven unpublished letters from Jones to Shelburne in the possession of the present marquis of Lansdowne.

National Library of Wales, Aberystwyth [Cit. N.L.W.]

Add. MSS 2598 C; 5733 D; 2409 C; 14,005 C; 4878 E; and 11,095 E; 6701 C; 4364 B; 4904 E; 4412 E and 54,760.

National Library of Scotland, Edinburgh [Cit. N.L.S.]

Add. MSS 5041 and 3386.

Sheffield Central Library [Cit. Burke Papers]

Burke papers, Wentworth, Woodhouse MSS. (By permission of Earl Fitzwilliam and the Trustees of the Wentworth Woodhouse Settled Estates.)

Bodleian Library, Oxford [Cit. Bodl. (Oxf.)]

Add. MSS 28,460; 25,434; 25,428; 25,442; and 30,162.
Add. C. 89; MS. Eng. poet. e. 25; MS Eng. poet. d. 53; MS Eng. poet. c. 51.

University Library, Cambridge [Cit. Camb.]

6958; oo–1–6; and 5877.

County Record Office, Warwick [Cit. Newdigate Papers]

Newdigate MSS 1636 and 2141.

Althorp Park, Northampton [Cit. Spencer Papers]

Spencer papers at the Muniment Room at Althorp Park, in the possession of the present Earl Spencer.

Asiatic Society of Bengal, Calcutta [Cit. *Transactions*]

MS Proceedings of the Society from 1784 to 1800.

Bar Library, High Court, Calcutta [Cit. Hyde Papers]

Justice Hyde's Manuscript Diary (relevant volumes only).

National Archives of India, Delhi [Cit. N.A.I.]

Public Consultations (Original).

Bibliothek der Ryksuniversitet, Leiden [Cit. B.P.L.]

Schultens–Jones Correspondence, B.P.L. 254. XIII.

William L. Clements Library, Ann Arbor, Michigan [Cit. Lacaita–Shelburne Papers]

Lacaita–Shelburne Papers.

American Philosophical Society, Philadelphia [Cit. A.P.S.]
  Letters from Jones to Benjamin Franklin and one letter to Arthur Lee.

Historical Manuscript Commission [Cit. H.M.C.]
  14. R. Appendix pt. IV.
  12. R. Appendix pt. IX and pt. X.
  13. R. Appendix pt. III and pt. VIII.

II. THE PUBLISHED WORKS OF
SIR WILLIAM JONES

Histoire de Nader Chah connu sous le nom de Thahmas Kuli Khan, Empereur de Perse, traduite d'un manuscrit Persan, par ordre de sa majesté le Roi de Danemark, avec des notes chronologiques historiques géographiques et un traité sur la poésie. London, 1770.

A grammar of the Persian language. London 1771.

Dissertation sur la litérature Orientale. London, 1771.

Lettre à Monsieur A... du P... London, 1771.

Poems consisting chiefly of translations from the Asiastick languages to which are added two essays, 1. On the poetry of the Eastern nations. 2. On the arts commonly called imitative. Oxford, 1772.

The history of the life of Nader Shah, King of Persia. Extracted from an Eastern manuscript which was translated into French by order of His Majesty the King of Denmark, with an Introduction containing, 1. A description of Asia, according to the Oriental geographers, 2. A short history of Persia from the earliest time to the present century: and an Appendix, consisting of an essay on Asiastick poetry and the history of the Persian language. To which are added pieces relative to the French translation. London, 1773.

Poeseos Asiaticae commentariorum, Libri sex, cum appendice. London, 1774.

The speeches of Isaeus in causes concerning the law of succession to property at Athens, with a prefatory discourse, notes, critical and historical, and a commentary. London, 1779.

An Address to the University of Oxford [Gough. Oxf. 90(2)]. Oxford, 1780.

An inquiry into the legal mode of suppressing riots with a constitutional plan of future defence. London, 1780.

Another edition of the same work, together with *A speech on the nomination of candidates to represent the county of Middlesex,* and *An oration intended to have been spoken in the theatre at Oxford. IX July MDCCLXXIII (1773).* London, 1782.

Another edition of the same work in *The three tracts by Sir William Jones.* London, 1819.

Another edition. London, 1819.

A speech on the nomination of candidates to represent the county of Middlesex. London, 1780.

An essay on the Law of Bailments. London, 1781.

A plan for national defence. London, 1782.

A speech to the assembled inhabitants of the counties of Middlesex and Surrey, the cities of London and Westminster, and the borough of Southwark. London, 1782.

The principles of government in a dialogue between a scholar and a peasant written by a member of the Society for Constitutional Information. London, 1782.

England's Alarm! on the prevailing doctrine of libel as laid down by the Earl of Mansfield, in a letter to his Lordship, by a country gentleman to which is added by way of appendix, the celebrated dialogue between a gentleman and a farmer, written by Sir William Jones, with remarks thereon, and on the case of the Dean of St Asaph, by M. Dawes. London, 1788.

The principles of government in a dialogue between a gentleman and a farmer, by the late Sir William Jones. Re-published with notes and historical elucidations, by T. S. Morgate. London, 1797.

Another edition of the same work (1800).

Another edition. London, 1818.

Another edition in the *Three tracts by Sir William Jones,* printed for E. Wilson. 1819.

The Mahomedan law of succession to the property of Intestates in Arabick. London, 1782.

The Moallakat or seven Arabian poems which were suspended on the Temple at Mecca with a translation, a preliminary discourse and notes, critical, philosophical, explanatory. London, 1782.

A letter to a patriot Senator (by Sir W.J.). London, 1783.

A discourse on the institution of a society for inquiring into the history, civil and natural, the antiquities, arts, sciences, and literature of Asia, delivered at Calcutta January 15th. 1784: A charge to the grand jury at Calcutta, December 4th. 1783: and *A hymn to Camdeo, translated from Hindu into Persian, and from Persian into English.* London, 1784.

Sacontala or the fatal ring, an Indian drama, by Calidas, translated from the original Sanscrit and Pracrit. Calcutta, 1789.

Al Sirajiyyah: or the Mohamedan Law of Inheritance; with a commentary. Calcutta, 1792.

Institutes of Hindu law, or the ordinances of Menu, according to the gloss of Culluca, comprising the Indian system of duties, religious and civil. London, 1796.

Bibliography

The discourses and other papers addressed to the Asiastick Society:

'A discourse on the institution of a society, for inquiring into the history, civil and natural, the antiquities, arts, sciences and literature', *As.R.* vol. I, pp. ix–xvi.

'A dissertation on the orthography of Asiastick words in Roman letters', *ibid.* pp. 1–56.

'On the Gods of Greece, Italy and India', *ibid.* pp. 221–75.

'On the literature of the Hindus, from the Sanscrit, communicated by Goverdhan Caul, with a short commentary', *ibid.* pp. 340–55.

'A conversation with Abraham, an Abyssinian, concerning the city of Gwender and the sources of the Nile', *ibid.* pp. 383–6.

'On the course of the Nile', *ibid.* pp. 387–8.

'The second anniversary discourse', *ibid.* pp. 405–14.

'On the Hindus', *ibid.* pp. 414–32.

'On the Arabs', *As.R.* vol. II, pp. 1–17.

'On the Tartars', *ibid.* pp. 19–41.

'On the Persians', *ibid.* pp. 43–66.

'Remarks on the Island of Hinzuan or Johanna', *ibid.* pp. 77–107.

'On the chronology of the Hindus', *ibid.* pp. 111–47.

'On the cure of the Elephantiasis and other disorders of the blood', *ibid.* pp. 153–8.

'On the Indian game of chess', *ibid.* pp. 159–65.

'On the second classical book of the Chinese', *ibid.* pp. 195–204.

'On the antiquity of the Indian zodiack', *ibid.* pp. 289–306.

'The design of a treatise on the plants of India', *ibid.* pp. 345–52.

'On the Chinese', *ibid.* pp. 365–81.

'A supplementary essay on Indian chronology', *ibid.* pp. 389–403.

'On the Spikenard of the Ancients', *ibid.* pp. 405–417.

'On the borderers, mountaineers and islanders of Asia', *As.R.* vol. III, pp. 1–16.

'A royal grant of land in Carnata', *ibid.* pp. 39–53.

'On the musical modes of the Hindus', *ibid.* pp. 55–87.

'On the mystical poetry of the Persians and Hindus', *ibid.* pp. 165–83.

'Gita govinda or the songs of Jayadev', *ibid.* pp. 185–207.

'The lunar year of the Hindus', *ibid.* pp. 257–93.

'On the origin and families of nations', *ibid.* pp. 479–92.

'On Asiatick history, civil and natural', *As.R.* vol. IV, pp. 1–17.

'On the loris, or slow-paced lemur', *ibid.* pp. 135–9.

'Additional remarks on the Spikenard of the Ancients', *ibid.* pp. 109–18.

'Questions and remarks on the astronomy of the Hindus', *ibid.* pp. 159–63.

'On the philosophy of the Asiaticks', *ibid.* pp. 165–80.

'Botanical observations on select Indian plants', *ibid.* pp. 237–312.

The works of Sir William Jones (ed. Anna Maria Jones), 6 vols. London, 1799.

Supplementary volumes of the works of Sir William Jones, 2 vols. London, 1801.

The works of Sir William Jones (ed. John Shore, Baron Teignmouth), 13 vols. London, 1807.

Memoirs of the life, writings and correspondence of Sir William Jones, by John Shore, Baron Teignmouth. London, 1804.

Letters of Sir William Jones chronologically arranged from Lord Teignmouth's collection, 2 vols. London, 1821.

Discourses delivered before the Asiatick Society: and miscellaneous papers on the religion, poetry, literature, etc. of the nations of India, by Sir William Jones with *an essay on his name, talents and character by Right Honourable Lord Teignmouth* (ed. J. Elnes), 2 vols. 1821.

Dissertations and miscellaneous pieces relating to the arts, sciences and literature of Asia, by Sir W. Jones, and many others. Dublin, 1793.

The poetical works of Sir William Jones (ed. T. Park), 2 vols. London, 1808.

The poetical works of Sir William Jones, 2 vols. London, 1810.

The works of the English poets from Chaucer to Cowper (ed. A. Chalmers), vol. XVIII. London, 1810.

Sir William Jones's Poems (ed. J. Benthall). Cambridge, 1961.

The catalogue of the library of the late Sir William Jones. London, 1831.

III. CONTEMPORARY WORKS

d'Anville, J. B. *Antiquité géographique de l'Inde, et de plusieurs autres contrées de la Haute Asie*. Paris, 1775.

Bernier, F. *Travels in the Mogul Empire* (trans. A. Constable). London, 1913.

Blackstone, W. *Commentaries on the laws of England*, 4 vols. 12th ed. Cambridge, 1793.

Blanchard, W. *The proceedings in the case of the King against the Dean of St Asaph*. London, 1783.

Boulanger, N. A. *The origin and progress of despotism in the Oriental and other empires, of Africa, Europe and America* (trans. J. Wilkes). Amsterdam, 1764.

Burnet, J. (Lord Monboddo). *Origin and progress of language*, 6 vols. Edinburgh, 1783.

Burke, E. *The works of the Right Honourable Edmund Burke*, vols. 1-3. Oxford, 1906.

Burke, E. *Correspondence of the Right Honourable Edmund Burke* (ed. Earl Fitzwilliam and Richard Bourke), 4 vols. London, 1844.

Cartwright, E. *A memoir of the life, writings and mechanical inventions of Edmund Cartwright.* London, 1843.

Cartwright, F. D. *The Life and Correspondence of Major Cartwright.* London, 1826.

Cartwright, J. *Take your choice.* London, 1776.

Colebrooke, H. T. *A digest of Hindu Law on Contracts and Successions.* 1798.

Courtenay, J. *A Poetical Review of the Literary and Moral character of Samuel Johnson.* London, 1786.

Devonshire, Duchess of. 'Selections from the letters of Georgiana, Duchess of Devonshire', *Anglo-Saxon Review* (September 1899).

Dow, A. *The History of Hindostan*, 3 vols. London, 1768–72.

Erskine, T. *The speeches of the Hon. Thomas Erskine* (ed. J. Ridgway), vol. I. London, 1870.

Emin, J. *The Life and Adventures of J.E., An Armenian written in English by himself*, 2nd ed., Calcutta, 1918.

Ferguson, A. *An essay on the history of Civil Society.* London, 1767.

Fielding, H. *An enquiry into the causes of the late increase of robbers.* Dublin, 1751.

Forbes, J. *Oriental Memoirs*, 2nd ed., 2 vols. London, 1834.

Forrest, G. W. *Selections from the state papers of the Governor-General:* (*a*) Warren Hastings (2 vols.) London, 1910. (*b*) Lord Cornwallis (2 vols.) London, 1926.

Fortesque, J. *The Correspondence of George the Third. 1760–1783*, vol. VI. London, 1928.

Foster, Sir William. *Early Travels in India 1583–1619.* Oxford, 1921.

Foster, Sir William. *The Embassy of Sir Thomas Roe 1615–19.* Oxford, 1926.

Franklin, Benjamin. *The works of Benjamin Franklin*, vol. VIII. Boston, 1840.

Gibbon, E. *The Memoirs of the life of Edward Gibbon* (ed. G. B. Hill). London, 1900.

Gibbon, E. *The decline and fall of the Roman empire*, vols. 4–6 (ed. J. B. Bury). London, 1896–1900.

Gladwin, F. *The Ayine Akbary or the Institutes of the Emperor Akbar.* London, 1777.

Gurney, J. *The whole proceedings on the trial of the King against Shipley.* London, 1784.

Halhed, N. *A Code of Gentoo Laws.* London, 1776.

Halhed, N. *A grammar of the Bengal language.* Hoogly, 1778.

Hamilton, A. *A new account of the East Indies, being the remarks of Captain A.H. who spent his time there from 1688 to 1723*, 2 vols. Edinburgh, 1727.

Bibliography

D'Herbelot. *Bibliothèque Orientale ou dictionnaire universel*. Paris, 1697.

Herder, J. G. *Outlines of a philosophy of the history of man*. (trans. T. Churchill). London, 1800.

Hickey, W. *Memoirs of William Hickey*, vols. II–IV (ed. A. Spencer). London, 1913.

Hodges, W. *Travels in India*. London, 1793.

Holwell, J. Z. *Interesting events relative to the provinces of Bengal and the empire of Indostan*. London, 1765.

Holwell, J. Z. *A review of the original principles, religious and moral of the ancient Bramins*. London, 1779.

Howell, T. B. *State Trials*, vol. XXI.

Impey, Elijah Barvell. *Memoirs of Sir Elijah Impey*. London, 1850.

India. *The present State of the British interest in India*. London, 1773.

India. *The several petitions of the British inhabitants of Bengal to the Governor-General and to the council of directors of the East India Company and to Parliament*. London [1785].

India. *Select Committee on considering the Administration of Justice in Bengal, Behar and Orissa*. Ninth Report, London, 1785.

Jesuits. *Travels of the Jesuits into various parts of the world* (ed. John Lockman). London, 1743.

Jesuits. *Lettres édifiantes*, vol. XIV. Paris, 1781.

Johnson, S. *Boswell's Life of Johnson* (ed. G. B. Hill), 4 vols. Oxford, 1897.

Johnson, S. *Johnsonian Miscellanies* (ed. G. B. Hill). Oxford, 1897.

Johnson, S. *Letters of Samuel Johnson*, 2 vols. (ed. G. B. Hill). Oxford, 1897.

Kenyon, Sir George. *John Locke's direction concerning education*. Oxford, 1933.

Locke, J. *Two Treatises of Government* (ed. P. Laslett). Cambridge, 1960.

Locke, J. *Some thoughts concerning education*. 1693.

London Society for Constitutional Information. *Proceedings*. 1782.

London Society for Constitutional Information. *Tracts published and distributed gratis by the Society*. 1783.

London Society for Constitutional Information. *List of Members*. 1782.

Macartney, Lord. *The private correspondence of Lord Macartney, governor of Madras (1781–85)* (ed. for the Royal Historical Society by C. Collin Davies). London, 1950.

Marshall, J. *John Marshall in India* (ed. S. A. Khan). Oxford, 1927.

Maurice, T. *Memoirs of the author of the Indian Antiquities*, 2 vols. London, 1819–20.

Middleton, C. *The history of the life of Marcus Tullius Cicero*, 3 vols. London, 1741.

Mill, J. *The History of British India*, 6 vols. London, 1826.

Milton, J. *Of Education*. London, 1644.

Montesquieu, *The Spirit of Laws*, 2 vols. (trans. T. Nugent). London, 1909.

Newton, Sir Isaac. *The chronology of Ancient Kingdoms amended to which is prefixed a short chronicle from the first memory of things in Europe, to the conquest of Persia by Alexander the Great*. London, 1728.

Nichols, J. *Literary anecdotes of the eighteenth century*, vols. III and IV. London, 1803.

Nichols, J. *Illustrations of the literary history of the eighteenth century*, vol. 7. London, 1848.

Orme, R. *A History of the military transactions of the British nation in Indostan*. 4th ed. Madras, 1861.

Parr, S. *The Works of Samuel Parr* (ed. J. Johnstone), 8 vols. London, 1828.

Parr, S. *Bibliotheca Parriana, a catalogue of the library of the late Samuel Parr*. London, 1827.

Pope, A. *Minor Poems* (ed. N. Ault, completed by J. Bull). London, 1954.

Priestley, J. *A comparison of the Institutions of Moses with those of the Hindoos and other Ancient nations*. Northumberland, 1799.

Purchas, S. *Purchas, his pilgrimage; or relations of the world and religions observed in all age etc*. London, 1613.

Rennel, J. *Memoirs of a map of Hindoostan or the Mogul's empire*. London, 1783.

Rennel, J. *Memoirs etc*. London, 1788.

Reynolds, H. R. *A letter to the Right Reverend the Lord Bishop of London on the law of marriage*. London, 1841.

Richardson, J. *A dissertation on the languages, literature, and manners of the Eastern nations*. Oxford, 1777.

Robertson, W. *An historical disquisition concerning the knowledge Ancients had of India and the progress of trade prior to the discovery of the passage to it by the Cape of Good Hope*. London, 1791.

Ross, C. *Correspondence of Charles, First Marquis Cornwallis*, 3 vols. London, 1859.

Rousseau, J. J. *The Social Contract and Discourses* (ed. G. D. H. Cole). London, 1955.

Sassetti, F. *Lettere di Fillipo Sassetti*. Milan, 1874.

Scott, Sir Walter. *Familiar Letters of Sir Walter Scott*, 2 vols. David Douglas. Edinburgh, 1894.

Scrafton, L. *Reflections on the Government of Indostan with a Short Sketch of the history of Bengal*. London, 1770.

Shelburne, Lord. *Life of William, Earl of Shelburne*, by Lord Fitzmaurice. 2 vols. London, 1912.

Shore, J., Baron Teignmouth. *Memoirs of the Life and Correspondence of Baron Teignmouth, by his Son* (Charles Shore), 2 vols. London, 1843.

Stephens, Thomas. *The Christian Puranna*. Mangalore, 1907.

Thrale, H. L. *Thraliana. The Diary of Mrs Hester Lynch Thrale* (later Mrs Piozzi). *1776–1809* (ed. C. Balderston). London, 1951.

Tucker, J. *A Sequel of Sir William Jones pamphlet on the principles of government in a dialogue between a freeholder in the County of Denbigh, and the Dean of Gloucester*. London, 1784.

Twining, T. *Travels in India a hundred years ago* (ed. Rev. William H. G. Twining). London, 1893.

Voltaire. *Fragments sur l'Inde, sur le général Lalli, et sur le Comte de Morangies*. Paris, 1763.

Voltaire. *An essay on universal history, the manners and spirit of nations* (English transl.). Dublin, 1769.

Voltaire. *The general history and state of Europe from the time of Charlemagne to Charles I* (English transl.). London, 1754.

Walpole, H. *Memoirs of the reign of George II*, 3 vols. (ed. Lord Holland). London, 1846.

Walpole, H. *Memoirs of the reign of George III*, 2 vols. (ed. Sir D. le Marchant). London, 1845.

Walpole, H. *Horace Walpole's Correspondence* (ed. W. S. Lewis), vols. 12, 15, 28 and 29. Oxford, 1944–55.

Weber, H. *Metrical Romances of the 13th, 14th and 15th centuries published from ancient manuscripts*. Edinburgh, 1810.

Wilkins, Sir Charles. *A Translation of a Royal Grant of Land by one of the Ancient Raajas of Hindostan*. Calcutta, 1781.

Wilkins, Sir Charles. *The Bhagvat-Geeta or dialogues of Kreeshna and Arjoon in eighteen lectures*. London, 1785.

Wilkins, Sir Charles. *The Heetopodes of Veeshnoo Sharma*. London, 1787.

Wilmot, J. *Memoirs of the life of the Right Honourable Sir John Eardley Wilmot* (2nd ed.). London, 1811.

Wyvil, Rev. Christopher. *Political papers etc.*, vol. 1. York, 1794.

IV. PERIODICALS

A.B.	*Annual Biography.*
A.R.	*Annual Register.*
	Archaeologia.
A.M.	*Asiatick Miscellany.*
As.R.	*Asiatick Researches.*
B.P.P.	*Bengal Past and Present.*
B.S.O.A.S.	*Bulletin of the School of Oriental and African Studies.*
E.R.	*Edinburgh Review.*
G.M.	*Gentleman's Magazine.*

Bibliography

Hist. et Mém....	*Histoire et Mémoires de l'Académie des Inscriptions et Belles Lettres.*
J.A.O.S.	*Journal of the American Oriental Society.*
J.A.S.B.	*Journal of the Asiatick Society of Bengal.*
J.H.I.	*Journal of the History of Ideas.*
J.R.A.S.	*Journal of the Royal Asiatick Society of Great Britain.*
	London Magazine.
M.P.	*Modern Philology.*
M.R.	*Monthly Review.*
N. & Q.	*Notes and Queries.*
	Penny Magazine.
	Philosophical Transactions.
	The Calcutta Gazette (I have only used the *Selections from Calcutta Gazettes* by W. S. Seton-Kerr, London, 1864).
	Transactions of the Royal Asiatic Society of Great Britain.

V. SECONDARY SOURCES

Acharya, B. K. *Codification in British India.* Calcutta, 1914.

Ahmad, A. *Studies in Islamic Culture in the Indian Environment.* Oxford, 1964.

Allan, J. *Catalogue of the Coins of Gupta Dynasties.* London, 1914.

Aldridge, A. O. *Man of Reason, the Life of Thomas Paine.* London, 1960.

Appleton, W. W. *A Cycle of Cathay.* New York, 1951.

Arberry, A. J. 'Persian Jones', *Asiatick Review*, vol. 40 (April 1944), pp. 186–96.

Arberry, A. J. *Asiatic Jones: The Life and Influences of Sir William Jones (1746–94).* London, 1946.

Aronson, A. *Europe looks at India: A Study in Cultural Relations.* Bombay, 1946.

Asiatic Society of Bengal. *Centenary Review of the Asiatic Society of Bengal 1784–1883.* Calcutta, 1885.

Asiatic Society of Bengal. *150th Jubilee of the Royal Asiatic Society of Bengal (1784–1934) and the Bicentenary of Sir William Jones (1746–1946).* Calcutta, 1946.

Asiatic Society of Bengal. *Sir William Jones: Bicentenary of his Birth Commemoration Volume 1746–1946.* Calcutta, 1948.

Aspinal, A. *Cornwallis in Bengal.* Manchester, 1931.

Ballhatchet, K. *Social Policy and Social Change in Western India, 1817–1830.* London, 1957.

Bartold, V. V. *La découverte de l'Asie* (traduit du Russe et annoté par B. Nikitine). Paris, 1947.

Bibliography

Basham, A. L. *The Wonder that was India*. London, 1956.

Batavian Society for Arts and Sciences. *Centenary Review*. Batavia, 1878.

Bayne-Powell, R. *The English Child in the Eighteenth Century*. London, 1939.

Bearce, G. D. *British Attitudes towards India, 1784–1858*. London, 1961.

Becker, C. L. *The Heavenly City of the Eighteenth-century Philosophers*. New Haven, 1935.

Bengal. *Bengal Obituary*. Calcutta, 1848.

Bernal, J. D. *Science in History*. London, 1954.

Blechynden, K. *Calcutta Past and Present*. London, 1905.

Bloch, M. *Feudal Society* (trans. L. Manyon), 2 vols. London, 1965.

Blunt, R. *Mrs Montagu—'Queen of the Blues'*. London (n.d.).

Bonfante, C. 'Ideas on the Kinship of the European Languages from 1200–1800', *Journal of World History*, vol 1, pp. 679–99.

Bréal, M. *Grammaire comparée des langues Indo-Européennes*, vol. I. Paris, 1866.

Briggs, A. *The Age of Improvement*. London, 1959.

Brown, F. K. *Fathers of the Victorians*. Cambridge, 1961.

Browne, E. G. *A Literary History of Persia*, 4 vols. Cambridge, 1929.

Buckland, C. E. *Dictionary of Indian Biography*. London, 1906.

Bryant, Donald C. *Burke and his Literary Friends* (Washington University Studies, no. 9). Dec. 1939.

Busteed, H. E. *Echoes from Old Calcutta*. Calcutta, 1888.

Butterfield, H. *Origins of Modern Science*. London, 1949.

Butterfield, H. *History and Man's Attitude to the Past: their Role in the Story of Civilisation*. London, 1961.

Cambridge. *The Cambridge History of the British Empire (C.H.B.E.)*, vol. IV. Cambridge, 1928.

Cambridge. *The Cambridge History of India (C.H.I)*, vols. I and III. Cambridge, 1927–35.

Cambridge. *The New Cambridge Modern History (N.C.M.H)*, vols. II, V and VII. Cambridge.

Cannon, G. H. *Sir William Jones, Orientalist. An Annotated Bibliography of His Works*. Honolulu, 1952.

Cannon, G. H. *Oriental Jones*. London, 1964.

Christie, Ian R. 'The Marquis of Rockingham and Lord North's offer of a coalition, June–July 1780', *English Historical Review (E.H.R.)*, vol. 69 (July 1954), pp. 388–407.

Christie, Ian R. *The End of North's Ministry*. London, 1958.

Christie, Ian R. *Wilkes, Wyvil and Reform*. London, 1962.

Club. *Annals of the Club 1764–1914*. London, 1914.

Collingwood, R. G. *The Idea of History*. Oxford, 1961.

Bibliography

Conant M. P. *The Oriental Tale in England in the Eighteenth Century.* New York, 1908.

Copeland, J. W. *Checklist of Burke Correspondence.* Cambridge, 1955.

Cronin, V. *A Pearl to India, the Life of Roberto de Nobili.* London, 1959.

Daniel, N. *Islam and the West.* Edinburgh, 1960.

Davies, C. C. *A Historical Atlas of the Indian Peninsula.* Bombay, 1959.

Dawson, W. R. *The Banks Letters.* London, 1958.

Derrett, J. D. M. 'Sanskrit legal treatises compiled at the instances of the British', in *Z. f. vergleichende Rechtswissenschaft,* Band 63, pp. 72–117. Stuttgart, 1961.

Eggeling, J. *Catalogue of Sanskrit Manuscripts in the Library of India Office,* vol. VI. London, 1899.

Elton, O. *A Survey of English Literature 1730–1780,* 2 vols. London, 1928.

Embree, A. T. *Charles Grant and British Rule in India.* London, 1962.

Evans, J. *A History of the Society of Antiquaries.* London, 1956.

Fairchild, H. N. *The Noble Savage, a Study in Romantic Naturalism.* New York, 1928.

Feiling, K. *Warren Hastings.* London, 1954.

Firminger, W. K. (ed.). *The Fifth Report,* 3 vols. Calcutta, 1917.

Fortwilliam-India House Correspondence, vol. IV (ed. C. S. Srinivaschari). Delhi, 1962.

Furber, Holden (ed.). *The Private Records of an Indian Governor-Generalship.* Cambridge (Mass.), 1933.

Furber, Holden. *John Company at Work.* Cambridge (Mass.), 1948.

Gillispie, C. *Genesis and Geology.* Cambridge (U.S.A.), 1951.

Goldley, A. D. *Oxford in the Eighteenth Century.* London, 1908.

Goldziher, I. 'Additional notes to the Hungarian bibliography of Eastern studies in the last century', *Egyetenes Philologicae Kö zlony.* Budapest, 1880.

Guha, R. *A Rule of Property for Bengal.* Paris, 1963.

Habib, I. 'An examination of Wittfogel's theory of Oriental Despotism', *Enquiry,* no. 6, pp. 54–73.

Hill, C. *The Century of Revolution.* London, 1961.

Hewitt, R. M. *A Selection from His Literary Remains* (ed. J. de Sola Pinto). Oxford, 1955.

Hobsbawm, E. J. *The Age of Revolution, Europe 1789–1848.* London, 1962.

Holdsworth, Sir William. *A History of English Law,* vols. 1, 5, 8, 11 and 12. London, 1937.

Kiernan, R. H. *The Unveiling of Arabia.* London, 1937.

Koebner, R. 'Despot and Despotism: vicissitudes of a political term', *Journal of the Warburg and Courtauld Institute,* vol. XIV, nos. 3–4, pp. 275–300.

Larkin, Rev. Paschal. *Property in the Eighteenth Century with Special Reference to England and Locke*. Cork, 1936.

Lach, Donald F. *Asia in the Making of Europe*, vol. I, bks I and II. Chicago, 1965.

Lehman, W. C. 'John Millar, historical sociologist: some remarkable anticipations of modern sociology', *British Journal of Sociology* (*B.J.S.*), vol. 3 (1950), pp. 30–46.

Leslie, C. R. and Taylor, T. *The Life and Times of Sir Joshua Reynolds*, vol. I. London, 1865.

Lewis, B. *British Contributions to Arabic Studies*. London, 1941.

Lockhart, L. *Nadir Shah, a Critical Study based mainly upon Contemporary Sources*. London, 1938.

Lohuizen, J. E. van. 'Sir William Jones', *Orientalia Netherlandica*. Leiden, 1946.

London; Royal India Society. *Proceedings of the Sir William Jones Bicentenary Conference*. (University College, Oxford, September 2–6, 1946). Oxford, 1946.

Macoby, S. *English Radicalism 1763–1785*. London, 1955.

Macpherson, C. B. *The Political Theory of Possessive Individualism from Hobbes to Locke*. Oxford, 1963.

Majumdar, R. C. and others. *The Classical Age*. Bombay, 1956.

Mallet, C. E. *A History of the University of Oxford*, 3 vols. Oxford, 1924–7.

Manuel. F. E. *The Eighteenth Century Confronts the Gods*. Harvard, 1959.

Marsh, N. S. 'Sir William Jones', *University College Records, 1954–5*. Oxford, 1955.

Misra, B. B. *The Central Administration of the East India Company 1773–1834*. Manchester, 1960.

Misra, B. B. *The Indian Middle Classes*. London, 1961.

Morris, H. *Sir William Jones*. London, 1901.

Morris, H. *The Life of Charles Grant*. London, 1904.

Morton, T. C. *Decisions of the Supreme Court of Judicature*. Calcutta, 1851.

Muhamoud, F. M. *The Oriental Tale in England in the Early Nineteenth Century* (Ph.D. thesis in London University).

Mukherjee, S. N. 'The tradition of Rāma Gupta and the Indian nationalist historians', *East and West*, vol. 13, no. I (1962), pp. 49–52.

Mukherjee, S. N. (ed.). *South Asian Affairs*, no. 2 (St Antony's Papers, no. 18). Oxford, 1966.

Müller, F. Max. *Chips from a German Workshop*, 4 vols. London, 1898.

Namier, Sir Lewis. *The Structure of Politics at the Accession of George III*. London, 1961.

Bibliography

Namier, Sir Lewis. *England in the Age of the American Revolution.* London, 1930.

Namier, Sir Lewis. *Monarchy and the Party System.* London, 1952.

Nicolson, Sir Harold. *The Age of Reason (1700–1789).* London, 1960.

Neff, E. *The Poetry of History.* New York, 1947.

Nida, E. A. *Linguistic Interludes.* California, 1947.

Nussbaum, F. L. *The Triumph of Science and Reason.* New York, 1953.

Oaten, E. F. *European Travellers in India.* London, 1909.

Olson, A. *The Radical Duke.* Oxford, 1962.

Pargiter, F. E. *The Purāṇa Text of the Dynasties of the Kali age.* Oxford, 1913.

Pascal, R. 'Property and Society', *Modern Quarterly*, March 1938, vol. I, no. 2, pp. 167–79.

Peardon, T. P. *The Transition in English Historical Writing 1760–1830.* New York, 1933.

Penderson, H. *Linguistic Science in the Nineteenth Century.* Cambridge (Mass.), 1931.

Philips, C. H. (ed.). *Historians of India, Pakistan and Ceylon.* London, 1960.

Plumb, J. H. *England in the Eighteenth Century.* London, 1957.

Pocock, J. G. A. 'Burke and the ancient constitution—a problem in the history of ideas', *Historical Journal*, II, 2 (1960), pp. 125–43.

Raychaudhuri, D. P. *Sir William Jones and his Translation of Kalidasa's Sakuntala.* Calcutta, 1928.

Raychaudhury, H. C. *Political History of Ancient India (P.H.A.I.).* Calcutta, 1953.

Reichwein, A. *China and Europe. Intellectual and Artistic Contacts in the Eighteenth Century* (trans. J. C. Powell). London, 1925.

Robbins, C. *The Eighteenth-century Commonwealthman.* Harvard, 1959.

Robertson, C. G. *Select Statutes.* London, 1949.

Roscoe, Henry. *Lives of Eminent British Lawyers.* London, 1830.

Roy, Rammohan. *The English Works of Raja Rammohan Roy*, 6 parts. Calcutta, 1945–51.

Rudé, G. F. E. 'The Gordon Riots, a study of the roiters and their victims', *Transactions of the Royal Historical Society*, 5th series, vol. VI, pp. 93–114.

Rudé, G. E. F. 'The London mob of the eighteenth century', *Historical Journal*, vol. II, no. I.

Rudé, G. F. E. *Wilkes and Liberty.* Oxford, 1962.

Sastri, K. A. N. *The Age of Nandas and Mauryas.* Benares, 1952.

Saville, J. *Democracy and the Labour Movement—Essays in Honour of Dona Torr.* London, 1954.

Bibliography

Schwab, R. *La renaissance orientale*. Paris, 1950.

Slessarev, V. *Prester John, a Popular Legend*. University of Minnesota, 1961.

Sencourt, R. *India in English Literature*. London, 1923.

Shackleton, R. *Montesquieu—a Critical Biography*. Oxford, 1961.

Sinor, D. *Orientalism and History*. Cambridge, 1954.

Smith, B. *European Vision and the South Pacific, a Study in the History of Art and Ideas*. Oxford, 1960.

Smith, V. A. *The Oxford History of India*. 3rd. edn. T. G. P. Spear. Oxford, 1958.

Spear, T. G. P. *The Nabobs*. Oxford, 1932.

Stephen, Sir Leslie. *History of English Thought in the Eighteenth Century*, 2 vols. London, 1902.

Stokes, E. *The English Utilitarians and India*. Oxford, 1963.

Sutherland, L. S. *The East India Company in Eighteenth-century Politics*. Oxford, 1952.

Sutherland, L. S. *The City of London and the Opposition to Government 1768-1774*. London, 1959.

Tawney, C. H. and Thomas, F. W. *Catalogue of Two Collections*. London, 1903.

Twiss, H. *The Public and Private Life of Lord Chancellor Eldon*. London, 1844.

Veitch, G. S. *The Genesis of Parliamentary Reform*. London, 1913.

Vivekananda Swami. *The Complete Works of Swami Vivekananda*, vols. 1, 2 and 3. Mayavati, 1923-32.

Ward, W. R. *Georgian Oxford, University Politics in the Eighteenth Century*. Oxford, 1955.

Waley, Arthur. 'Anquetil-Duperron and Sir William Jones', *History Today*, vol. 2 (1952), pp. 23-33.

Wellek, R. *A History of Modern Criticism*, vols. I and II. London, 1955.

Weitzman, S. *Warren Hastings and Philip Francis*. Manchester, 1929.

Western, J. R. *The English Militia in the Eighteenth Century*. London, 1965.

Willey, Basil. *The Eighteenth-century Background*. London, 1950.

Willey, Basil. *The Seventeenth-century Background*. London, 1953.

Williams, E. *Slavery and Capitalism*. London, 1954.

White, R. J. (ed.). *The Conservative Tradition*. London, 1950.

Whiteway, R. S. *The Rise of the Portuguese Power in India*. London, 1889.

Winternitz, M. *A History of Indian Literature*, vol. I. Calcutta, 1921.

Wittfogel, K. *Oriental Despotism*. London, 1957.

Ziauddin, M. *A Grammar of the Braj Bhakha by Mirza Khan* (1676 A.D.). Santiniketan, 1935.

INDEX

Index

Davis, S., 87, 103
Deism, Deists, 4–5, 10, 15, 78, 112
Demosthenes, 20, 25, 30
Derrett, J. D. M., 129
Devonshire, Duchess of, 28, 34, 71, 86
Duke of, 34
Diderot, 6, 42
Diwani of Bengal, 16, 127–8
Doblen, Sir W., 66, 67
Dow, A., 13–14, 15, 16, 46, 78, 105
Dundas, H., 130
Dunning, J. (Lord Ashburton), 32, 71, 72, 125
Duperron, A., 24, 38, 94, 141

Emin, J., 137
Enlightenment, *see under* Age of Reason
Erskine, T., 53, 55, 58

Ferguson, A., 83
Feudal, Feudalism, 13, 14–15, 46, 61–3
Fitch, R., 8
Ford, Dr, 78
Fox, C. J., 26, 33, 50, 55
Francis, Sir P., 2, 80
Franklin, B., 27, 52, 53

Garrick, D., 29, 31, 33
George II, 49
George III, 60, 71
Ghulam Hussain, 90, 106, 139
Gibbon, E., 22, 26, 31, 37, 42, 57
Gladwin, F., 77, 87
Govardhana Kaul, 102, 139
Grant, C., 89, 139
Guignes, J. de, 102, 105, 107, 109

Habib, I., 12
Halhed, N., 29, 46, 77, 79, 140
Hamddulla, 76, 90, 126
Hargrave, F. H., 70
Harrow, 19, 20–1, 29, 30
Hastings, W., 31, 48, 79–80, 83, 84, 85, 89, 102, 115, 123, 124, 137

and Jones, 89, 123–4
and Oriental Studies, 79–80
Herbelot, d', 6, 46
Herder, J., 43, 83
Herodotus, 36
Hickey, W., 124
Hindu, Hinduism, 7, 11, 14, 15, 16, 78, 97, 98, 99, 101, 102, 103, 104, 105, 106, 107, 111, 116, 117, 119, 126
law, 74, 127–31, 137–8, 139–40
Hobbes, T., 5, 58
Holwell, T. Z., 15, 16, 78
Hyde, J., 134

Indio-European languages, family of, 91, 92, 99
Isaeus, 26, 31, 32, 33

Jagannatha Tarkapanchanan, 90, 138, 139, 140
Jains, 8, 110
Jebb, J., 50
Jesuits, 5, 9–10, 15, 95, 96
Johanna, King of, 75–6, 126
Johnson, S., 18, 22, 31, 32
Jones, H., 138
Jones, W., the mathematician, 17–18
Jones, Sir W.
and the Asiatick Society, 2, 81–90, 121, 140–1
and the Indians, 3, 47, 90, 114, 139
and James Mill, 111–12, 121, 139
and Wales, 17
mother of, 17–19, 66–7
childhood of, 18–19
at Harrow, 19–22
at Oxford, 22–4
with the Spencer family, 24–30
and Anna Maria Shipley (Lady Jones), 27, 72, 73–4, 113–14, 122, 138–9
models his life after Cicero, 30–1
joins Johnson's club, 31
elected Fellow of Royal Society, 31

Index

Jones, Sir W. (*cont.*)
  as a lawyer, 32–4
  as an Orientalist in England, 35–48
  and the Judgeship in Bengal, 34, 47, 70–2
  and the Oxford election, 66–9
  knighted, and leaves for India, 72–3
  and Johanna, 75–6, 126
  in Benares, 89
  in Krishnagar, 90, 94–5, 113–14, 123
  death, 139
  views on
    adult franchise, 60, 63–4
    America, 25, 66, 69–70
    aristocracy, 61
    Blackstone, 25, 56–8
    Burke, 59, 61
    Christianity, 26, 76, 112, 118–19
    Comparative Law, 32, 33, 40
    education, 23–5
    English Common Law, 58–60, 136
    English constitution, 25–6, 59–61, 120
    feudal system, 61–3
    Gibbon, 26, 42
    Gordon Riots, 64–5, 135
    Hinduism, 118–19
    History, 36–41, 96–7
    Indian civilizations, 116–17, 120–1
    Indian law, 47–8, 126–30, 137–8, 139–40
    Indian literature, 47, 119–20
    Indian natural sciences, 120
    Kālidāsa, 115
    learning languages, 93–4
    Locke, 25, 51
    Milton, 28–9, 51
    Mosaic history, 98–101, 104, 108
    Nadir Shah, 40–41, 44
    Oriental despotism, 40–1, 47–8, 125–6, 136–7
    poetry, 42–5
    property, 61–4
    Rousseau, 42
    slavery, 48, 66, 75, 133–5
    Voltaire, 36–7, 42

Kālidāsa, *see Śakuntalā*

Land
  laws, 1, 32
  rights in, 9, 13, 14, 16, 140
Langton, Captain, 31, 34, 51
Leibniz, 6, 92
Lennox, C., Duke of Richmond, 50
Linnaeus, 98, 113
Locke, J., 4, 5, 12, 14, 18, 25, 51, 55, 56, 58, 66, 134
Loyola, I., 9

Macartney, Lord, 27
Macaulay, Lord, 2
Macpherson, J., 55, 124
Mahdi, M., 39–40, 41
Manu, 10, 94, 101, 104, 135
Marco Polo, 7
Marsden, W., 86
Maurice, T., 33
Mill, J., 6, 111–12, 119, 121, 139
Millar, J., 62–3
Milton, J., 23, 28–9, 51, 112
Mirza, the Syrian, 22, 23
Montagu, E., 28, 68
Montesquieu, 5, 13, 40
Mughal, 9, 11, 12, 14, 15, 16, 41, 42, 47, 74
Muslim (Islam, Muhammedan), 7, 14, 15, 47, 49, 74, 85, 89, 106, 122, 126, 127, 128, 129, 131, 132, 135, 138, 139
  Law, 74, 85, 122, 126, 127–9, 131, 132, 138
  and the West, 15

Nadir Shah, 27, 39–41, 44, 46
  biographies of, 30, 31, 37, 39, 85
Namier, Sir L., 1
Newdigate, Sir R., 66, 67
Newton, I., 4–5, 18, 37, 97, 100, 104, 119

Index

Niebuhr, C., 39
Nobile, de, 10
North, Lord, 69, 70
   Regulation Act, 1773, 80, 128

Orient (Oriental Studies), 2, 7, 16,
   17, 23, 27, 31, 33, 35, 45, 46,
   55, 78–81, 82, 83, 86
Oriental despotism, 9, 13–15, 40–1,
   124, 137
Orme, R., 14, 46, 71, 78
Oxford, 19, 22–4, 29, 30, 31, 32, 34,
   36, 38, 51, 52, 57, 64, 66, 71
   election, 66–9

Paine, T., 59
Palibothra, *see* Pātaliputra
Pāṇini, 92, 99
Paradise, J., 24, 52
Pargitar, F. E., 102
Parnell, J., 21
Parr, S., 21, 34, 65
Pāṭaliputra, 105–6, 107, 108, 111
Persia, Persian, 9, 16, 23, 37, 36,
   37, 38, 41, 43, 44, 45, 46, 47,
   77, 78, 79, 92, 93, 94, 95, 98,
   102, 106, 116, 129
Philosophes, 5, 6, 11, 16, 42, 97
Physiocrats, 5, 14
Pitt, W. (younger), 50, 130
Pope, A., 4, 19
Prester John, 7
Price, Richard, 50, 51, 59, 118
Priestley, J., 118
Property, 5, 12, 13, 62, 63, 66, 126,
   128, 131–2, 133, 136
   in land, 9, 12, 14, 15, 63, 65, 132
   in person, 63–4
   and franchise, 63–6
   see also under Jones, Sir W.

Radhakanta Sharman, Pandit, 90,
   102, 104, 110, 114, 135, 137,
   138, 139
Ramlochan, Pandit, 90, 102, 115,
   135, 139
Rennel, J., 105–6
Reviczki, Count, 27, 28, 29, 35

Reynolds, Sir J., 31, 81, 123
Richardson, J., 97
Robertson, W., 105
Rockingham, Duke of, 69, 71
Roe, Sir T., 9, 13, 15
Roger, A., 10, 115
Romantic Movement, The, 6, 42,
   43, 44, 96, 111, 112, 141
Romantic Statesmen in India, 6,
   141
Rous, J., 129–30
Rousseau, J. J., 6, 42, 43, 60, 111
Roy, Raja Rammohan, 141
Rudé, G., 64

Śakuntalā, 3, 91, 114–15, 121, 141
Sandrocottas, *see* Candragupta
Sanskrit, 10, 16, 46, 77, 87, 89, 91,
   94–6, 99, 105, 106, 108, 110,
   114, 115, 118, 129
Sasseti, F., 95
Schlegel, F., 96
Scott, W. (Lord Stowell), 67, 68
Scrafton, L., 15
Shakespeare, W., 18, 28
Shelburne, Lord, 50, 65, 71
Shipley, A. M., *see under* Jones,
   Sir W.
Shipley, Bishop of St Asaph, 27,
   31, 51, 53, 86
Shipley, W., Dean of St Asaph, 21,
   53, 55, 58, 65
Shore, J. (Lord Teignmouth), 49,
   77, 78, 79, 90, 124, 138, 139
Smith, V., 41
Spencer family, 27, 28, 29, 30, 71
Spencer, G. J. (Viscount Althorp),
   20, 24, 25, 26, 28, 29, 30, 31–2,
   88, 115
Spencer, Lady G., 22, 24, 25, 29,
   30, 34, 64
Stephens, T., 10, 95
Stokes, E., 1

Tacitus, 36
Terry, E., 8–9
Thucydides, 36
Thurlow, Lord, 70–2

198

Index

Tory, 68
Tucker, Josiah (Dean of Gloucester), 55, 59, 72
Turk's Head, Soho, 31–2, 34, 35
Turner, S., 85

Utilitarianism, 139, 140. *See also under* Bentham, J., *and* Mill, James

Vedānta, 11, 118, 141
Vergennes, C. G. Comte de, 52, 53
Vivekananda, Swami, 141
Voltaire, 5, 6, 7, 14–15, 36, 37, 38, 40, 42, 45, 45, 62, 118, 126

Walpole, H., 4, 28, 68, 121
Watson, R., 86
Whig philosophy, 3, 25, 66, 124, 136
Whigs, 49, 60, 61, 68, 69
  'real', 51
Wilberforce, W., 66
Wilkes, J., 49, 50, 52, 65
Wilkin, C., 10, 77, 78, 79, 85, 86, 94, 110, 115
Wyvill, C., 50

Xavier, F., 9

Yeates, T., 61